Communications
in Computer and Information Science   1190

Commenced Publication in 2007
Founding and Former Series Editors:
Phoebe Chen, Alfredo Cuzzocrea, Xiaoyong Du, Orhun Kara, Ting Liu,
Krishna M. Sivalingam, Dominik Ślęzak, Takashi Washio, Xiaokang Yang,
and Junsong Yuan

Editorial Board Members

More information about this series at http://www.springer.com/series/7899

Guido Juckeland · Sunita Chandrasekaran (Eds.)

Tools and Techniques for High Performance Computing

Selected Workshops, HUST, SE-HER and WIHPC
Held in Conjunction with SC 2019
Denver, CO, USA, November 17–18, 2019
Revised Selected Papers

 Springer

Editors
Guido Juckeland ⓘ
Helmholtz-Zentrum Dresden-Rossendorf
Dresden, Germany

Sunita Chandrasekaran ⓘ
University of Delaware
Newark, DE, USA

ISSN 1865-0929   ISSN 1865-0937 (electronic)
Communications in Computer and Information Science
ISBN 978-3-030-44727-4   ISBN 978-3-030-44728-1 (eBook)
https://doi.org/10.1007/978-3-030-44728-1

Preface

The current proceedings combine 12 papers from three workshops co-located with the International Conference for High Performance Computing, Networking, Storage and Analysis (SC 2019). The workshops are HPC User Support Tools (HUST), Software Engineering for HPC-Enabled Research (SE-HER), and the Workshop on Interactive High Performance Computing (WIHPC). A description of each of the workshop is as follows:

The HUST workshop, held by Chris Bording (IBM Research, Hartree Centre), Elsa Gonsiorowski (Lawrence Livermore National Laboratory), and Karen Tomko (Ohio Supercomputing Center), has been the ideal forum for new and innovative tools such as XALT, SPACK, and Easybuild which have been widely announced to the broader HPC community. This has created communities and special interest groups surrounding these tools, many of which now hold their own BoFs, workshops, and tutorials at SC, ISC, and other HPC conferences. HUST will continue to provide a necessary forum for system administrators, user support team members, tool developers, policy makers, and end users. The workshop provided a forum to discuss support issues and we will provide a publication venue for current support developments. Best practices, user support tools, and any ideas to streamline user support at supercomputing centers are in the scope. HUST submitted four papers in total. For further details, please refer to the workshop website: https://hust-workshop.github.io/.

Developers who build research software for HPC or High Performance Data Analysis/Analytics (HPDA) face software engineering (SE) challenges at scales not often addressed by traditional SE approaches. For example, HPC and HPDA software developers must solve reliability, availability, and maintainability problems at extreme scales, consider reproducibility, understand domain specific constraints, deal with uncertainties inherent in scientific exploration, and efficiently use compute resources. SE researchers have developed tools and practices to support development tasks, including: requirements, design, validation and verification, testing, continuous integration, and maintenance. Because of the scale of HPC and HPDA, there is a need to adapt these SE tools/methods that are standard elsewhere. SE-HER 2019, held by Jeffrey C. Carver (University of Alabama), Anshu Dubey (Argonne National Laboratory), Neil Chue Hong (Software Sustainability Institute and Edinburgh Parallel Computing Center), and Daniel S. Katz (University of Illinois at Urbana-Champaign), brought together members of the SE and HPC/HPDA communities to present findings relative to these problems and to generate an agenda to advance software engineering tools and practices for HPC/HPDA software. For further details, please refer to the workshop website: http://SE4Science.org/workshops/seher19/.

Interactive exploration and analysis of large data sets, intelligent simulation ("cog-sim") workflows that combine interactive analysis and AI techniques with modeling and simulation, interactive preparation and debugging of large-scale scientific simulations, in-situ visualization, and application steering are all compelling scenarios for exploratory science, design optimizations, and signal processing. However, a range of technical, organizational, and sociological challenges must be overcome to make these interactive workflows mainstream in HPC centers: What simulation scenarios or problem domains can benefit most from interactivity? How can we simplify the toolchain? What center policies are needed to support highly interactive workflows? WIHPC 2019, held by Michael Ringenburg (Cray Inc.), John Stone (University of Illinois at Urbana-Champaign), and Albert Reuther (MIT-Massachusetts Institute of Technology) on interactive high performance computing brought together domain scientists, tool developers, and HPC center administrators to identify the scientific impact and technical challenges of highly interactive access to HPC resources. For further details, please refer to the workshop website: https://sites.google.com/view/interactive-hpc/home.

Review Process

Papers from each workshop were peer reviewed with an average of three reviews per paper.

These proceedings include 12 papers in total, 4 from each of the 3 workshops. Each workshop put together a Steering and Program Committee of researchers and scientists spanning academia, national labs, and industries to drive the workshop and help with selecting high-quality papers.

February 2020   Guido Juckeland
                                                              Sunita Chandrasekaran

Organization

Annual Workshop on HPC User Support Tools (HUST)

Organizers

Chris Bording	IBM Research, Hartree Centre, UK
Elsa Gonsiorowski	Lawrence Livermore National Laboratory, USA
Karen Tomko	Ohio Supercomputing Center, USA

General Chair

Chris Bording	IBM Research, Hartree Centre, UK

Program Committee Chairs

Elsa Gonsiorowski	Lawrence Livermore National Laboratory, USA
Karen Tomko	Ohio Supercomputing Center, USA

Program Committee

Daniel Ahlin	PDC Center for High Performance Computing, Sweden
David Bernholdt	Oak Ridge National Laboratory, USA
Fabrice Cantos	National Institute of Water and Atmospheric Research (NIWA), New Zealand
Eric Engquist	Rice University, USA
Christopher Harris	Pawsey Supercomputing Center, Australia
Mozhgan Kabiri-Chimeh	University of Sheffield, UK
Paul Kolano	NASA, USA
Kevin Manalo	PACE, Georgia Institute of Technology, USA
Robert McLay	TACC, USA
Abhinav Thota	Indiana University, USA

International Workshop on Software Engineering for HPC-Enabled Research (SE-HER)

Organizers

Jeffrey C. Carver	University of Alabama, USA
Anshu Dubey	Argonne National Laboratory, USA
Neil Chue Hong	Software Sustainability Institute and Edinburgh Parallel Computing Center, UK
Daniel S. Katz	University of Illinois at Urbana-Champaign, USA

Program Committee

Mark Abraham	KTH Royal Institute of Technology, Sweden
Lorena Barba	George Washington University, USA
Christian Feld	Juelich Supercomputing Center, Germany
Carina Haupt	German Aerospace Center (DLR), Germany
Kenneth Hoste	University of Gent, Belgium
Valerie Maxville	Curtin University, Australia
Damian Rouson	Sourcery Institute, USA
Manodeep Sinha	Swinburne University, Australia
Sophie Voisin	Oak Ridge National Laboratory, USA
Alexander Wagner	University of Tsukaba, Finland

Workshop on Interactive High-Performance Computing (WIHPC)

Organizers and Program Committee

Sadaf Alam	CSCS, Switzerland
Nicola Ferrier	Argonne National Laboratory, USA
Peter Messmer	NVIDIA, USA
Albert Reuther	MIT Lincoln Laboratory, USA
Michael Ringenburg	Cray Inc., USA
John Stone	University of Illinois at Urbana-Champaign, USA

Sponsor Logos

Contents

WIHPC – Workshop on Interactive High-Performance Computing

HUST - Annual Workshop on HPC User Support Tools

Buildtest: A Software Testing Framework with Module Operations for HPC Systems

Shahzeb Siddiqui$^{(\boxtimes)}$ ⓘ

Pfizer Inc. Groton & Labs, 445 Eastern Point Road, Groton, CT 06340-5146, USA
shahzebmsiddiqui@gmail.com

Abstract. HPC support teams are often tasked with installing scientific software for their user community and the complexity of managing a large software stack gets very challenging. Software installation brings forth many challenges that requires a team of domain expertise and countless hours troubleshooting to build an optimal software state that is tuned to the architecture. In the past decade, two software build tools (Easybuild, Spack) have emerged that are widely accepted in HPC community to accelerate building a complete software stack for HPC systems. The support team are constantly involved in fulfilling software request for end-users which leads to an ever-growing software ecosystem. Once a software is installed, the support team hands it off to the user without any testing because scientific software requires domain expertise in order to test software. Some software packages are shipped with a test suite that can be run at post build while many software have no mechanism for testing. This poses a knowledge gap between HPC support team and end-users on the type of testing to do. Some HPC centers may have developed in-house test scripts that are suitable for testing their software, but these tests are not portable due to hardcoded paths and are often site dependent. In addition, there is no collaboration between HPC sites in building a test repository that will benefit the community. This paper presents buildtest, a framework to automate software testing for a software stack along with several module operations that would be of interest to the HPC support team.

1 Introduction

HPC computing environment is a tightly coupled system that includes a cluster of nodes and accelerators interconnected with a high-speed interconnect, a parallel filesystem, multiple storage tiers, a batch scheduler for users to submit jobs to the cluster and a software stack for users to run their workflows. A software stack is a collection of compilers, MPI, libraries, system utilities and scientific packages typically installed in a parallel file-system. A module tool like environment-modules [1, 2] or Lmod [3] is generally used for loading the software environment into the users' shell environment.

Software are packaged in various forms that determine how they are installed. A few package formats are: binary, Makefile, CMake, Autoconf, github, PyPi, Conda, RPM, tarball, rubygem, MakeCp, jar, and many more. With many packaging formats, this creates a burden for HPC support team to learn how to build software since each one has a unique build process. Software build tools like Easybuild [3, 4] and Spack [5] can build

© Springer Nature Switzerland AG 2020
G. Juckeland and S. Chandrasekaran (Eds.): HUST 2019/SE-HER 2019/WIHPC 2019,
CCIS 1190, pp. 3–27, 2020.
https://doi.org/10.1007/978-3-030-44728-1_1

up to 1000+ software packages by supporting many packaging formats to address all sorts of software builds. Easybuild and Spack provide end-end software build automation that helps HPC site to build a very large software stack with many combinatorial software configurations. During the installation, some packages will provide a test harness that can be executed via Easybuild or Spack which typically invokes a make test or ctest for packages that follow ConfigureMake, Autoconf, or CMake install process.

Many HPC sites rely on their users for testing the software stack, and some sites may develop in-house test scripts to run sanity check for popular scientific tools. Despite these efforts, there is little or no collaboration between HPC sites on sharing tests because they are site-specific and often provide no documentation. For many sites, the HPC support team don't have the time for conducting software stack testing because: (1) lack of domain expertise and understaffed, (2) no standard test-suite and framework to automate test build and execution. Frankly, HPC support teams are so busy with important day-day operation and engineering projects that software testing is either neglected or left to end-users. This demands for a concerted effort by HPC community to build a strong open-source community around software stack testing.

There are two points that need to be addressed. First, we need a framework to do automatic testing of installed software stack. Second, is to build a test repository for scientific software that is community driven and reusable amongst the HPC community. An automated test framework is a harness for *automating* the test creation process, but it requires a community contribution to accumulate this repository on per-package basis. Before we dive in, this paper will focus on conducting sanity check of the software stack so tests will need to be generic with simple examples that can be compiled easily. In future, buildtest will focus on domain-specific tests once there is a strong community behind this project.

In this paper, we will introduce the buildtest framework in Sect. 2 followed by several module operations in Sect. 3. In Sect. 4 we will present future work and followed by Sects. 5 and 6 with related work and conclusion.

2 Buildtest

2.1 Motivation

There are many build automations tools [6] for compiling source code into binary code, the most used tool is the **make** [7] utility found in most Linux systems. Build scripts like **configure, cmake** [8] and **autoconf** [9] can generate files used by **make** for installing the software. **Makefile** is a file used by make program that shows how to compile and link a program which is the basis for building a software package. One can invoke **make test** which will run the target named **test** in Makefile that dictates how tests are compiled and run. Makefile is hard to interpret and requires in-depth experience with shell-scripting and strong understanding of how package is built and tested. Note that package maintainers must provide the source files, headers, and additional libraries to test the software and **make test** simply automates the test compilation and execution. Tools like configure, cmake and autoconf are insufficient for testing because HPC software stack consist of applications packaged in many formats and some are make-incompatible.

We wanted a framework that hides the complexity for compiling source code and provide an easy markup language to define test configuration to create the test. This leads to buildtest, a framework that automates test creation by using test configuration written in YAML syntax. YAML was picked given its simplicity and it lowers the barrier for new contributors to start sharing test configuration in order to build a comprehensive test suite that will work with buildtest.

2.2 Inception

Pfizer is multinational pharmaceutical corporation headquartered in New York City with their research headquarter in Groton, CT. The company develops and produces medicines that help patients' lives. Pfizer has two HPC clusters and a diverse user community comprised of chemists, computational scientists, statisticians, bioinformatics, data scientists, AI engineers and many more. In 2017, one of the clusters was going to be physically moved to another data center with growing capacity, this required a considerable effort by many groups in testing the entire compute environment. Shahzeb Siddiqui was tasked with testing the software ecosystem by focusing on the most important application due to time constraints. During this period, several dozen test scripts were developed in shell-script that targeted core HPC tools such as compilers, MPI, R, Python, etc. A single master script was used to run all the tests which led to **buildtest**. Originally buildtest was implemented in bash and due to several language limitations, it was ported to Python. In September 2018, buildtest was ported from Python 2 to Python 3. The project was started on Feb 24th, 2017 and source code and documentation can be found on GitHub [10].

2.3 Framework

Buildtest [10, 11] is a python framework for automating software stack testing by utilizing test configuration (YAML) to generate test script. The framework is tightly integrated with Lmod module system to allow the framework to load modules properly when building test. Buildtest can use a single test configuration and build a test with multiple modules seamlessly. Some additional features of buildtest include listing software and modules, module load testing, building test with user collections, building job scripts for LSF & SLURM scheduler, sanity check on binary for system packages and modules, and support for benchmark.

Buildtest was designed on the premise of reusable and easy to read test configuration that can be shared by the HPC community. YAML was chosen as the configuration markup language because it's compatible with many programming languages [25] including Python via **pyyaml** package. buildtest repository contains the source code for buildtest, documentation in **Re**Structured **T**ext (RST) using sphinx documentation builder, and test configuration with source files to build the tests.

2.4   Integration with Lmod Spider

In order to test the software stack, one must load the appropriate modules via module command and run a series of commands such as compiling source files into object files to build an executable and finally run the executable with a set of arguments. For instance, a simple test script shown below will build a C program (**hello.c**) via gcc compiler and run the executable (**hello**) with a set of arguments. Shown below is an example test script

```
#!/bin/bash
module load GCC/5.4.0
gcc -o hello hello.c
./hello hello world
rm ./hello
```

This example is only applicable for testing **GCC/5.4.0** module which is not suitable in a software stack that consists of multiple versions of each software. It will be a repetitive process when one needs to write the same test for another version by simply changing the **module load** command. Furthermore, module load needs to be done properly if multiple modules need to be loaded, the order matters! Luckily, Lmod provides a tool called **spider** [12] that provides details on all modules in your system with meta-data on each module file.

Spider is used to help build spider cache that is used by HPC sites to keep their modules up to date. The **spider** utility is different from **module spider** while both achieve the purpose of finding all modules in the system, their use-case will differ. Spider provides the complete metadata of all modules in json format which can be retrieved by executing the following:

```
$ spider -o spider-json $MODULEPATH | python -m json.tool
```

The spider utility can be found in the directory defined by the environment variable $LMOD_DIR that is typically defined when installing Lmod as a package (rpm, deb). For Redhat/Centos distribution, if Lmod is installed as a package, then $LMOD_DIR will be set to the following:

```
$ echo $LMOD_DIR
/usr/share/lmod/lmod/libexec
```

Figure 1 represents the spider output for a single record (**gompi**) in Lmod 7, with the key **fullName** in yellow indicates the full canonical name of the module. The top-level key in dictionary is a list of unique software name (i.e. gompi) followed by inner dictionary with full path to module file and metadata for modulefile inside the dictionary.

```
 1        "gompi": {
 2           "/gpfs/apps/easybuild/2019/SkyLake/redhat/7.5/modules/all/gompi/2018b.lua": {
 3              "pV": "000002018.*b.*zfinal",
 4              "Description": "GNU Compiler Collection (GCC) based compiler toolchain,\n including O
 5              "whatis": [
 6                 "Description: GNU Compiler Collection (GCC) based compiler toolchain,\n including
 7                 "Homepage: (none)"
 8              ],
 9              "wV": "000002018.*b.*zfinal",
10              "help": "\nDescription\n===========\nGNU Compiler Collection (GCC) based compiler too
11    e: (none)\n",
12              "parentAA": [
13                 [
14                    "eb/2019"
15                 ]
16              ],
17              "hidden": false,
18              "Version": "2018b",
19              "fullName": "gompi/2018b"
20           }
21        },
```

Fig. 1. Example json record for gompi in Lmod 7 (Color figure online)

Parent modules are modules that alter MODULEPATH to access modules from another module tree, in Fig. 1 the module **eb/2019** exposes a module tree where **gompi/2018b** is found. Recall that order of module load is important, the **parentAA** key provides this information that is used by buildtest to load parent modules before loading the requested module. It's worth mentioning parentAA is a nested list that contains a list of parent combinations where each parent combination is a list of modules to load. If your system has more than one route to reach a module-tree then you are likely to have multiple parent combinations. Figure 2 shows the json record from Lmod 6 for **zlib/.1.2.8** with multiple parent combination.

```
 4        "full": "zlib/.1.2.8",
 5        "full_lower": "zlib/.1.2.8",
 6        "help": "\nDescription\n===========\nzlib is designed to be a free, general-purpose, lega
 7        "markedDefault": false,
 8        "name": "zlib",
 9        "name_lower": "zlib",
10        "parent": [
11           "default:eb/2017:GCC/5.4.0-2.27:OpenMPI/2.0.0",
12           "default:medsci:hpc/eb-2017-core:GCC/5.4.0-2.27:OpenMPI/2.0.0"
13        ],
```

Fig. 2. Multiple parent combination from Lmod 6

There is a slight difference in the data structure in Lmod 6 and 7, for instance key **full** in Lmod 6 is replaced with **fullName** and key **parent** in Lmod 6 is replaced with **parentAA** in Lmod 7. The parent key is a single list whereas parentAA is a nested list. Each parent combination in **parent** key is a string separated by a colon that makes up a list of parent modules to load.

In order to load module **zlib/.1.2.8**, any parent combination will work, for demonstration purposes let's try the first parent combination as shown below:

```
$ module list
No modules loaded
$ module load eb/2017 GCC/5.4.0-2.27 OpenMPI/2.0.0
zlib/.1.2.8
$ module list
Currently Loaded Modules:
  1) eb/2017              7) OpenMPI/2.0.0
  2) GCCcore/.5.4.0       8) OpenBLAS/0.2.19-LAPACK-3.6.0
  3) binutils/.2.27       9) FFTW/3.3.4
  4) GCC/5.4.0-2.27      10) ScaLAPACK/2.0.2-OpenBLAS-0.2.19-
LAPACK-3.6.0
  5) numactl/2.0.11      11) zlib/.1.2.8
  6) hwloc/1.11.3
```

Buildtest will use spider to figure out how to load any module and inject them into test scripts. In Sect. 2.7 we will present how buildtest creates the test scripts from configuration file and how it deals with modules.

2.5 Setup

To get started with buildtest, simply clone the project from github by running:

```
$ git clone git@github.com:HPC-buildtest/buildtest-
framework.git
```

To use buildtest you will need Python 3.6 or higher and Lmod in your system. You will need to install buildtest dependencies by running:

```
$ pip install docs/requirements.txt
```

Upon completion, you will need to initialize the environment and setup auto-complete on buildtest argument by running:

```
$ source sourceme.sh
$ eval "$(register-python-argcomplete buildtest)"
```

sourceme.sh will initialize buildtest by adding buildtest program in your $PATH and set $BUILDTEST_ROOT to root of buildtest repo which will be used for referencing full path to test configuration. buildtest commands are organized into subcommands, so in order to learn more about any command just run:

```
$ buildtest <subcommand> --help
```

Commands for building and running test is controlled by **buildtest build** and **buildtest run**. The process of building and running test is separated so that the execution of test can be run independently from the build process.

The root of buildtest repository contains a configuration file **settings.yml** that is used to configure buildtest. This file is copied to **$HOME/.buildtest/settings.yml** by buildtest if file is not present. The user can modify buildtest configuration through this file, and some options can be overridden by environment variables. The configuration file is shown in Fig. 3 and some of the options will be covered in the paper or refer to the documentation on **Configuring Buildtest** [13].

```
1   # Delete Build Directory before writing tests.  Valid Options: [True, False]
2   BUILDTEST_CLEAN_BUILD: False
3   #
4   # # binary test support. Valid options [True, False]
5   BUILDTEST_BINARY: False
6   #
7   # # Configure shell when running test.
8   # # Valid options:  [bash, csh, sh].
9   # # Default: [sh]
10  BUILDTEST_SHELL: sh
11  #
12  # # Configure whether to force purge modules in test creation. Defaults to "module purge".
13  # # When set to True, it will write "module --force purge" in test script. Useful if your
14  # # site has sticky modules
15  BUILDTEST_MODULE_FORCE_PURGE: False
16  #
17  # # list root of module tree where modules are installed. Specify multiple module tree as a list
18  BUILDTEST_MODULEPATH: []
19  #
20  # # control output of Lmod spider.
21  # # Valid values are
22  # # current: retrieve modules whose abspath is a subdir of directories defined in BUILDTEST_MODULEPATH
23  # # all: retrieve all records
24  BUILDTEST_SPIDER_VIEW: current
25  #
26  # # control how parent modules are retrieved.
27  # # Valid option: first, all
28  BUILDTEST_PARENT_MODULE_SEARCH: first
29  #
30  # # criteria for success threshold when running job.
31  # # Valid Option: [0.0-1.0]
32  BUILDTEST_SUCCESS_THRESHOLD: 1.0
33  #
34  # # directory where buildtest logs will be written.
35  BUILDTEST_LOGDIR: /tmp/$USER/buildtest/logs
36  #
37  # # directory where test scripts will be generated
38  BUILDTEST_TESTDIR: /tmp/$USER/buildtest/tests
39  #
40  # # directory where buildtest will write .run files
41  BUILDTEST_RUN_DIR: /tmp/$USER/buildtest/run
```

Fig. 3. Buildtest configuration file

2.6 Architecture Overview

Figure 4 presents an architecture overview of how test scripts are created in buildtest. The test configuration and source files are stored in github. The buildtest build must specify a test configuration as input to the builder. Buildtest will parse the YAML keys, detect the programming language by checking the source file extension to figure out the compiler. Currently, buildtest supports GNU and Intel compiler and minimal support for MPI limited to OpenMPI and MPICH.

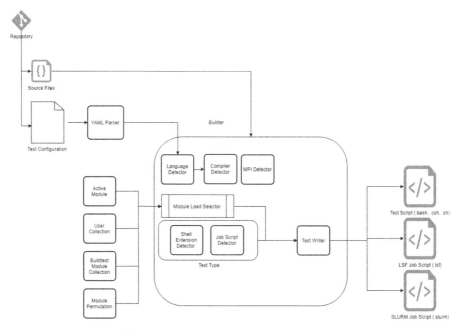

Fig. 4. Buildtest build architecture overview

Currently, buildtest can set module load inside test script by utilizing active modules, user collection, buildtest module collection, and module permutation. For active modules, just load the modules in your user environment before building the test and buildtest will insert the active modules in the test script. Buildtest can operate with user collection and its own module collection system for loading modules in test script. Module Permutation is used when running a test against all versions of a software (e.g. single test against all version of gcc). Section 3 will discuss in further detail on the different module load integration. The Module Load Selector will determine how to load modules from one of the four module load types. By default, buildtest will write test script in one of the shell extension (.bash, .csh, .sh) that can be configured in buildtest configuration file. buildtest will detect if test is a job script which will have a different shell extension. Currently, buildtest supports LSF and SLURM job script which will have the .lsf or .slurm extension.

The test configuration and source files are located under **toolkit** directory found at the root of buildtest repo. The actual location is in a sub-directory **toolkit/buildtest/suite** and tests are categorized by their functionality that is called suite in buildtest. Figure 5 presents the structure of **suite** directory. In this case **suite** refers to compilers, cuda, mpi and openmp. Each suite will be further sub-divided into sub-directory to categorize tests by a name. For instance, mpi suite has two test names **examples** and **matrixmux**. This was done for ease of management for project-maintainers and contributors. If anyone wants to contribute, they need to create a sub-directory in one of the suites and add the test configuration and source files.

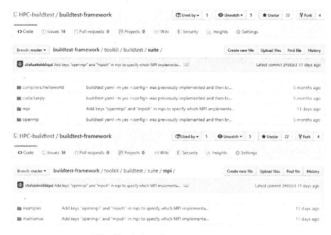

Fig. 5. Suite directory structure

Figure 6 shows the location of test configuration and source files. Test configuration must be named with **.yml** extension and all source code must be placed under **src** directory.

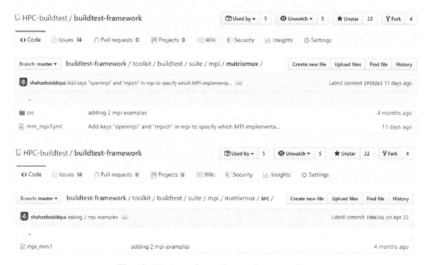

Fig. 6. Test configuration and source files

2.7 Building Test

When building a test, buildtest will detect system details, read the test configuration (YAML), validate the keys, detect the compiler, and finally write a shell script in a unique path. In buildtest this can be done as follows:

```
$ buildtest build -c <test configuration>
```

Let's dive into a simple C++ compilation of hello world using gnu compiler. Shown below is a test configuration in YAML syntax.

```
compiler: gnu
flags: -O3
maintainer:
    - shahzeb siddiqui shahzebmsiddiqui@gmail.com
source: hello.cpp
testblock: singlesource
```

First line **compiler:gnu** is used to indicate buildtest we will use gnu compiler. Note we don't specify which compiler wrapper (gcc, gfortan, g++) since buildtest figures this out based on file extension. Second line **flags: -O3** is compiler flags used to build the source file specified in line 5 **source: hello.cpp**. Each yaml file has a list of maintainers to determine source of author which follows a git commit format (First, Last, email). Last line, **testblock: singlesource** is used in buildtest to support single source compilation, this directs buildtest to invoke the appropriate python class. Depending on the choice for testblock, a set of keys will be available that can be used when writing test configuration. For more details on list of YAML keys refer to the documentation [14].

To build the above test you can run the following command:

```
$ buildtest build -c
$BUILDTEST_ROOT/toolkit/buildtest/suite/compilers/hellowo
rld/hello_gnu.yml
```

During this build, buildtest will do the following:

1. Read the yaml file and check the YAML keys
2. Detect shell extension (sh, bash, csh) and test script will be named as the yml file with the shell extension
3. Detect the compiler wrapper and file extension
4. Issue module purge and add any module command if provided
5. Build the source file and name executable based on source file with **.exe** extension
6. Lastly, buildtest will run the executable and remove it upon completion.

Shown below is the generated test script, in this example **eb/2018** module was loaded in the current session before building test.

```
#!/bin/sh
module purge
module load eb/2018
cd /home/ec2-user/buildtest/suite/compilers/helloworld
g++ -O3 -o hello.cpp.exe /home/ec2-user/buildtest-
frame-
work/toolkit/buildtest/suite/compilers/helloworld/src/hel
lo.cpp
./hello.cpp.exe
rm ./hello.cpp.exe
```

2.8 Building Job Scripts

Buildtest supports a set of keys for LSF and SLURM scheduler. The keys are named with the equivalent option provided by **bsub** and **sbatch** program. Figure 7 highlights how to write an LSF job-script which starts at line 3 in yellow. This test will build using 4 tasks, requesting 200 MB of memory using the sandybridge resource with a 1 h walltime.

```
1       compiler: gnu
2       flags: -O2
3       lsf:
4         M: 200M
5         R: sandybridge
6         W: 01:00
7         n: '4'
8       maintainer:
9       - shahzeb siddiqui shahzebmsiddiqui@gmail.com
10      source: hello.c
11      testblock: singlesource
```

Fig. 7. LSF test configuration example

Buildtest has verbose option (**-v**) to show extra output during the build with up to 2 levels of verbosity. Shown below is the complete build for LSF:

```
$ buildtest build -c
$BUILDTEST_ROOT/toolkit/buildtest/suite/compilers/hellowo
rld/hello_lsf.yml -vv
```

```
compiler: gnu
flags: -O2
lsf:
  M: 200M
  R: sandybridge
  W: 01:00
  n: '4'
maintainer:
- shahzeb siddiqui shahzebmsiddiqui@gmail.com
source: hello.c
testblock: singlesource
```

```
Key Check PASSED for file /home/ec2-user/buildtest-
frame-
work/toolkit/buildtest/suite/compilers/helloworld/hello_l
sf.yml
Source File /home/ec2-user/buildtest-
frame-
work/toolkit/buildtest/suite/compilers/helloworld/src/hel
lo.c exists!
Programming Language Detected: c
LSF Keys Passed
Compiler Check Passed
Writing Test: /tmp/ec2-
us-
er/buildtest/tests/suite/compilers/helloworld/hello_lsf.y
ml.lsf
Changing permission to 755 for test: /tmp/ec2-
us-
er/buildtest/tests/suite/compilers/helloworld/hello_lsf.y
ml.lsf
```

```
#!/bin/sh
#BSUB -M 200M
#BSUB -R sandybridge
#BSUB -W 01:00
#BSUB -n 4
module purge
cd /tmp/ec2-
user/buildtest/tests/suite/compilers/helloworld
gcc -O2 -o hello.c.exe /home/ec2-user/buildtest-
frame-
work/toolkit/buildtest/suite/compilers/helloworld/src/hel
lo.c
./hello.c.exe
 rm ./hello.c.exe
```

Notice the tag **#BSUB** is automatically set from appropriate LSF keys defined in test configuration. The one-one relation between keys and equivalent #BSUB command is easy to remember for those familiar with #BSUB directive. The test script is written with **.lsf** extension to indicate that test should be submitted to batch scheduler. Upon creation, one can use buildtest to send all job scripts to scheduler by utilizing the following:

```
$ buildtest run -j -S <test-suite>
```

For example, we have 3 tests in the **mpi** test suite, two of them are slurm jobs that will be submitted to SLURM scheduler and one test will be run locally. As shown, buildtest will dispatch the jobs (job id: 17, 18) via **sbatch** and let scheduler take care of execution. Buildtest provides a run file (**.run**) extension that contains a summary of the results including test output.

```
$ buildtest run -S mpi -j
Running All Tests from Test Directory: /tmp/ec2-
user/buildtest/tests/suite/mpi
===================================================
                    Test summary
Package:  mpi
Executed 3 tests
Passed Tests: 3 Percentage: 100.0%
Failed Tests: 0 Percentage: 0.0%
SUCCESS: Threshold of 100.0% was achieved
Writing results to /tmp/ec2-
user/buildtest/run/buildtest_15_29_19_08_2019.run
Submitted batch job 17
Submitting Job: /tmp/ec2-
us-
er/buildtest/tests/suite/mpi/examples/mpi_ping.c.slurm.ym
l.slurm to scheduler
Submitted batch job 18
Submitting Job: /tmp/ec2-
us-
er/buildtest/tests/suite/mpi/examples/mpi_ping.c_ex1.yml.
slurm to scheduler
```

3   Module Operations

Buildtest is tightly coupled with Lmod utility called spider that helps buildtest acquire details on modules that will dictate how to load modules inside test scripts. With the help of spider, buildtest can implement some interesting module operations that will benefit HPC sites that manage large software stacks.

The following module operation are available in buildtest

1. Module Load Testing
2. Module Difference between two module trees
3. Reporting Easybuild & Spack Modules
4. Building test with user and module collection
5. Building test with Module Permutation
6. Reporting Unique Software and Modules

3.1 Module Load Test

Any large HPC facility that supports 1000+ modules can affirm that it is extremely difficult for the support team to keep track of all modules and whether they are working properly. One way to test all modules is to run **module load** for every module. This can be a very tedious operation if done manually, luckily buildtest has a feature to automate **module load** testing for the entire stack. To execute module load test in buildtest just run the following:

```
$ buildtest module loadtest
```

Buildtest will make use of MODULEPATH to seek out all module trees when testing modules. In buildtest, this is managed by variable BUILDTEST_MODULEPATH which is a list of module trees separated by colon.

Shown below is a snapshot of **module load** test in buildtest:

```
$ buildtest module loadtest
module load RHEL6-apps
RUN: 1/3 STATUS: PASSED - Testing module: RHEL6-apps
────────────────────────────────────────────────────────────
module load deprecated
RUN: 2/3 STATUS: PASSED - Testing module: deprecated
────────────────────────────────────────────────────────────
module load eb/2018
RUN: 3/3 STATUS: PASSED - Testing module: eb/2018
────────────────────────────────────────────────────────────
Writing Results to /tmp/modules-load.out
Writing Results to /tmp/modules-load.err
────────────────────────────────────────────────────────────

                    Module Load Summary
Module Trees:
['/nfs/grid/software/moduledomains', '/etc/modulefiles',
'/usr/share/modulefiles',
'/usr/share/lmod/lmod/modulefiles/Core']
PASSED:                                3
FAILED:                                0
```

In the above test, a module load command is issued against each module file by retrieving the full module name defined in json data structure discussed in Sect. 2.4. Buildtest will check the exit status of each command, a non-zero will report as FAILED test and zero indicates PASSED. Finally, buildtest will write the results in the filesystem and summarize the total PASSED/FAILED results, including the list of module trees that were tested.

The test above shows modules tested in module trees which is how this system was configured at startup (i.e. /etc/profile.d/) however these modules are parent modules which serve other software stacks. This system may have up to 1000 modules, in order to test all modules and all sub trees you can set the following variable **BUILDTEST_SPIDER_VIEW=all** in configuration file or as an environment variable and run the test as follows:

```
$ BUILDTEST_SPIDER_VIEW=all buildtest module loadtest
```

HPC Support Team will benefit from this feature which automates module load testing for all modules in their cluster. The test can reveal any broken modules in their system and take corrective action to fix the issue. This type of testing is best suited with CI tools like Jenkins that can trigger notification to support team on faulty modules and take proactive actions to fix issues before it reaches production.

3.2 Module Tree Difference for Parallel Software Stack in Heterogeneous Cluster

buildtest can report differences between module trees, this is particularly useful when building architecture specific software stack in a heterogeneous cluster. In this scenario, the support team must check that the software stack is same for all module trees. To report difference between module trees, use the option **–diff-trees** and specify two module trees separated by commas as follows:

```
$ buildtest module --diff-trees <tree1>,<tree2>
```

If there is no difference between two trees, buildtest will not report any modules. Shown below we compare Broadwell and IvyBridge stack installed in shared filesystem in separate paths

```
$ buildtest module --diff-trees
/clust/app/easybuild/2018/Broadwell/redhat/7.3/modules/al
l,/clust/app/easybuild/2018/IvyBridge/redhat/7.3/modules/
all
No difference found between module tree:
/clust/app/easybuild/2018/Broadwell/redhat/7.3/modules/al
l  and module tree:
/clust/app/easybuild/2018/IvyBridge/redhat/7.3/modules/al
l
```

In Fig. 8 we see difference between two module trees that illustrate modules **FOUND/NOT FOUND** in the two module trees. The tabular output is very intuitive in spotting missing modules if you are supporting architecture tree for a heterogeneous cluster. Asymmetries in module trees across multiple architecture will break user work-flows that span across architectures. buildtest will report difference based on full module name retrieved from json data structure via spider.

```
$ buildtest module --diff-trees /clust/app/easybuild/2018/commons/modules/all,/usr/share/lmod/lmod/modulefiles/Core
                    Comparing Module Trees for differences in module files
                    ------------------------------------------------------------
Module Tree 1:  /clust/app/easybuild/2018/commons/modules/all
Module Tree 2:  /usr/share/lmod/lmod/modulefiles/Core
ID       |      Module                                         |   Module Tree 1   |   Module Tree 2
---------|--------------------------------------------------|-------------------|--------------------
1        |    lmod/6.5.1                                       |   NOT FOUND       |   FOUND
2        |    EasyBuild/3.6.0                                  |   FOUND           |   NOT FOUND
3        |    Java/1.8.0_152                                   |   FOUND           |   NOT FOUND
4        |    CUDA/9.1.85                                      |   FOUND           |   NOT FOUND
5        |    settarg/6.5.1                                    |   NOT FOUND       |   FOUND
6        |    Anaconda3/5.1.0                                  |   FOUND           |   NOT FOUND
7        |    IGV/2.3.98-Java-1.8.0_152                        |   FOUND           |   NOT FOUND
8        |    git-lfs/2.4.0                                    |   FOUND           |   NOT FOUND
9        |    CUDA/7.5.18                                      |   FOUND           |   NOT FOUND
10       |    CUDA/8.0.61                                      |   FOUND           |   NOT FOUND
11       |    cuDNN/7.1-CUDA-9.1.85                            |   FOUND           |   NOT FOUND
12       |    EasyBuild/3.5.3                                  |   FOUND           |   NOT FOUND
13       |    Anaconda2/5.1.0                                  |   FOUND           |   NOT FOUND
```

Fig. 8. Module difference between two module trees

3.3 Reporting Easybuild and Spack Modules

Easybuild and Spack will write module files as part of the software build. If your site utilizes these tools, then buildtest can report easybuild and spack modules. This can be useful to differentiate which modules are autogenerated as opposed to those that were written manually or sites that support both Easybuild and Spack modules will want to distinguish modules between the two build tools. Every easybuild module will contain a text in module file as follows:

```
Built with Easybuild version 3.7.1
```

The version number may differ in your modulefile depending on the version of easybuild-framework you are using at the time of building the software. To find easy-build modules use the command **buildtest module –easybuild**. Buildtest will find the substring in all module files in all module trees. Shown below is a snapshot of all easybuild modules detected in the system.

```
Module:
/clust/app/easybuild/2018/Broadwell/redhat/7.3/modules/al
l/zlib/1.2.11-GCCcore-6.4.0.lua is built with Easybuild
Total Easybuild Modules: 404
Total Modules Searched: 824
```

Similarly, every spack module will have a string to denote the module via spack along with a timestamp.

```
Module file created by spack
(https://github.com/spack/spack) on 2019-04-11
11:38:31.191604
```

buildtest module –spack can be used to retrieve spack modules and if one wants to retrieve all records from spider you can set **BUILDTEST_SPIDER_VIEW=all**. The default value of BUILDTEST_SPIDER_VIEW is **current** which means it will search for modules found in sub-directories defined by BUILDTEST_MODULEPATH which is a subset of records from the spider output. Shown below is a retrieval of all spack modules in the system

```
$ BUILDTEST_SPIDER_VIEW=all buildtest module --spack
Module:
/nfs/grid/software/RHEL7/medsci/modules/all/ffmpeg/3.2.4-
n6ulc43.lua is built with Spack
Total Spack Modules: 1
Total Modules Searched: 824
```

3.4   User Collections and Buildtest Module Collections

User collections [15] is a Lmod feature to allow users to reference a set of modules by a collection name. This feature is commonly used to load a set of modules with a single collection name. Lmod provides a several commands for managing user collections including **module save, module restore,** and **module describe**.

To save a user collection, just load the modules of interest and run **module save <collection name>**. User collections are stored in $HOME/.lmod.d/<collection> and they can be retrieved by running **module -t savelist.** Shown below is an example of 2 user collections.

```
$ module -t savelist
default
intelmpi
```

To restore a collection, run **module restore <collection name>,** in buildtest this can be used in test script to build a test with any user collection. This method is effective when dealing with lots of modules to run a workflow. In buildtest this can be done by using **buildtest build –collection <collection-name>** or short option **-co**. To demonstrate we will build a test with intelmpi collection by running:

```
$ buildtest build -c
$BUILDTEST_ROOT/toolkit/buildtest/suite/compilers/hellowo
rld/hello_intel_fortran.yml -co intelmpi
```

The generated test is as follows:

```
#!/bin/sh
module restore intelmpi
cd /tmp/ec2-
user/buildtest/tests/suite/compilers/helloworld
ifort -O3 -o hello.f90.exe /home/ec2-user/buildtest-
frame-
work/toolkit/buildtest/suite/compilers/helloworld/src/hel
lo.f90
./hello.f90.exe
rm ./hello.f90.exe
```

If you take note, the second line **module restore intelmpi** is inserted in test script. Buildtest will rely on Lmod to restore the module collection assuming the collection can be restored properly.

User collections are commonly used in running complex workflow that require many software modules to be loaded in the user environment. Collection names must be unique which can pose a challenge when managing dozens of user collections. Users must be creative in naming their collections to avoid name conflict. Buildtest supports managing user collections without relying on Lmod collection by tracking module collection in a json file: **$BUILDTEST_ROOT/vars/default.json**

To utilize buildtest module collection, buildtest provides options to add, remove, list, and update collection via **buildtest module collection** subcommand. First, we start out by loading a set of modules via module load. For example, we have **eb/2018** and **CUDA/9.1.85** modules actively loaded.

```
$ module list
Currently Loaded Modules:
  1) eb/2018   2) CUDA/9.1.85
```

Next, we add the modules to buildtest collection via **buildtest module collection -a**, this will add the modules into a collection stored in json file.

```
$ buildtest module collection -a
{
    "collection": [
        [
            "eb/2018",
            "CUDA/9.1.85"
        ]
    ]
}
Updating collection file: /home/ec2-user/buildtest-
framework/var/default.json
```

Instead of viewing the json file, buildtest provides an option to view module collection via **buildtest module collection -l**

```
$ buildtest module collection -l
0: ['eb/2018', 'CUDA/9.1.85']
```

Whenever a module collection is added, the index number is incremented by 1 starting with index 0. Shown below, we have three module collections that are represented by an index number followed by a list of modules.

```
$ buildtest module collection -l
0: ['eb/2018', 'CUDA/9.1.85']
1: ['eb/2018', 'GCCcore/6.4.0', 'binutils/2.28-GCCcore-
6.4.0', 'GCC/6.4.0-2.28']
2: ['eb/2017', 'icc/.2017.1.132-GCC-5.4.0-2.27',
'GCCcore/.5.4.0', 'binutils/.2.27', 'ifort/.2017.1.132-
GCC-5.4.0-2.27', 'impi/2017.1.132', 'imkl/2017.1.132',
'intel/2017.01']
```

Buildtest makes use of module collection index to load the appropriate collection name which can be done by **-mc <index>** or long option **--module-collection.** Let's build a test using index 2 from module collection by running:

```
$ buildtest build -mc 2 -c
$BUILDTEST_ROOT/toolkit/buildtest/suite/compilers/hellowo
rld/hello_intel_fortran.yml
```

Shown below is the generated test script

```
#!/bin/sh
module load eb/2017 icc/.2017.1.132-GCC-5.4.0-2.27
GCCcore/.5.4.0 binutils/.2.27 ifort/.2017.1.132-GCC-
5.4.0-2.27 impi/2017.1.132 imkl/2017.1.132 intel/2017.01
cd /tmp/ec2-user/buildtest/suite/compilers/helloworld
ifort -O3 -o hello.f90.exe /home/ec2-user/buildtest-
frame-
work/toolkit/buildtest/suite/compilers/helloworld/src/hel
lo.f90
./hello.f90.exe
rm ./hello.f90.exe
```

In the above test, buildtest will read default.json and insert the modules from index 2 into the test script. Buildtest supports user collection from Lmod and buildtest module collection to pick modules when building test. User collections are written in $HOME/.lmod.d which means if data is accidently deleted, it will result in error when running **module restore**, this is not the case when using buildtest module collection.

3.5 Module Permutation

So far, we have shown how buildtest can generate test with loading modules via user collections, buildtest module collection, or active modules before building the test script.

Once a test is working with a version, it makes sense to build test against all versions of the same software to validate all versions.

Imagine, you have multiple versions of intel compiler and you want to test compilation of a program against all intel versions. Buildtest keeps record of modules in a modified json structure due to difference between Lmod 6 and 7 in a file named: **$BUILDTEST_ROOT/vars/modules.json**

Currently, buildtest stores full name and parent modules for each module, which was done since key names changed in Lmod version 6 and 7 and there is no guarantee these keys will be retained for future release. To build a test with module permutation, use the **–modules** option as shown below:

```
$ buildtest build -c <configuration> --modules <software>
```

In module permutation, one test script is written per module version, so for instance a system with 2 intel modules as shown below, will have 2 test scripts generated during module permutation. In example below, we retrieve all intel modules and their corresponding versions using the **module spider** command

```
$ module -t spider intel
intel/2018.3
intel/2018b
```

For purpose of demonstration we will show a snapshot of module permutation of intel modules with a test configuration.

```
$ buildtest build --modules intel -c
$BUILDTEST_ROOT/toolkit/buildtest/suite/compilers/hellowo
rld/hello_intel_fortran.yml
Each test will be built with 2 module permutations
Module Permutation List
                                                   _____

module load medsci/.2019.1 intel/2018.3
module load eb/2019 intel/2018b
Writing Test:
/tmp/siddis14/buildtest/tests/suite/compilers/helloworld/
hel-
lo_intel_fortran.yml_0xb689c79defc3132c21d272ef2f9081d.sh
Writing Test:
/tmp/siddis14/buildtest/tests/suite/compilers/helloworld/
hel-
lo_intel_fortran.yml_0xd908367ea8d8207d89949e7c504786c1.s
h
Writing 2 tests for /gpfs/home/siddis14/buildtest-
frame-
work/toolkit/buildtest/suite/compilers/helloworld/hello_i
ntel_fortran.yml
```

Buildtest will utilize a 128bit random number when generating test script to avoid name conflict. Also note that a single test script is generated per intel module and the parent modules are loaded first. By default, buildtest will use the first parent combination when loading modules, however buildtest can permute with all parent modules if the following is set:

```
BUILDTEST_PARENT_MODULE_SEARCH=all
```

This will create a permutation of a single module with all parent combinations.

3.6   Report Unique Software and Modules

An end-user or HPC support team would want to know details of all installed software in the cluster and breakdown of software by versions and path to all module files. This information can be useful for documentation purposes typically maintained by the HPC support team that can assist users in knowing the complete software ecosystem. Recall, the spider command from Lmod has access to all module information that was shown in Fig. 1. The output of spider is very extensive that is not suited well when invoked in a console. Buildtest will process the details from spider and present the output in a tabular format that is human readable. To retrieve a unique list of software run the following:

```
$ buildtest list --software
```

Buildtest will retrieve the top-level key from spider that is the software name whose modulefile is found in module trees defined by BUILDTEST_MODULEPATH. Figure 9 shows a list of unique software modules alphabetically sorted with a total count of software packages

Fig. 9. List unique software names

To get a complete list of all unique software, buildtest needs to retrieve all records from spider which can be tweaked by setting **BUILDTEST_SPIDER_VIEW=all**. By default, it is set to **current** and retrieves modules that are found in sub-directories defined in BUILDTEST_MODULEPATH.

Buildtest can retrieve full module name and module file path which can be used to see a snapshot of all module versions. This can be fetched by running:

```
$ buildtest list --modules
```

Figure 10 reports a list of modules, versions and full path and it will color code Lua modules and count all Lua and non-Lua modules. The output is alphabetically sorted by full name of module that is convenient when spotting multiple versions and path to module file.

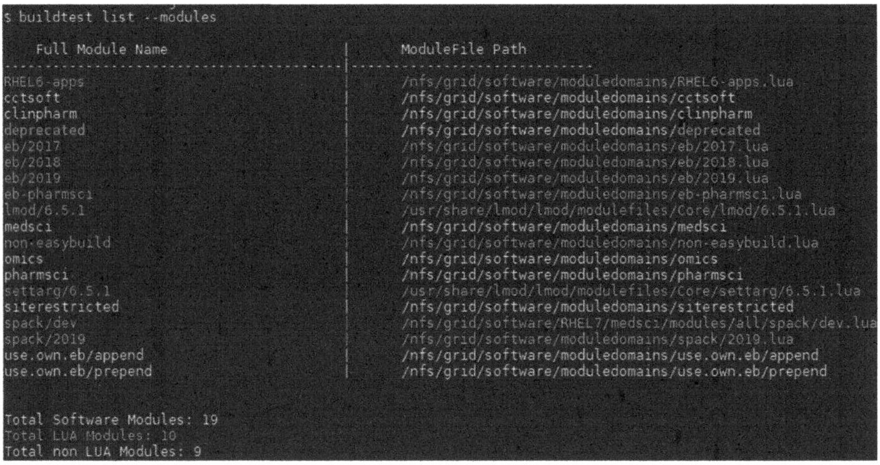

Fig. 10. Listing full module name with path to modulefile

4 Future Work

In this paper, we only showcased single source compilation and scheduler examples, however support for building MPI is in active development [23] and it currently supports OpenMPI, and MPICH. Buildtest will need to detect MPI flavor through configuration file and map it to the correct MPI launcher. In IntelMPI, **mpiexec.hydra** is the MPI launcher but if you are using SLURM then it is recommended to use **srun** but you may use **mpirun** or **mpiexec.hydra** though not recommended [16]. MVAPICH2 and MPICH2 use mpiexec.hydra while OpenMPI uses mpirun, but if you have LSF then **blaunch** is responsible for launching MPI tasks [17]. This can get complicated when supporting multiple MPI implementation with different schedulers. Furthermore, each mpi runtime launcher has slightly different options so test configuration will need to be explicit in the runtime launcher (orterun, mpiexec.hydra, mpirun, srun, blaunch) when launching MPI jobs.

Buildtest already retrieves scheduler information like queue names, node names, and application profiles (LSF) for only reporting purposes. Buildtest can utilize the scheduler information for tweaking job scripts on the fly with different run parameters. Since scheduler configuration is site specific, buildtest will need to expose these options on the command-line as part of the build phase to control how job scripts are built.

Currently, buildtest supports compilation of single source programs with a limited set of YAML keys to compile serial code, multi-threaded, and MPI code. This method can be extended to add additional testblock for other types of compilation such as CUDA, Python, R, etc. Currently, buildtest supports OSU microbenchmark [24], in future we can extend support for other benchmarks like STREAM, HPCG, and HPL.

Community feedback is important in best managing a test repository for buildtest, several ideas are discussed in the wiki article [18] including categorizing test by application, components, and archiving tests. Buildtest will need a better handle on what types of test are accepted in main repository, because a huge influx of contributions can dilute the purpose of tests and cause overhead for project maintainers. A few ideas are discussed such as voting on test using Like/Dislike, test satisfaction score, and a test limit count on the repository. Other topics are discussed in wiki including how to deal with tests for unpopular or obscure software, whether to introduce vendor tests that may conflict license agreement and adding a list of maintainers for every test.

5 Related Work

A few tools have emerged in the field of software testing for HPC software stack including Automatic Testing of Installed Software (ATIS) [19], **HPC SoftWare TEST**ing Framework (hpcswtest) [20] and ReFrame [21, 22]. ATIS is focused on sanity test for mpi wrappers where tests were executed using ctest and visualized in CDASH. There has been no activity on this project since 2014 and the main author has deprecated the project. hpcswtest was developed by Idaho National Lab (INL) Scientific Computing Department to test sanity check of HPC software stack. The program is written in C++11 with some scripts in python2. A json configuration file hpcswtest.json is used for configuring the project with system details including scheduler configuration and list of modules that are site-specific. Due to limited documentation and no active contribution since March 2018, this project has ceased development.

ReFrame is regression framework implemented in Python that focuses on sanity and performance check of applications. ReFrame is developed by Swiss National Supercomputing Center (CSCS) and has been in production since 2016 to test Piz Daint system. Unlike buildtest, ReFrame makes use of Python class when writing test, which adds a learning curve for users to contribute to ReFrame. ReFrame has a considerable test collection that test numerical libraries, GPUs, microbenchmarks (osu, stream, hpcg, dgemm). In ReFrame, module names are specified in python test class, and tests are subject to break due to module load error if module names are changed over time or module configuration leads to a different module load order. Buildtest will face same issue, however this problem can be fixed by rebuilding the test because buildtest relies on **spider** and is the source of truth for module load. Reframe has a large collection (300+) of tests for Piz-Daint system unlike buildtest that supports up to 30+ tests that is partly due to lack of community contribution. Reframe supports sanity checking for numerical results against reference output which is not present in buildtest. Both, buildtest and Reframe have support with workload manager, buildtest supports LSF and SLURM while Reframe supports SLURM and PBS/Torque.

Buildtest has a robust module integration that allows for greater flexibility when testing software. Furthermore, buildtest provides many software stack utilities and a few module operations that are useful for HPC support team in managing their software stacks. Currently, ReFrame does not support the software stack operations and module integration with spider that buildtest provides.

6 Conclusion

Scientific software is evolving at a rapid pace with new tools being installed in HPC systems. HPC Software Stack consist upwards of 1000+ software modules with new versions requested by end users every day. The HPC sites must collaborate closely and actively contribute to build a collection of tests that will benefit the HPC community and software providers. Some tools have emerged in the open-source community in HPC Software Testing that requires active contributors in the open-source community to sustain these projects including buildtest.

In this paper, we present buildtest, a tool that automates test creation by utilizing YAML style test configuration. Buildtest comes with a repository of tests (test configuration, source files) that can be used as a basis for building a test suite for every software that is installed in HPC cluster. Buildtest is tightly integrated with Lmod **spider** utility which provides some interesting features like reporting unique software and modules, module load testing, difference between module trees, building tests with users & module collection and module permutation.

In order to sustain an open-source project like buildtest, we need an active community that contributes to this project. This can be achieved by targeting the community that support open-source tools like Lmod, Easybuild, and Spack.

References

1. Furlani, J.L.: Modules: providing a flexible user environment. In: Proceedings of the Fifth Large Installation Systems Administration Conference (LISA V), pp. 141–152 (1991)
2. Furlani, J.L., Osel, P.W.: Abstract yourself with modules. In: Proceeding of the Tenth Large Installation System Administration (LISA 1996), pp. 193–204 (1996)
3. Geimer, M., Hoste, K., McLay, R.: Modern scientific software management using EasyBuild and Lmod. In: 2014 First International Workshop on HPC User Support Tools (2014). https://doi.org/10.1109/hust.2014.8
4. Hoste, K., Timmerman, J., Georges, A., Weirdt, S.D.: EasyBuild: building software with ease. In: 2012 SC Companion: High Performance Computing, Networking Storage and Analysis (2012). https://doi.org/10.1109/sc.companion.2012.81
5. Gamblin, T., et al.: The Spack package manager. In: Proceedings of the International Conference for High Performance Computing, Networking, Storage and Analysis - SC 2015 (2015). https://doi.org/10.1145/2807591.2807623

6. List of build automation software. https://en.wikipedia.org/wiki/List_of_build_automation_software

7. GNU make. https://www.gnu.org/software/make/manual/make.html

8. CMake Documentation. https://cmake.org/documentation/

9. Autoconf. https://www.gnu.org/software/autoconf/

10. Buildtest. https://github.com/HPC-buildtest/buildtest-framework

11. Buildtest Documentation. https://buildtest.readthedocs.io/en/latest/

12. The spider tool. https://lmod.readthedocs.io/en/latest/136_spider.html

13. Configuring buildtest. https://buildtest.readthedocs.io/en/latest/configuring_buildtest.html

14. Show Keys. https://buildtest.readthedocs.io/en/latest/introspection.html#show-keys

15. User Collections. https://lmod.readthedocs.io/en/latest/010_user.html#user-collections

16. MPI and UPC User Guide. https://slurm.schedmd.com/mpi_guide.html#intel_mpi

17. Best Practices Using MPI under IBM Platform LSF. https://www.ibm.com/developerworks/community/wikis/form/anonymous/api/wiki/99245193-fced-40e5-90df-a0e9f50a0fb0/page/359ab0d9-7849-4c6a-8cb8-7a62050b5222/attachment/5c2eb892-b60e-4601-8548-2e836818c0a5/media/Platform_BPG_LSF_MPI_v2.pdf

18. Buildtest, Managing a Test Repository. https://github.com/HPC-buildtest/buildtest-framework/wiki/Managing-a-Test-Repository

19. Besseron, X.: Automatic Testing of Installed Software. FOSDEM 2014. https://archive.fosdem.org/2014/schedule/event/hpc_devroom_automatic_testing/

20. Idaho National Laboratory: hpcswtest. https://github.com/idaholab/hpcswtest

21. Swiss National Supercomputing Center (CSCS): ReFrame. https://github.com/eth-cscs/reframe

22. ReFrame Documentation. https://reframe-hpc.readthedocs.io/en/stable/

23. Build Examples. https://buildtest.readthedocs.io/en/devel/build_subcommand/build_examples.html

24. OSU Microbenchmark. https://buildtest.readthedocs.io/en/devel/benchmark_subcommand/osu.html

25. YAML. https://yaml.org/

Using Malleable Task Scheduling to Accelerate Package Manager Installations

Samuel Knight[1]([✉]), Jeremiah Wilke[1], and Todd Gamblin[2]

[1] Sandia National Laboratories, Livermore, CA 94550, USA
{sknight,jjwilke}@sandia.gov
[2] Lawrence Livermore National Lab, Livermore, CA 94550, USA
gamblin2@llnl.gov

Abstract. Package managers, containers, automated testing, and Continuous Integration (CI), are becoming an essential part of HPC development workflows. These automated tools often require software recompilation. However, large stacks such as those deployed on HPC clusters can have combinatorial dependencies, and may take a system several days to compile. Despite the use of simple parallelization (such as 'make -j'), build execution time often do not scale with system resources. For such cases, it is possible to improve overall installation time by compiling parts of software stack independently, each scheduled on a subset of available cores. We apply malleable-task scheduling algorithms to better exploit available parallelism in build system workflows and improve stack build time overall. Using a prototype implementation in the Spack package manager, malleable-task scheduling can improve build times by more than 2x.

1 Introduction

Scientific applications require unique software stacks that run in specialized hardware environments. Historically, scientists installed this software manually: an error-prone and difficult to reproduce process. Common issues including incompatible dependencies and source code regressions require the installer to become familiar with each part of the software stack and complete the installation over many iterations which can take days or even weeks.

Scientists have strict software requirements for deploying their codes on HPC systems in order to support specialized hardware, and application needs. Common package managers, including pip, YUM, ZYpper, and APT distribute most or all of their packages as pre-built binary files onto system paths. Distributing binaries is greatly advantageous in terms of installation speed but at the cost of a configurable software stack, which often requires codes to be manually compiled in deployment. Using root paths is also not conducive to a shared

Under the terms of Contract DE-NA0003525, there is a non-exclusive license for use of this work by or on behalf of the U.S. Government.

G. Juckeland and S. Chandrasekaran (Eds.): HUST 2019/SE-HER 2019/WIHPC 2019,
CCIS 1190, pp. 28–48, 2020.
https://doi.org/10.1007/978-3-030-44728-1_2

multi-tenant system like an HPC because users do not usually have access to elevated privileges and the use of root paths would not allow for multiple different software stacks. The Spack package manager [6] has recently become a popular tool among HPC users for automating software installation. It supports a rich specification syntax to define aspects of the software stack's dependencies features, then compiles and installs it from source in a local directory.

Spack generates a dependency graph from a specification provided from the command line or in a YAML file, then iteratively builds each dependency. Thus, installation times grow as software stacks increase in complexity. Stacks that include multiple versions of a foundational dependency, such as compilers or communication libraries, may see their build times multiply. On the scale of hundreds of packages, stacks can take tens of hours to install. These build times can cause severe bottlenecks for workflows, such as continuous integration or building containers. Despite the installation time, Sect. 2.1 observes many individual build systems poorly utilize the resources available on modern nodes. This key insight suggests there are cases where the total installation time of a software stack can be reduced.

Prior research into graph scheduling has produced algorithms for scheduling *malleable tasks*, which are granular units of work whose execution times can be reduced with the addition of processor cores. Malleable tasks are a good analog for build systems, and this class of graph scheduling algorithm will serve as a foundation for the scheduler improvements in the Spack package manager. This paper will demonstrate through theory and application, how a package manager can use build history to greatly improve software stack installation time.

2 Build Systems

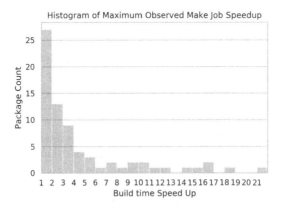

Fig. 1. Maximum observed package build time speedup for xSDK dependencies on a 28-core node.

2.1   Build Systems and Spack Package Manager

HPC codes commonly are written in compiled languages, primarily C/C++ and Fortran. These languages use build systems which consist of several layers of tools, the most foundational of which is the compiler toolchain. The majority of projects use Autotools or CMake (Fig. 2) to automate sanity checking, dependency discovery, and Makefile generation. This practice creates a pipelined build system consisting of a configuration, build, then installation step. Thus build systems are not monolithic executions, but several pipelined phases.

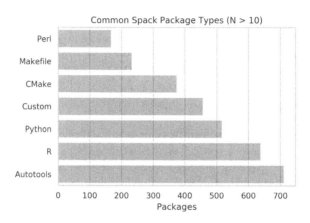

Fig. 2. Package types identified by base-class. A package is identified as *Custom* if it uses the most generic base class.

Spack is a Python-based package manager, specifically designed for HPC environments [8]. A Spack package consists of a directory with a Python script named *package.py*. The Python script contains a derived class with information about the package, such as known versions, build variants, patches, conflicts, and dependencies defined in its scope. The class may inherit one of several base classes that represent common build systems, which simplifies package writing and maintenance by encouraging code reuse. The package class logically divides separate parts of the installation into different functions called *phases*. For example, a package derived from the *CMakePackage* class will include the phases *cmake* (configure), *build*, and *install*.

A *Spec* is a representation of installation constraints. Specs fed to Spack through the command line are abstract, meaning its dependency tree is only partially resolved. At installation time, Spack will resolve an abstract spec's dependencies and variants in a process called *concretization*. The concretized spec is represented as a *Directed Acyclic Graph* (DAG). Spack then installs each package in a depth-first traversal of the DAG, which ensures each package is installed after their respective dependencies. When possible, Spack will instruct the build system to spread compilation across all of the available cores (i.e. 'make -j' within a package).

3   Parallel Builds and Task Scheduling

3.1   Theory

Each build system has a sequence of phases - usually configure, build, and install. Some phases will be able to improve execution time by distributing work across multiple cores. Even when Makefile build systems try to improve installation time by executing independent steps on multiple cores, build systems often do not tend to scale well across multicore nodes. Build systems include slow serial configuration steps. Even when parallelism is available in the build phase, the build system is not always able to efficiently spread tasks from the parallel build tree across the available cores. Most package managers install dependencies sequentially with each package receiving all of the available cores. However, this does not efficiently utilize resources. Figure 1 shows the maximum observed speedup of xSDK [3,5] dependencies. 55% of the packages are not able to exceed even a 3x speedup with 28 cores while only a few are able to exceed a 10x speedup.

While good speedups are often obtained on a few cores, the speedup quickly levels off quickly and additional cores make little difference. For example, GNU GMP (Fig. 3) initially scaled well, but could not exceed a speedup of 12x on a 32 core system. Thus build systems follow an Amdahl's law of diminishing returns as more cores are used to parallelize a workload. A potentially more efficient strategy than assigning all cores to a single package would be to partition cores between independent packages in the stack.

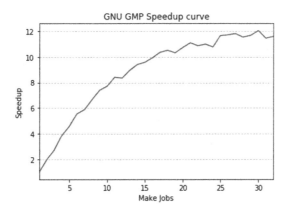

Fig. 3. Speedup curve for installation GMP demonstrates a plateau as more cores are added.

Rather than using a basic sequential schedule, we therefore want to derive a task parallel schedule based on the package dependency graph (DAG). For a directed graph $G = <V,E>$ where V is a set of weighted vertices (hereafter called tasks) and E a set of connecting edges, there is some *critical path* from an

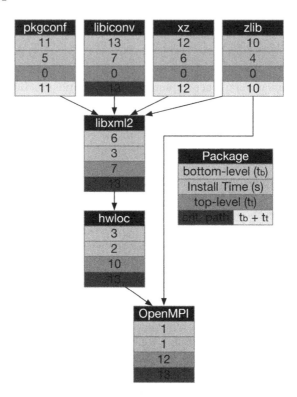

Fig. 4. Package DAG representation of OpenMPI with simplified times. Includes key metrics t_t, t_b, and an indicator of critical path. Arrows indicate direction of execution.

entry task to a leaf task where the combined weights of the vertices and edges are maximized. Since the critical path is the longest chain of tasks by weight, it defines a lower bound for the execution time of a given DAG. A critical path for an example DAG is shown in Fig. 4.

A scheduling algorithm must minimize total graph execution time, or *makespan*, by scheduling tasks along the critical path as soon as possible, and by (depending on the model) increasing resources that can improve task execution time, such as allocating more cores or faster processors. Many task scheduling algorithms assume a single core per task or fixed compute time per task, meaning the critical path length is fixed [12]. Alternatively, schedulers can execute using a variable core allotment, reducing the critical path length by assigning more cores. These tasks are denoted *malleable, moldable, multitask,* or *M-task* in the literature (Table 1).

Table 1. List of symbols.

Symbol	Definition
T	Set of all tasks
t_i	ith task in set of all tasks
$t_i(p_i)$	Execution time of ith task with p processors
p_i	No. processors allotted to ith task
w_i	ith Task work area $(t_i(p) \times p)$
t_s	Start time of ith task
t_f	Finish time of ith task
t_{ser}	Serial proportion of task execution
t_{sc}	Whether a task is scalable
t_t	Task top-level
t_b	Task bottom-level
V	Set of vertices
E	Set of edges
P	Set of processors
W	Precedence levels

3.2 Prior Work

Creating an optimal schedule that minimizes execution time of an arbitrary task graph has been demonstrated NP-hard in most cases [7], and much of the research into the topic propose tractable algorithms or heuristics tailored to constrained scenarios.

Optimal Task Schedulers. Early scheduling algorithms often define tasks as fixed-time single process executions. Optimal polynomial time algorithms have been demonstrated for three cases [12]: unit-weight tasks in free trees [10], an arbitrary DAG on two processors [4, 16], and interval ordered DAGs with unit-weight tasks [9]. None of these algorithms account for weighted edges, which would represent the communication cost between tasks.

Multicore Task and Data Aware Schedulers. As computing networks grew larger and shared-memory regions began hosting multiple processor cores, proposed algorithms began to include schedulers that account for communication cost, locality, and spreading single tasks across multiple cores. Two Step Allocation and Scheduling (TSAS) [15] and Two Level scheduling (TwoL) attempt to schedule task graphs while taking into account task and data communication cost. *Critical Path Reduction* (CPR) [14] prioritizes scheduling for tasks along the critical path by greedily selecting improved schedules with single core allotment changes. CPR was demonstrated to produce superior schedules, but has a higher time complexity than the other two-step allocation methods by $O(V)$. The same authors proposed *Critical Path and Allocation* (CPA), a two-step scheduler that iteratively allocates cores to tasks along the critical path in order of greatest reduction of computational area until the critical path reaches average global computational area, then creates a schedule once in the final step [13]. CPA has a significantly lower time complexity than the other two-step schedulers, at the price of a larger makespan. *Modified CPA (MCPA)* was proposed as an improvement to CPA that uses the same area reduction strategy, while also reducing processor allotment to task-parallel regions of the DAG with a precedence tracking step [2]. MCPA's schedule creation time is similar to CPA, but produces schedules that are often comparable to CPR when the graph is balanced.

Several proposed algorithms tend to create better schedules than CPR, but have a higher time complexity. IAES was a similar iterative allotment procedure to CPR, but also tried to remove holes by shrinking tasks when a schedule fails to improve [11]. Tests showed IAES tended to produce superior schedules with unbalanced DAGs. LoC-MPS proposed by Vydyanathan et al. [17] deployed several novel strategies, such as back filling to remove schedule holes, and testing concurrency ratio to prevent processor allotment changes from being too greedy.

4   Scheduling Algorithm

4.1   Task Execution Time Heuristic

The scheduling algorithm must anticipate how a change in the number of cores allotted to a task affects its execution time. The execution time will either scale (usually with the assistance of a parallel Makefile), or run in fixed time despite the addition of more cores. No matter how well a build system scales, there will be a lower bound to the task's execution time determined by the longest segment of serial execution according to Amdahl's law [1]. Build times should not increase with additional cores, unlike some scheduling models that include intra-task communication and could increase in execution time. To simplify the hard problem of finding near-optimal schedules, we select approximations appropriate for build systems and package managers. We assume individual build systems do not cross memory boundaries onto multiple nodes.

Using Amdahl's law, we can create a simple model of a scalable task's execution time,

$$t(p) = ((1 - t_{ser})/p + t_{ser})t(1)$$

where t_{ser} is the serially executed proportion of the task. Since $t(1)$ and t_{ser} are task-intrinsic constants, $t(p)$ can be condensed into a first degree asymptotic polynomial function,

$$t(p) = k_A/p + k_B$$

Constants k_A and k_B are calibrated by timing task's execution time with different core allotments and using linear least-squares to fit the function to the samples.

While a polynomial approximation can be made fit to any set of measurements with aggressive enough parameters, it can cause unexpected predictions when extrapolating past the boundaries of the dataset. In this application, the risk is diminished because the lower bound cannot decrease below 1 core, and the upper bound converges asymptotically to k_B. A fitted curve heuristic provides two benefits over using raw measurements. First, the fitted curve can be accurately interpolated, which allows for sparse sampling. Second, a fitted curve prevents measurement jitter from violating the assumption that build times cannot increase as the number of cores increase. Violating this assumption can trap schedulers in local minimums, degrading schedule quality (Table 2).

Table 2. Summary of algorithms described in Sect. 4.

Algorithm/Complexity	Description
CPR (Critical Path Reduction) $O(EV^2P + V^3P(logV + PlogP))$	Greedy scheduler that iterates many possibly schedules
F-CPR (Filtered CPR) $O(EV^2P + V^3P(logV + PlogP))$	CPR with minimum improvement threshold ("filter") for pruning search space
CPA (Critical Path and Allocation) $O(V(V + E)P)$	Allots cores on critical path until it reaches average processor area
MCPA (Modified CPA) $O(V(VW + E)P)$	CPA with additional checks for task parallelism amongst independent tasks
MLS (M-task List Scheduling) $O(E + Vlog(V) + VPlogP)$	Basic scheduling algorithm for assigning task start times
R-MLS (Reuse MLS) $O(E + VPlogP)$	MLS with memoization to reduce CPR's time complexity

4.2   CPR and MCPA Implementation

CPR and MCPA reduce the execution time of a schedule by prioritizing the execution of tasks along the critical path. These schedulers measure tasks using two functions: *b-level* (t_b, bottom level) is the longest path by weight from a given task to an exit task including that task's execution time, and *t-level* (t_t, top level) is the longest path from the current task to an entrance task excluding the task's execution time (see Fig. 4). $t_b + t_t$ is maximized for tasks along the critical path. Figure 4 is a simple example that assumes fixed times for each task (build). For the malleable task schedulers we consider here, the t- and b-levels change as cores are assigned or removed.

CPR and MCPA follow a *two step* process. The first step iteratively increases the core allotment to tasks along the critical path using their respective strategies, and the second creates a schedule using a common *M-task list scheduling* (MLS) procedure which determines the start times of each task based on core allotment determined in the first step. The remainder of this section includes descriptions of these algorithms' reference implementations, and proposed modifications to improve their application in this use case. For illustration, we apply these algorithms to an example DAG, a subset of the DAG for Trilinos (Fig. 5). Synthetic (rather than empirical) compute times are used to illustrate the example. Scheduling strategies are compared to a baseline sequential scheduler (Fig. 6) that builds a single package at a time across all cores using 'make -j'.

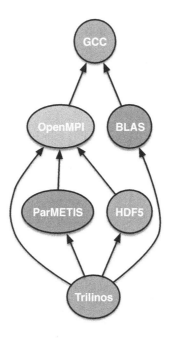

Fig. 5. Task graphs for example installation of Trilinos showing direct software dependencies.

CPR Implementation. CPR (see pseudocode) uses a greedy strategy to create a schedule. The outer loop assembles a list of candidate tasks, and will continue until the inner loop cannot improve the schedule. The inner loop selects the most critical task from the list, adds a core, and checks if the schedule produced by MLS has a smaller makespan. If the makespan does not decrease, the core is removed from that task, and the task is removed from the list of candidates. If the inner loop successfully reduces the makespan or there are no more tasks to try, the inner loop escapes to the outer loop. CPR is a "thorough" algorithm, yielding good results for many different DAGs by iteratively trying many possible schedules at the cost of extra computational complexity. Despite CPR's complexity, it is still a greedy approach which can get trapped in a suboptimal schedule (local minimum).

The publication proposing CPR [14] does not specify how to select between tasks with the same maximized $t_t + t_b$ during the selection step (indicating multiple candidate tasks are along a critical path). This distinction is important, since the ordering affects decisions made by a greedy algorithm. Here we select tasks based on best compute area improvement for tie breaking, selecting the next task based on biggest improvement of execution time when one core is added. CPR was applied to the DAG in Fig. 5 with synthetic timings to produce the schedule in Fig. 6.

```
procedure CPR(Proc count P, set<Task> tasks)
    for all tᵢ ∈ tasks do
        pᵢ ← 1
    end for
    Schedule T ← MLS()
    repeat
        X ← set of tasks where pᵢ < P
        repeat
            t ← t with max t.t_level + t.b_level
            t.nproc ← t.nproc + 1
            Schedule T' ← MLS()
            if Length(T') < Length(T) then
                T ← T'
            else
                t.nproc ← t.nproc - 1
                Remove t from X
            end if
        until T is modified or X is empty
    until T is unmodified
end procedure
```

MCPA Implementation. MCPA (see pseudocode) tries to allot more cores to tasks along the critical path that maximize compute area reduction. Cores are assigned iteratively until the global average compute area is greater than the compute area of the critical path. Average compute area is defined as

$$A_p = \frac{1}{p} \sum_{t_i \in T} w(i, n_i) \times n_i$$

When the critical path length L_{cp} is less than A_p, the average processor is doing *more* work than is on the critical path.

MCPA limits the total cores that can be allocated across each *precedence level*, a cross-sectional slice of independent tasks assigned via a breadth-first traversal. Tasks do not scale perfectly, which means compute area *increases* with more cores as the number of "core-seconds" overall increases, despite a

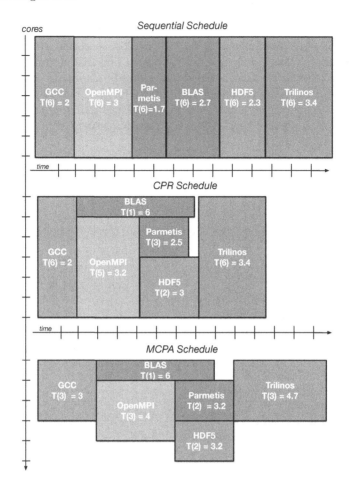

Fig. 6. Comparison of sequential scheduler with malleable-task schedules using CPR and MCPA. Box heights indicate the number of processors used. Box widths indicate the time taken. MCPA fails to allocate cores to GCC and Trilinos, leading CPR to have a shorter schedule makespan. Additional passes (with increased complexity) would correct issues with MCPA. CPR performs much better than sequential schedule, while MCPA has only a minor improvement.

reduction in task execution time. This illustrates a tradeoff between intra-task versus inter-task parallelism. When available, inter-task parallelism generally provides "ideal speedups" across independent tasks, while intra-task parallelism has diminishing returns with additional cores. MLS is only invoked once as a final step, ensuring a much lower time complexity than CPR. Limiting core allocations to precedence levels and only running MLS once improve schedule creation time complexity, but also result in poorer results than CPR Fig. 6. MCPA fails to allocate all possible cores to the tasks, producing a longer makespan than CPR. While in this simple example it is obvious how to improve the MCPA schedule,

procedure MCPA(In: Proc count P, In-Out: set<Task> tasks)
    for all t ∈ tasks **do**
        t.ncores = 1
    end for
    $computeTandBLevels(tasks)$
    while $L_{cp} > A_p$ **do**
        $CP \leftarrow$ set of tasks on current critical path
        $ValidT \leftarrow \varnothing$
        for all t ∈ CP **do**
            if cores available at t's precedence level **then**
                $ValidT \leftarrow t$
            end if
        end for
        $t_{opt} \leftarrow bestWorkArea(ValidT)$
        $t_{opt}.ncores \leftarrow t_{opt}.ncores + 1$
        $computeTandBLevels(tasks)$
    end while
end procedure
procedure BESTWORKAREA(set<Task> tasks)
    $t_{opt} \leftarrow NULL$
    $G_{opt} \leftarrow \inf$
    for all $t_i \in tasks$ **do** find max work area gain G
        $G_i \leftarrow \frac{w_i(n_i)}{n_i} - \frac{w_i(n_i+1)}{n_i+1}$
        if $G_i > G_{opt}$ **then**
            $t_{opt} \leftarrow t_i$
            $G_{opt} \leftarrow G_i$
        end if
    end for
end procedure

adding more available cores to tasks in the general case without introducing new resource (scheduling) dependencies is nontrivial.

MLS Implementation. MLS (see pseudocode) takes a list of tasks with core allotments and assigns start times such that they execute within a limited core constraint and without violating dependency precedence. It iterates through each task in order of highest priority according to a heuristic (this implementation, as well as MCPA's implementation uses maximum t_b). MLS maintains a sorted list of earliest idle times for each processor core and schedules the task to run on the first idle cores. The start time (t_s) and end time (t_f) are determined either by the latest idle time among the selected cores, or by the latest completion time of the task's dependencies,

$$t_s = \max(\max_{d \in t_{dep}}(d_f), \max(p_{idle}))$$
$$t_f = t_s + t(p)$$

This implementation of MLS also includes a step to avoid the creation of idle holes in the schedule selecting cores with later idle times when it does not increase the candidate task's start time.

---

procedure MLS(Proc count P, set<Task> tasks, set<Core> cores)
    tasks ← sort tasks by b-level
    for all $c \in cores$ **do**
        $c.idle\_time \leftarrow 0$
    end for
    for all $t \in tasks$ **do**
        $sortedCores \leftarrow$ sorted cores by idle time
        $selectedCores \leftarrow sortedCores[0:p(t)]$
        $offset \leftarrow 0$
        $t.start\_time \leftarrow$ latest $selectedCores$ or dependency end time
        $t.end\_time \leftarrow t.start\_time + t.exec\_time$
        while $sortedCores[p(t)+ \text{offset} +1] \leq t.start\_time$ **do**
            offset ←offset+1
        end while
        for $i \leftarrow$offset$, p(t)$+offset **do**
            $sortedCores[i] \leftarrow t.end\_time$
        end for
    end for
end procedure

Improving CPR Schedule Creation and Execution Time. CPR's greedy strategy can lead to suboptimal schedules. Tasks which scale poorly with additional cores may trap the assigned cores in a local minima. Evaluating tasks with poor scaling is also costly with CPR's high time complexity. Instead of evaluating every task, the outer loop could filter tasks that don't scale out of the candidate task list with the following heuristic,

$$t_{sc} = \begin{cases} Scalable & \text{if } t_c(n)/t_c(1) < threshold, \\ Unscalable & \text{otherwise} \end{cases}$$

This has the potential to both prune the search space and avoid sub-optimal local minima. Benchmarks in Sect. 6 will use an n of 8 and a *threshold* of 0.8, meaning a task is rejected for evaluation if execution time does not improve at least 20% with 8 cores. As we will see later in results, though, more tuning of this method is required.

Multi-node Schedules. The implemented two-step scheduling algorithms cannot create schedules with tasks that use processors across memory boundaries. However, a trivial change to MLS could allow for scheduling tasks across disjoint sets of processors, which is feasible in this model provided the cluster is provisioned with a network file system so build systems have access to dependencies compiled on other nodes.

After selecting the next task, the MLS reference implementation will try to find a set of processors that will allow for the earliest scheduling. Instead of searching one list of processors, the list scheduler can select cores on each node, and choose the node with the earliest start time. A tie breaker includes a test for which node's allotment creates the smallest idle processor time hole, measured as the sum of the time difference between the selected cores' idle time and the task start time on each node.

5   Methodology

The workflow begins by collecting installation times from a fork of Spack containing the scheduler enhancements (Fig. 7). The fork builds a database that records the spec, phase, number of cores used and execution time. The second step uses the timings database to measure schedule creation times and makespans, and a third step will create a package DAG schedule and install it in a timed live run. The results from the steps 2 and 3 are the basis for the figures and conclusions.

Table 3. Benchmarked software stacks. Each stack consists of a single root package and its dependencies.

Stack	Packages	Phases
Python 2.7.16	14	45
Tk 8.6.8	21	80
Rust 1.33.0	43	149
R 3.5.3	68	248
xSDK 0.4.0	72	222

Table 4. Benchmark node configurations, including processor, memory and hardware used in crucial filesystem mount points.

	Node A	Node B
Hardware cores	32	28
Memory	512 GB	256 GB
Build mount	SATA III SSD	PCIe NVMe
Install mount	SATA III SSD	NFS
OS mount	SATA III SSD	NFS

Scheduler performance was benchmarked on two node configurations (Table 4). Node A resembles a large workstation with a local filesystem. Node B has network filesystem mountpoints that are hosted by a storage appliance, which more closely resembles a cluster node.

The stacks used for benchmarking (Table 3) consist of a single Spack package with its full dependency tree. Using a single package is not a requirement for any of these algorithms however, and a stack in production could consist of an arbitrary number of top level packages. Times are normalized against a sequential installation where each dependency is built one at a time across every available core. Schedules produced by CPR, Filtered CPR (F-CPR), and MCPA were benchmarked to compare their performance.

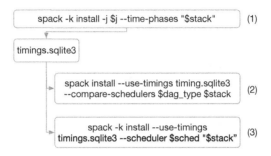

Fig. 7. Steps for timing installations. (1) Generate timings database by profiling installations with multiple core counts. (2) Print makespan and creation time comparisons. (3) Run live installations with each scheduler.

6 Results and Discussion

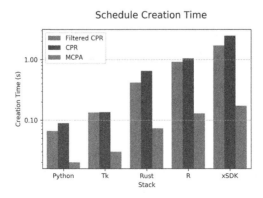

Fig. 8. Schedule creation times for benchmarked package dependency graphs.

Table 5. Schedule creation times compared to execution times for the CPR method on Node B.

Stack	Execution time (s)	CPR creation time (s)
Python	879.21	0.09
Tk	385.46	0.13
Rust	4563.35	0.65
R	1478.01	1.05
xSDK	4293.00	2.49

6.1   Schedule Creation Time

CPR and F-CPR create schedules more slowly than MCPA for every tested stack (Fig. 8). Despite this, every schedule was created quickly enough to run faster than sequential installation (Table 5). F-CPR's schedule creation time improvement was limited since most packages were reasonably scalable and little pruning was done. Despite F-CPR's reduction of inner loop iterations, it must still run MLS many times on an overall larger DAG making it more expensive than MCPA. These creation times come from a Python implementation, and could be reduced by using an optimized Python extension or another language.

6.2   Schedule Execution Time

CPR consistently produces the fastest builds (Fig. 9). In most cases, F-CPR also creates schedules with comparable build execution times. F-CPR generally produces a better schedule than MCPA with the exception of Tk. MCPA generally produces slower builds than CPR; despite this, it consistently out-performs the Simple Parallel execution time. Interestingly, the scaling behavior for Node A and Node B are almost identical, despite installation times on Node B running about 30% slower. This indicates the file system differences did not cause a significant divergence in task execution behavior in this test. Ideally, the times estimated by the heuristic should match the observed build times. For the Node B configuration, the predicted schedule speedups are in excellent agreement with the observed ties (Fig. 9). Rust diverged from the expected speedup by about 10% for CPR and F-CPR on Node A, however.

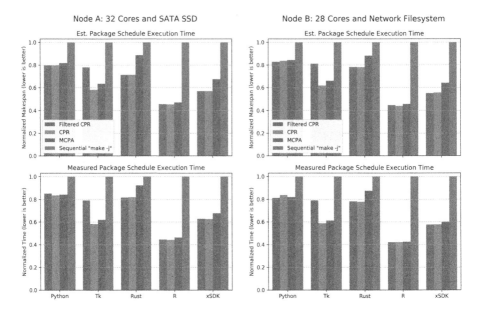

Fig. 9. Estimated schedule execution time using makespan for package-task DAGs, and tested with a live run. Values normalized to execution time of the package's respective sequential execution time.

6.3   Scheduler Choice and DAG Size

For all of the packages considered here, the quality of the CPR schedules produced outweighs the extra time complexity. For a very large graph, CPR's superlinear scaling will eventually make schedule creation time too costly to produce execution time improvements over a sequential installation. However, this threshold may not be possible to pass with the largest single-root-package dependency trees currently available in Spack.

MCPA would become a more practical alternative at the scale of hundreds or thousands of tasks. While F-CPR cannot improve time complexity, it does reduce schedule creation overhead relative to CPR. For DAG sizes where scheduling overhead is reaching the limits of CPR's performance, MCPA and F-CPR can be used together, and the faster of the two schedules is selected.

6.4   Improving Schedule Creation Times

CPR heavily iterates over MLS, changing one task's core allotment each time a schedule is created. This is not an efficient use of MLS, since each new schedule will contain identical placements from the beginning of the task list to the first task where reordering has occurred. An improved Reuse MLS (R-MLS) algorithm tabulates its task placement decisions into a data structure. Subsequent schedule creations replay the decisions until it reaches a task with a modified allotment or a change in task ordering, then continues the scheduling procedure

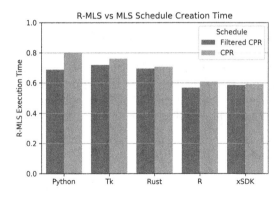

Fig. 10. Schedule creation time of CPR implementations using R-MLS and normalized against MLS execution time.

from that iteration. Reuse does not improve MLS's worst case time complexity, but constrains it to cases where the modified task is near the front of the list due to a high t_b. After its first invocation, R-MLS will have a time complexity between $O(E + V(logV + PlogP))$ [14] when a high t_b task changed from the last schedule, and $O(VP)$ when a low t_b task changed.

The original paper includes a $V(logV)$ step to sort the task list by priority. The sort can actually be done in $O(V)$ time by saving the previously sorted list, since only single task changes need to be updated after the first iteration. Thus R-MLS's worst-case time complexity can be reduced to $O(E + VPlogP)$ after the first iteration. It should be noted that these strategies cannot improve MCPA's time complexity because R-MLS relies on information reuse between iterations, and MCPA only invokes the list scheduler once.

CPR and F-CPR create schedules much more quickly with R-MLS. Figure 10 records a 40% creation time improvement with R and xSDK stacks. Since R-MLS produces identical schedules, there is no downside to its use over MLS for CPR.

7   Future Work

7.1   Task Cost Heuristic

The task cost heuristic used here assumes ideal scaling with the addition of cores. Makefile builds do not scale optimally due to the limited parallelism between build targets, and traversal through the build tree is interspersed with serialized linking steps. Fitting a curve that accounts for parallel speedup decay may result in more optimal schedules.

Another open question is heuristic portability, which may be inconsistent across different node configurations. If a build node is in every aspect half of the speed the sampled node, the build node can be expected to make a schedule that is just as optimal as it would be on the original node, but execute in twice the time.

However, the heuristic breaks down when different components operate at different speeds. In particular, the difference between CPU performance and filesystem bandwidth/latency will affect each task differently. A build node with a filesystem significantly slower than the sampled node (such as an NFS mount-point compared to a local SSD), may disproportionately affect the execution time and scalability of more I/O bound tasks. Thus an improved heuristic could find a way parameterize a specific platform's hardware configuration on execution time.

7.2 Package Fetching

Before installing a package, Spack executes a step to download an archive. This paper did not explore ways of mitigating this delay for two reasons: environments that build packages regularly are likely have a mirror or up-to-date cache that will preempt the download step, making the time cost of a fetch negligible, and execution time of fetches without a cache will go over the internet, which cannot be reliably predicted. However, this is still a relevant use-case and it will have a real affect in many one-off builds. Although adding a fetching step to the DAG is trivial (attach a leaf dependency to each package task), fetching should use a different schedule model that does not try to optimize on core allotment.

7.3 Hyperthreading

The possible benefits of hyper-threading was not explored in this paper. Most architectures support 2–4 threads per hardware core. A relevant research question could explore the affect of over-provisioning core allotments to build systems. This could benefit total execution times, by more consistently saturating resources that bottleneck build times.

7.4 Phase Tasks and Build System Tasks

Tasks in the dependency graph can be defined at one of two levels of granularity. In the first case, each task represents the installation of one package, with connecting edges representing its dependents and dependencies. However, most build systems in Spack consist of several pipelined steps, called *phases* in Spack. Of these phases, the *build* phase (or *install* phase for Makefile projects that do not define a build step) is often the only part that can be improved by the allotment of multiple cores. Any core allotment greater than one that spends time executing unscalable phases will be idle and are wasted.

In theory, more optimal schedules can be created which use tasks consisting of individual phases of a build, instead of monolithic software packages that contain both serial and parallel segments (see Fig. 11). Each package task decomposes into 2.4 times as many phase tasks on average (Table 6). The structure of the DAG, meaning the regions where dependencies fan out or form choke points will not change, since a package consists of a serial chain of phases.

Table 6. Occurrence of packages by phase count.

Phase count	Packages
1	1078
2	538
3	806
4	717
5	1
Mean	2.37

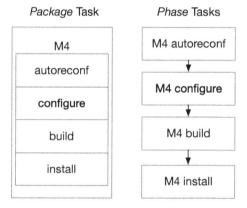

Fig. 11. Task representation of GNU M4. A package task includes all phases, and a phase tasks consist of serially-connected phases.

An even finer level of granularity would be extending task-parallel scheduling to reorder and reschedule within the CMake or Automake build systems. This could involve, e.g. malleable tasks at the directory level or single tasks at the object-file level. While CPR was the best choice for our Spack use case, a lower complexity scheduler may prove more useful if task graphs are extended to include individual build directories or object files.

8   Conclusion

This paper demonstrates that build systems can severely underutilize modern multiprocessor nodes. Build systems also vary widely in terms of their multicore speedup, with the majority never reaching a 3x speedup on a 32 core system. In a package manager workflow that depends on the execution of tens or even hundreds of build systems, the results shown in Sect. 6 demonstrate it is possible to substantially improve execution time by selectively reducing the core allotment to individual build systems and executing them in parallel. Two algorithms, CPR and MCPA were used to build common software stacks. CPR produced high quality schedules, while MCPA can be used to produce schedules for very large stacks at a lower time complexity.

References

1. Amdahl, G.M.: Validity of the single processor approach to achieving large scale computing capabilities. In: Proceedings of the April 18–20, 1967, Spring Joint Computer Conference, AFIPS 1967 (Spring), pp. 483–485. ACM, New York (1967). https://doi.org/10.1145/1465482.1465560, http://doi.acm.org/10.1145/1465482.1465560
2. Bansal, S., Kumar, P., Singh, K.: An improved two-step algorithm for task and data parallel scheduling in distributed memory machines. Parallel Comput. **32**(10), 759–774 (2006). https://doi.org/10.1016/j.parco.2006.08.004. http://www.sciencedirect.com/science/article/pii/S0167819106000524
3. Bartlett, R., et al.: xSDK foundations: toward an extreme-scale scientific software development kit. Supercomput. Front. Innov. **4**(1) (2017). http://superfri.org/superfri/article/view/127
4. Coffman Jr., E.G., Graham, R.L.: Optimal scheduling for two-processor systems. Acta Informatica **1**(3), 200–213 (1972). https://doi.org/10.1007/BF00288685
5. xSDK contributors: xsdk home (2019). https://xsdk.info/
6. Spack Contributors: Spack (2019). https://spack.io/. Accessed 27 Feb 2019
7. Du, J., Leung, J.Y.T.: Complexity of scheduling parallel task systems. SIAM J. Discrete Math. **2**(4), 473–487 (1989). https://doi.org/10.1137/0402042
8. Gamblin, T., et al.: The Spack package manager: bringing order to HPC software chaos. In: Proceedings of the International Conference for High Performance Computing, Networking, Storage and Analysis, SC 2015, pp. 40:1–40:12. ACM, New York (2015). https://doi.org/10.1145/2807591.2807623, http://doi.acm.org/10.1145/2807591.2807623
9. Papadimitriou, C.H., Yannakakis, M.: Scheduling interval-ordered tasks. SIAM J. Comput. **8**, 405–409 (1979). https://doi.org/10.1137/0208031
10. Hu, T.C.: Parallel sequencing and assembly line problems. Oper. Res. **9**(6), 841–848 (1961). http://www.jstor.org/stable/167050
11. Huang, K.C., Wu, W.Y., Wang, F.J., Liu, H.C., Hung, C.H.: An iterative expanding and shrinking process for processor allocation in mixed-parallel workflow scheduling. SpringerPlus **5**(1), 1138 (2016). https://doi.org/10.1186/s40064-016-2808-y
12. Kwok, Y.K., Ahmad, I.: Static scheduling algorithms for allocating directed task graphs to multiprocessors. ACM Comput. Surv. **31**(4), 406–471 (1999). https://doi.org/10.1145/344588.344618. http://doi.acm.org/10.1145/344588.344618
13. Radulescu, A., van Gemund, A.J.C.: A low-cost approach towards mixed task and data parallel scheduling. In: International Conference on Parallel Processing 2001, pp. 69–76 (2001). https://doi.org/10.1109/ICPP.2001.952048
14. Radulescu, A., Nicolescu, C., van Gemund, A.J.C., Jonker, P.P.: CPR: mixed task and data parallel scheduling for distributed systems. In: IPDPS (2001)
15. Ramaswamy, S., Sapatnekar, S., Banerjee, P.: A framework for exploiting task and data parallelism on distributed memory multicomputers. IEEE Trans. Parallel Distrib. Syst. **8**(11), 1098–1116 (1997). https://doi.org/10.1109/71.642945
16. Sethi, R.: Scheduling graphs on two processors. SIAM J. Comput. **5**, 73–82 (1976). https://doi.org/10.1137/0205005
17. Vydyanathan, N., et al.: Locality conscious processor allocation and scheduling for mixed parallel applications. In: 2006 IEEE International Conference on Cluster Computing, pp. 1–10 (2006). https://doi.org/10.1109/CLUSTR.2006.311861

Enabling Continuous Testing of HPC Systems Using ReFrame

Vasileios Karakasis[1]([✉]), Theofilos Manitaras[1], Victor Holanda Rusu[1],
Rafael Sarmiento-Pérez[1], Christopher Bignamini[1], Matthias Kraushaar[1],
Andreas Jocksch[1], Samuel Omlin[1], Guilherme Peretti-Pezzi[1],
João P. S. C. Augusto[2], Brian Friesen[3], Yun He[3], Lisa Gerhardt[3],
Brandon Cook[3], Zhi-Qiang You[4], Samuel Khuvis[4], and Karen Tomko[4]

[1] Swiss National Supercomputing Centre, Via Trevano 131, 6900 Lugano, Switzerland
vasileios.karakasis@cscs.ch
[2] Università della Svizzera Italiana, Via Giuseppe Buffi 13, 6900 Lugano, Switzerland
[3] Lawrence Berkeley National Laboratory, 1 Cyclotron Road,
Berkeley, CA 94720, USA
[4] Ohio Supercomputer Center, 1224 Kinnear Road, Columbus, OH 43212, USA

Abstract. Regression testing of HPC systems is of crucial importance when it comes to ensure the quality of service offered to the end users. At the same time, it poses a great challenge to the systems and application engineers to continuously maintain regression tests that cover as many aspects as possible of the user experience. In this paper, we briefly present ReFrame, a framework for writing regression tests for HPC systems and how this is used by CSCS, NERSC and OSC to continuously test their systems. ReFrame is designed to abstract away the complexity of the interactions with the system and to separate the logic of a regression test from the low-level details, which pertain to the system configuration and setup. Regression tests in ReFrame are simple Python classes that specify the basic parameters of the test plus any additional logic. The framework will load the test and send it down a well-defined pipeline which will take care of its execution. ReFrame can be easily set up on any cluster and its straightforward invocation allows it to be easily integrated with common continuous integration/deployment (CI/CD) tools, in order to perform continuous testing of an HPC system. Finally, its ability to feed the collected performance data to well known log channels, such as Syslog, Graylog or, simply, parsable log files, make it also a powerful tool for continuously monitoring the health of the system from user's perspective.

1 Introduction

HPC systems are highly complex systems in all levels of integration; from the physical infrastructure up to the software stack provided to the end users. A small change in any of these levels could have an impact on the stability or the performance of the system. It is of crucial importance, therefore, not only to

© Springer Nature Switzerland AG 2020
G. Juckeland and S. Chandrasekaran (Eds.): HUST 2019/SE-HER 2019/WIHPC 2019,
CCIS 1190, pp. 49–68, 2020.
https://doi.org/10.1007/978-3-030-44728-1_3

make sure that the system is in a sane condition after every maintenance, but also to monitor its performance during production, so that possible problems are detected early enough and the quality of service is not compromised.

Regression testing can provide a reliable way to ensure the stability and the performance requirements of the system, provided that sufficient tests exist that cover a wide aspect of the system's operations from both the operators' and users' point of view. However, given the complexity of HPC systems, writing and maintaining regression tests can be a very time consuming task. A small change in the system configuration or the deployment may require adapting hundreds of regression tests at the same time. Similarly, porting a test to a different system may require significant effort if the new system's configuration is substantially different from that of the system that it was originally written for.

Most HPC sites use one or another type of regression testing to check some aspects of their system behavior. These efforts are usually custom, in-house solutions that tend to couple strongly the regression tests with the system configuration, increasing the maintenance burden significantly.

In this paper, we present ReFrame, a regression testing framework that tries to address these challenges. In fact, when designing ReFrame, we have set three major goals:

1. *Productivity.* The writer of a regression test should focus only on the logical requirements of the test and should not need to deal with any of the low level system details, e.g., how the test environment is loaded, how jobs are created and submitted, how output is parsed etc.
2. *Portability.* Configuring the framework to support new systems and system configurations should be easy and should not affect the existing tests. Also, adding support of a new system in a regression test should require minimal adjustments.
3. *Robustness and ease of use.* The new framework must be stable enough and easy to use by non-advanced users. When the system needs to be returned to users outside normal working hours, the personnel in charge should be able to run the regression suite and verify the sanity of the system with a minimal involvement.

Since recently, there are ongoing discussions and several exploratory projects in progress in the HPC community toward embracing well-established cloud technologies, such as containers, Continuous Integration and Continuous Deployment (CI/CD) and DevOps. An essential ingredient of such a convergence between classical HPC and the Cloud is robust testing. ReFrame can be easily integrated with well known CI/CD frameworks, such as Jenkins or Gitlab, and can be therefore used for continuously testing a system and, even for continuously deploying changes to the system. Also since ReFrame tests are written in a fully fledged programming language, they can adjust their behavior for different systems in a self-contained manner and with minimal changes, making it easy to create and maintain a suite of tests.

The rest of the paper is organized as follows: Sect. 2 presents the key design principles of the framework, Sect. 3 presents the syntax of a ReFrame test file and discusses how common tasks can be achieved. Section 4 presents some basic aspects of configuring and running ReFrame. Section 5 presents the use cases of ReFrame at CSCS, NERSC and OSC. Section 6 discusses related work and how ReFrame is positioned among other tools. Finally, Sect. 7 concludes the paper and presents the future development directions.

2   Framework Design

ReFrame is written entirely in Python3 and follows a layered design that abstracts away the system related details (Fig. 1). An API for writing regression tests is provided to the user at the highest level, allowing the description of the requirements of the test. The framework defines and implements a concrete pipeline that a regression test goes through during its lifetime and the user is given the opportunity to intervene between the different stages and customize their behavior if needed. All the system interaction mechanisms are implemented as backends and are not exposed directly to the regression test developer. For example, the exact same test could be run on a system using either native Slurm or Slurm+ALPS or PBS+mpirun. Similarly, the same test can run "as-is" on system partitions configured differently. The writer of a regression test need not also care about generating a job script, querying the status of the associated job or managing the files of the test. All of these are taken care of transparently by the framework without affecting the regression test. This not only makes a regression test easier to write, but it also increases its readability, since the intent of the test is made clear right from its high-level description.

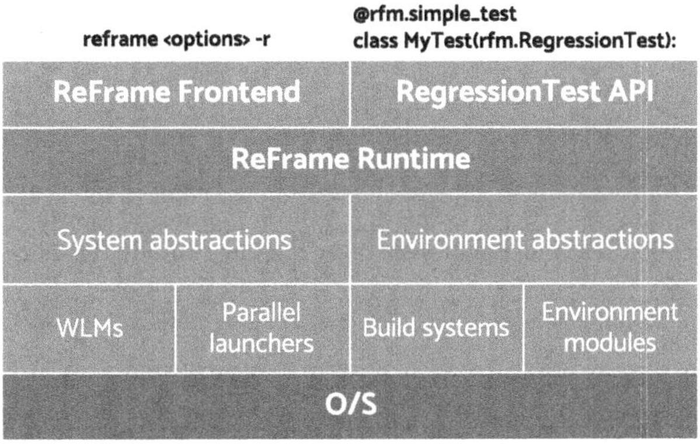

Fig. 1. ReFrame's layered architecture abstracts away the system details and allows to extend its functionality by implementing different backends.

ReFrame also defines several internal APIs that interface different framework components, such as job schedulers, parallel job launchers, build systems etc. This allows the easy extension of its functionality by implementing different, independent, backends which do not affect the framework's core infrastructure.

2.1 The Regression Test Pipeline

At the heart of ReFrame is the *regression test pipeline*. This is a set of well defined stages that each regression test goes through during its lifetime. Figure 2 depicts this pipeline in more detail. After initialization, each regression test will be tried for all the current system's partitions and all the programming environments supported by each partition. A test may choose to skip some systems, system partitions and/or programming environments. The tuple consisting of the regression test, the current partition and the current programming environment is called a *test case*. As soon as a test enters the pipeline, it will pass through all the stages sequentially, although some of them may be implemented as a "no-op" for certain types of tests. A detailed description of each of the pipeline stages can be found at the online documentation.

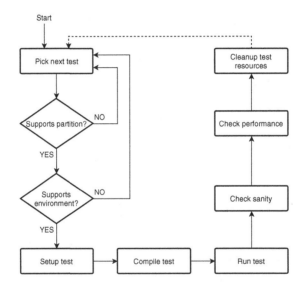

Fig. 2. The regression test pipeline. Every regression test run by ReFrame goes through these stages.

2.2 The Frontend

The frontend of ReFrame is responsible for loading, filtering and running a set of regression tests. It communicates with the different backends and drives the regression testing pipeline. ReFrame can run a test suite in two ways: serially or asynchronously.

The serial execution policy will run all the selected tests sequentially for all their supported programming environments and system partitions, whereas the asynchronous execution policy executes the run stage of the test asynchronously.

As soon as a test case is submitted for execution, ReFrame will not block and will continue by picking up the next test case to run. It will keep submitting new test cases until a user-defined concurrency limit is reached per partition. Internally, ReFrame keeps track of the currently running and ready tasks per partition and it regularly checks their status. As soon as a test case finishes, it resumes its execution from the sanity checking stage and runs it to completion. Meanwhile, it submits for execution to the corresponding partition any available ready tasks, so that it keeps the concurrency high.

2.3   Pluggable Backends

ReFrame's core does not assume anything about the underlying system setup. Instead it communicates with the system utilities through well defined internal APIs, which are implemented by various backends. ReFrame works internally with abstract base classes, whose concrete implementations are provided as backends. As a result, the functionality of the framework may be extended easily without touching its internal structure. Currently, ReFrame defines low-level abstractions for job schedulers, parallel job launchers, modules systems and build systems. Going into details about the internal APIs is beyond the scope of this paper, but we will briefly describe the different backends currently available in ReFrame:

Job Scheduler Backends

- `local`: This pseudo-scheduler simply launches OS processes on the current host asynchronously.
- `slurm`: A wrapper to the SLURM job scheduler [28].
- `pbs`: A wrapper to PBS scheduler. This backend should be suitable for any PBS-derived job scheduler, e.g., Torque.

Parallel Job Launcher Backends

- `local`: An empty launcher; no command is emitted.
- `srun`: The native Slurm job launcher.
- `srunalloc`: The native Slurm job launcher but with job allocation options emitted. This is useful in combination with the `local` job scheduler, since it allows you to submit jobs directly without a job script.
- `alps`: The Cray ALPS job launcher
- `mpirun, mpiexec`

Environment Modules Backends

- `nomod`: This is a pseudo modules system that simply implements the corresponding internal API as no-op. This is used for systems that do not normally have any modules system installed.
- `tmod`: The TCL implementation of the environment modules [10].
- `tmod4`: The TCL implementation version 4 of the environment modules [23].
- `lmod`: The Lua implementation of the environment modules [21].

Build Systems Backends. The build functionality inside ReFrame is abstracted away as well, so as to support different build processes seamlessly and expose an homogeneous and easy-to-use interface to the user. Build systems in ReFrame is a lightweight component that focuses more on the continuous integration aspect of compiling a code rather than the full installation process, which is the target of other more suitable tools, e.g., EasyBuild [15], Spack [11] etc. Currently, ReFrame supports the following build systems:

- `SingleSource`: This build system simply invokes the compiler on a single source file.
- `Make`: This build system invokes `make` on a directory.
- `Autotools`: This build system invokes the Autotools toolchain, i.e., `configure` and `make`.
- `CMake`: This build system invokes the CMake toolchain, i.e., `cmake` and `make`.

3   Writing a Regression Test in ReFrame

A regression test in ReFrame is simply a specially decorated Python class that ultimately derives from the `RegressionTest` base class. This class has several attributes that the user may set in order to control the behavior of his test. In this section, we will only present some basic aspects of the user API, in order to give the reader an idea of how a ReFrame test looks like. For a complete and detailed description of the API, the reader is referred to ReFrame's online documentation.

The following listing assumes a simple performance test that compiles and runs a CUDA-based dense matrix-vector multiplication code and checks its output and performance:

```
import reframe as rfm
import reframe.utility.sanity as sn


@rfm.simple_test
class Example7Test(rfm.RegressionTest):
    def __init__(self):
        self.descr = 'DMV CUDA performance test'
        self.valid_systems = ['daint:gpu']
        self.valid_prog_environs = ['PrgEnv-gnu',
                                    'PrgEnv-cray']
        self.sourcepath = 'example_dmv_cuda.cu'
        self.build_system = 'SingleSource'
        self.build_system.cxxflags = ['-O3']
        self.executable_opts = ['4096', '1000']
        self.modules = ['cudatoolkit']
        self.sanity_patterns = sn.assert_found(
            r'time for single dmv', self.stdout)
        self.perf_patterns = {
            'perf': sn.extractsingle(
                r'Performance:\s+(?P<Gflops>\S+) Gflop/s',
                self.stdout, 'Gflops', float)
```

```
        }
        self.reference = {
            'daint:gpu': {
                'perf': (50.0, -0.1, 0.1, 'Gflop/s'),
            }
        }
```

The base class of all regression tests in ReFrame is the `RegressionTest` class, so every user-defined test must eventually derive from this class. Every regression test class to be registered with ReFrame must be decorated with either the `@simple_test` or the `@parameterized_test` decorator. We will not cover the latter in this paper, but the reader is referred to the online documentation.

In a ReFrame test class, almost always, everything happens inside its constructor, which serves as the specification of the test. The important attributes in this code snippet are the following:

- `valid_systems`: This is the list of systems that this test can run on. A system is specified by its name and optionally a specific partition. In this example, this test is valid only for the `gpu` partition of the system named `daint`. Systems and their partitions are configured in ReFrame's configuration file. The test does not have to know about any irrelevant details. If the job scheduler in this system changes, the test will be still valid. Similarly, enabling this test for different systems should be as simple as extending this list and, perhaps, adapting some test-specific options. But no low-level system-specific details are exposed to the test.
- `valid_prog_environs`: This is a list of ReFrame programming environment names, that this test can be run with. These are just symbolic names that are resolved in ReFrame's configuration. The definition of a programming environment, e.g., modules that load it, can change without affecting the test. The framework will also take automatically care of any conflicts between the current environment and the requested ones and will make sure to resolve them transparently.
- `build_system`: This is the build system that will be used for building the code of this test. Each build system defines a set of attributes that can be set to control its behavior. In this example, we simply set the compilation flags.
- `sourcepath`: This is the source file to be compiled. It can also refer to a directory, in which case `make` will be invoked automatically.
- `executable_opts`: This is a list of options to be passed to the generated executable.
- `modules`: This is a list of additional environment modules to load before compiling and running this test. ReFrame will handle automatically any conflicts and the test does not need to know the underlying modules system used.
- `variables`: This is a dictionary of environment variables to be set before compiling and running this test.
- `sanity_patterns`: This a lazily evaluated expression that will validate the output of the test. Its evaluation is lazy because it does not happen at the time it is called inside the test's constructor, but rather during the "sanity checking" stage of the regression test pipeline. ReFrame provides a library of

useful *sanity functions* that a test can use directly to perform several tasks, e.g., extract and convert values from the output, calculate aggregate functions on the collected values, perform assertions etc. Users may also write their own sanity functions.

- `perf_patterns`: If this attribute is defined, then the test is considered as a performance test. It is essentially a dictionary of pairs of *performance variables* and lazily evaluated expressions, which will be used by ReFrame to extract the values of these performance variables from the output of the test. In the example shown, we extract the performance metric of Gflop/s that is printed in the standard output of the test.
- `reference`: This attribute stores the reference values for each performance variable/metric defined in `perf_patterns` for each of the supported systems or partitions. The reference information is a four-tuple consisting of the actual reference value and lower and upper thresholds expressed as fractional differences from the reference value and the measurement unit. In this example, the acceptable performance value for the `gpu` partition of the system `daint` for this test is 50 Gflop/s $\pm 10\%$. The reference dictionary is treated specially by ReFrame. In fact, the keys describing systems and system partitions define hierarchical scopes. When trying to resolve a performance variable, ReFrame will try several scopes in the `reference` dictionary and pick the most specific reference value. You may also define a global scope using the special '`*`' key, that would allow to run the test on unknown systems that you have not yet a reference.

There is a lot more to writing tests in ReFrame than the simple functional example that we have presented here, but it cannot be covered in this paper. The reader is referred to the online documentation for all the details and the reference guides. We will simply mention here that you can very easily differentiate the behaviour of the test (e.g., to change the compilation flags) based on the current system or the current programming environment. You may also create much more advanced sanity checking than the one presented here, purely in Python, without having to learn complex libraries or custom syntaxes. Using the `@parameterized_test` decorator you may ask ReFrame to generate families of tests by modifying individual parameters of your test. Finally, you need not take care about error handling when writing your test, since all errors are handled automatically by ReFrame's runtime.

4   Configuring and Running ReFrame

Configuring ReFrame for a new site is easy and straightforward. The site configuration comprises two basic sections: a section for configuring the systems and their partitions and another one for configuring the different programming environments. We will not cover in detail the configuration options of ReFrame; we will only outline some key configuration parameters. For configuring a new system in ReFrame, you just need to specify the modules system used (if any) and a set of hostname patterns of its login nodes that would allow ReFrame to recognize it automatically. Each system should have at least one system partition. The minimum information needed for a system partition to be configured is the job scheduler, the parallel job launcher and the programming environments to test. There are also additional options for (a) setting the required options to be passed to the backend scheduler in order to gain access to this partition, (b) specifying any necessary modules to be loaded every time ReFrame runs a test on this partition, (c) adjusting the concurrency limit for the asynchronous execution policy etc.

For programming environments, one can define the required modules that load them, set any additional environment variables and/or set the values for the basic compilers (C, C++ and Fortran) and corresponding default flags. Each programming environment is given a symbolic name, with which it is referenced also inside the tests. The same programming environment may also be redefined specially for different systems or system partitions. This allows users to reuse the same programming environment names for different systems and avoid changing their regression tests. The following listing shows a minimal configuration of a test system at CSCS.

```
site_configuration = {
    'systems': {
        'ault': {
            'descr': 'Ault␣TDS',
            'hostnames': ['ault'],
            'modules_system': 'lmod',
            'partitions': {
                'login': {
                    'scheduler': 'local',
                    'environs': ['PrgEnv-gnu'],
                    'descr': 'Login␣nodes',
                },
                'amdv100': {
                    'scheduler': 'nativeslurm',
                    'access':   ['-pamdv100'],
                    'environs': ['PrgEnv-gnu'],
                }
            }
        }
    }
    'environments': {
        'ault': {
            'PrgEnv-gnu': {
                'type': 'ProgEnvironment',
                'modules': ['gcc', 'cuda', 'openmpi'],
                'cc':   'mpicc',
                'cxx':  'mpicxx',
                'ftn':  'mpif90'
            }
        }
    }
}
```

For all possible configuration options and the exact syntax of the configuration file, the reader is referred to the online documentation.

4.1 Performance Logging

ReFrame takes particular care in logging the performance data of performance tests. More specifically, for each performance test case and for each of the performance variables defined in the `perf_patterns` attribute of a test, ReFrame logs the achieved value and the reference. The log record format is fully customizable and may contain lots of test-specific details (e.g., job id, test directories, test tags etc.) The logging mechanism of ReFrame is built upon the Python logging framework, so it inherits lots of its functionality. Apart from the log record formatting, more important is that multiple handlers can be registered at the same time to log the performance data differently. Currently, three types of performance logging are supported:

- File: ReFrame, by default, will create a log file per test, system and system partition and will start appending data to it. The default log record prints a timestamp, the full test case description (test name, system partition and environment), the job id, and all the related performance information.
- Syslog: ReFrame can send log records to as syslog interface via the Python `logging` module.
- Graylog: ReFrame is capable of sending performance log data to a Graylog [13] server. These data can then be plotted with tools for analyzing Graylog records.

4.2 Running ReFrame

ReFrame is run from the command-line and offers several options that control its behavior. The simplest way to invoke it is by running "`reframe -r`". This will load all tests found in a predefined location and run them. When invoking ReFrame, after loading the configuration, the frontend goes through three phases:

1. Discovery of regression tests.
2. Filtering of regression tests.
3. Action on regression tests.

There are options controlling each of these phases. During the first phase, ReFrame searches for Python files in either a predefined location or a user-specific one, parses them and, if they contain ReFrame tests, it loads them and instantiates the tests. The following command will load and run all the tests defined in `mytest.py`: `reframe -c mytest.py -r`. The `-c` option can also be passed a directory and with the `-R` option, ReFrame will recursively search for tests inside it.

The second phase is the filtering of the loaded tests. Currently, tests in ReFrame can be filtered by name, by supported programming environments and by tags. There are options controlling each of these possibilities, and they can also be combined together to form more complex selection criteria. Each ReFrame test may be associated with a set of tags by setting its `tags` attribute. Tags allow the user to create arbitrary groups of tests, which can be invoked at any time. The following command will execute all the tests found under `mytests/` and are tagged with `production`:

```
reframe -c mytests/ -R -t production -r
```

You may also use Python regular expressions as arguments to any of the test selection options.

The final phase of the frontend is the actual action to be taken on the selected tests. Two actions are supported: (a) list tests by passing the `-l` or `-L` options and (b) run tests by passing the `-r` option. Listing of tests is quite useful for preparing a ReFrame run, since you can check which tests were actually found and selected before running them. Additional information per test is also printed, such as the file that defines it, its supported programming environments, its tags, its maintainers etc. The *run* action runs the tests. By default, all test cases are executed sequentially, but the execution policy can be changed using the `--exec-policy` option.

Apart from these basic options described briefly here, ReFrame offers several more for controlling the execution of the tests, passing through options directly to the backend scheduler, manipulating the environment modules etc. For more information the reader is referred to ReFrame's help and to the online documentation.

4.3 Dealing with Test Failures

When a regression test or particularly a test case fails, ReFrame will print a "FAIL" mark for it and continue to execute the rest of the test cases. It will not print any specific failure information inline, since this would make tracking this information difficult in large outputs. Instead, it will print a summary of all the failures with all the required details at the end of its output. The information printed includes the test name, the current system partition, the current programming environment, the current pipeline stage, the stage directory of the test case, the error message and, optionally, a stack trace depending on the type of failure. ReFrame takes particular care in properly managing errors in the context of a test execution, so as to never print error information inline. Even programming errors in a test will not break the frontend.

5   Use Cases

ReFrame has been publicly released on May 2017 and is being actively developed. Since then it has gained visibility across large computing centers, which are considering integrating it in their production testing workflows. To our knowledge, private companies in the HPC sector are using it, too. In this section, we will briefly discuss the use cases of ReFrame at the Swiss National Supercomputing Centre (CSCS) in Switzerland, at the National Energy Research Scientific Computing Center (NERSC) and at the Ohio Supercomputer Center (OSC) in the United States.

5.1   ReFrame at CSCS

CSCS uses ReFrame for both functionality and performance tests for all of its production systems, namely Piz Daint (Cray XC40/XC50 hybrid system), Piz Kesch (Cray CS-Storm used by MeteoSwiss for weather prediction) and Monte Leone (HP DL 360 Gen 9). The same ReFrame tests are reused as much as possible across systems with minor adaptations. The test suite of CSCS (publicly available at the ReFrame repository) comprises tests for full scientific applications, scientific libraries, programming environments, compilation and linking, profiling and debugger tools, basic CUDA operations, performance microbenchmarks and I/O libraries. Using tags we have split the tests in three broad overlapping categories: production, maintenance and benchmarking tests. The first category comprises a large variety of tests and is run daily overnight using Jenkins. The maintenance suite is essentially a small subset of the production tests, comprising mostly application sanity and performance tests, as well as sanity tests for the programming environment and the scheduler. It is run before and after maintenance of the systems. The benchmarking tests are used to measure the performance of different computing and networking components and are run manually before major upgrades or when a performance problem needs to be investigated. We are currently working on a fourth category of tests that are intended to run frequently (e.g., every 10 min). The purpose of these tests is to measure the system behavior and performance as perceived by the users. Example tests are the time it takes to run basic Slurm commands and/or performance basic filesystem operations. Such glitches might affect the performance of running applications and cause users to open support tickets. Collecting periodically such performance data will help us correlate system events with user application performance. Finally, there is an ongoing effort to expand our ReFrame test suite to virtual clusters based on OpenStack. The new tests will measure the responsiveness of our OpenStack installation to deploy compute instances, volumes, and perform snapshots. We plan to make them publicly available in the near future.

Analyzing the Performance Data Produced by ReFrame. The performance data produced by all performance tests that are run through our ReFrame installation is logged directly to an internal Graylog server. We then either use Grafana [12] queries for plotting the performance evolution over time or we use custom scripts for extracting the data and performing more advanced analysis. Our ultimate goal is to identify performance variations over time and try to correlate this with other events on the system and/or reports from users. In the following, we describe very briefly our ongoing effort on characterizing the performance of the system based on the ReFrame logs using some data analysis techniques.

Figure 3a shows the performance data of a single GROMACS (GPU) test recorded over the past 12 months. This spiky performance "signal" is not something strange in a heavily shared HPC system. A first qualitative assessment allows to identify two to three main performance regimes in the time series based on the amplitude and frequency of the signal. However, due to the noise in the data, identifying quantitatively when the real performance degradation started is not as straightforward. We have been developing a set of tools recently with the intention to create a more automated way to determine performance changes in the system. We apply adaptive non-parametric clustering with regularization [14] to each individual ReFrame performance test, in order to identify performance *regimes* that are of particular interest.

A typical first step would be to reconstruct the signal of Fig. 3a using a rolling mean. Figure 3b shows two reconstructed signals created using different time windows. As the time window width increases, the noise will be smoothed out, but so will the information content with respect to the performance. Furthermore, the reconstructed signals still do not permit to clearly classify all performance regimes for every point in the series.

Using the aforementioned clustering approach on the raw performance signal, however, five clear performance clusters can be identified, which are shown in Fig. 3c. The sharp boundaries separating the performance clusters are a prerequisite for automation of the analysis process.

Adding variance to the analysis will give us three performance regimes, as shown in Fig. 3d, which is aligned to the initial perception by looking into the raw data. The important thing here is that clear regions where performance varies (either by its mean or its variance) can be identified, which allows an easier correlation with other tests or events. Another advantage of this method is that it does not impose any a priori probabilistic assumptions on the data. The performance and windowed variance signals were considered to be enough for this analysis since the majority of the problems should be reflected on the distribution's mean and the variance. The type of the tests' distributions are also important for characterising the overall computing system performance but it is not considered.

For future work, we plan to extend the analysis by adding outlier detection along with information about concurrent applications running on the same cabinet as the ReFrame test and also include the cabinet physical location in the analysis. The aim is to investigate the causality relation between performance drops and resource sharing in the cluster. The daily monitoring of the performance outliers, specially when multiple regression tests show unsatisfactory performance, can help identify faulty components of the system.

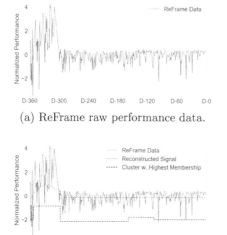

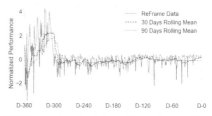

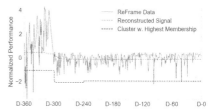

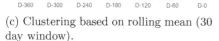

(a) ReFrame raw performance data.

(b) Reconstructed signal based on rolling mean for different window sizes.

(c) Clustering based on rolling mean (30 day window).

(d) Clustering based on rolling mean and variance.

Fig. 3. Progression from raw performance data obtained with ReFrame over the past 12 months to performance cluster indices with highest membership for a Gromacs GPU-only test.

5.2   ReFrame at NERSC

ReFrame at NERSC covers functionality and performance of its current HPC system "Cori", a Cray XC40 with Intel "Haswell" and "Knights Landing" compute nodes; as well as its smaller Cray CS-Storm cluster featuring Intel "Skylake" CPUs and NVIDIA "Volta" GPUs. The performance tests include several general-purpose benchmarks designed to stress different components of the system, including HPGMG [4,20,25] (both finite-element and finite-volume tests), HPCG [8], Graph500 [5], IOR [19], and others. Additionally, the tests include several benchmark codes used during NERSC system procurements, as well as several extracted benchmarks from full applications which participate in the NERSC Exascale Science Application Program (NESAP) [18]. Including NESAP applications ensures that representative components of the NERSC workload are included in the performance tests.

The functionality tests evaluate several different components of the system; for example, there are several tests for the Cray "DataWarp" software which enables users to interact with the Cori burst buffer. There are also several Slurm tests which verify that partitions and QoSs are correctly configured for jobs of varying sizes. The Cray programming environments, including compiler wrappers, MPI and OpenMP capability, and Shifter, are also included in these tests, and are especially impactful following changes in defaults to the programming environments.

The test battery at NERSC can be invoked both manually and automatically, depending on the need. Specifically, the full battery is typically executed manually following a significant change to the Cori system, e.g., after a major system software change, or a Cray Linux OS upgrade, before the system is released back to users. Under most other circumstances, however, only a subset of tests are typically run, and in most causes they are executed automatically. NERSC uses ReFrame's tagging capabilities to categorize the various subsets of tests, such that groups of tests which evaluate a particular component of the system can be invoked easily. For example, some performance tests are tagged as `daily`, others as `weekly`, `reboot`, `slurm`, `aries`, etc., such that it is clear from the test's Python code when and how frequently a particular test is run.

ReFrame has also been integrated into NERSC's centralized data collection service used for facility and system monitoring, called the "Data Collect" [27]. The Data Collect stores data in an Elasticsearch instance, uses Logstash to ingest log information about the Cori system, and provides a web-based GUI to display results via Kibana. Cray, in turn, provides the Cray Lightweight Log Manager [3] on XC systems such as Cori, which provides a syslog interface. ReFrame's support for syslog, and the Python standard `logging` library, enabled simple integration with NERSC's Data Collect The result of this integration with ReFrame to the Data Collect is that the results from each ReFrame test executed on Cori are visible via a Kibana query within a few seconds of the test completing. One can then configure Elasticsearch to alert a system administrator if a particular system functionality stops working, or if the performance of certain benchmarks suddenly declines.

Finally, ReFrame has been automated at NERSC via the continuous integration (CI) capabilities provided by an internal GitLab instance. More specifically, GitLab was enhanced due to efforts from the US Department of Energy Exascale Computing Project (ECP) [24] in order to allow CI "runners" to submit jobs to queues on HPC systems such as Cori automatically via schedulable "pipelines." Automation via GitLab runners is a significant improvement over test executed automated by cron, because the runners exist outside of the Cori system, and therefore are unaffected by system shutdowns, reboots, and other disruptions. The pipelines are configured to run tests with particular tags at particular times, e.g., tests tagged with `daily` are invoked each day at the same time, tests tagged `weekly` are invoked once per week, etc.

5.3   ReFrame at OSC

At OSC, we use ReFrame to build the testing system for the software environment [17]. As a change is made to an application, e.g. upgrade, module change or new installation, ReFrame tests are performed by a user-privilege account and the OSC staff members who receive the test summary can easily check the result to decide if the change should be approved.

ReFrame is configured and installed on three production systems (Pitzer, Owens and Ruby). For each application we prepare the following classes of ReFrame tests:

1. default version – checks if a new installation overwrites the default module file,
2. broken executable or library – i.e. run a binary with the `--version` flag and compare the result with the module version,
3. functionality – i.e. numerical tests,
4. performance – extensive functionality checking and benchmarking,

where we currently have functionality and performance tests for a limited subset of our deployed software.

All checks are designed to be general and version independent. The correct module file is loaded at runtime, reducing the number of Python classes to be maintained. In addition, all application-based ReFrame tests are performed as regression testing of software environment when the system has critical update or rolling reboot.

ReFrame is also used for performance monitoring. We run weekly MPI tests and monthly HPCG tests. The performance data is logged directly to internal Splunk server via Syslog protocol. The job summary is sent to the responsible OSC staff member who can watch the performance dashboards.

6   Related Work

Regression testing of HPC systems has long been an important matter among user support and operations teams of HPC centers. Several tools have been proposed in the past trying to accomplish this complex task. In this section, we present the tools and frameworks targeting HPC system testing and discuss briefly their advantages and shortcomings.

Another approach to system testing is BuildTest [26], also Python-based, which follows a slightly different path to handle regression testing. Tests in BuildTest are simple YAML files, but they are not completely self-contained as in ReFrame. Job scheduler related information is kept in separate YAML files and the tests do no specify environment modules. This can be viewed also as an advantage, since it decouples completely the test from the system, but on the other hand it makes harder to keep track of the requirements of a test. An inherent disadvantage of the YAML syntax for tests is that it imposes restrictions on the validation of the test results, since eventually you might have to move more complex test logic to an external script. Finally, BuildTest seems not to target explicitly performance tests, although it provides some basic microbenchmarks in its test suite.

Another tool that uses regression tests in YAML is the freshly released Pavilion2 from LANL [2]. One interesting feature is that you can extend the test syntax by writing plugins in Python that implement the new syntax element. This promises to make the framework easily extensible, but there is a possibility that the logic of a test is scattered between plugins and the YAML file. Since rather new, there is not yet a proof-of-concept on how this solution scales in terms of maintainability and portability to hundreds of tests.

A Python-based tool, similar to ReFrame, for tackling HPC regression testing is the Automated Testing System (ATS) [9] developed at LLNL. Tests in ATS are written in Python2 and common functionality is provided by the framework. It supports also homogeneous web reports, customizable tests with command line options, test dependencies and performance testing. However, there is no portable definition of programming environments and machine configurations require coding to set up. This makes writing even a simple test a not so straightforward process. This tool is no more actively developed.

The recently proposed Testpilot [7] is a user-centric regression testing framework which is used to verify the overall health of an HPC cluster. It is implemented as a combination of shell and Perl scripts and it consists of three "subtools" (Testpilotunit, Testpilotwing and Testpilotpatrol), which handle individual application testing, cluster regression testing and continuous assessment of a cluster health, respectively. Compared to ReFrame, it currently supports only PBS job schedulers, while the job scheduler-specific details are defined in each test and are not handled by the framework. Additionally, it does not fully support parallel execution of tests.

Another interesting approach is the JUBE framework developed at Jülich Supercomputing Centre [16]. This framework targets chiefly benchmarking rather than sanity checking and uses XML files for configuring new regression tests. Among others, it offers sandboxing of a regression test, statistical utilities for reporting the performance of the benchmarks and a parameter "template" mechanism that allows to run the same test multiple times with different parameters. However, since it does not target specifically sanity checking, it is not as straightforward to run the exact same check with multiple programming environments. The portability of a regression test across different systems is not very easy either, since the only way to differentiate the behavior of a regression test is by masking in or out parts of the checks using special XML tags.

Toward the standardization of the deployment and regression testing of HPC systems, is also the OpenHPC initiative [1]. OpenHPC offers a regression suite, written in M4 and shell scripting, for checking deployments according to its standards. Despite the clean structure of the regression suite, a concrete knowledge of the actual deployment is still required in order to write a regression test. Also, the way of checking and reporting the test result is left upon each test. Maintaining therefore a common uniform structure across all regression tests could incur further unnecessary maintenance overhead. Another shortcoming of the OpenHPC regression suite is that it assumes a "standard" cluster setup and deployment, which makes it difficult to adopt for different cluster solutions, such as for Cray sites.

A couple of proprietary tools are also available. IBM India has developed JACE [22], which couples with other IBM tools to handle regression testing. It is menu-driven, supports parallel execution and is job-script agnostic. Additionally, a centralized report database as well as Excel spreadsheet reports allow an easy analysis of regression test outputs. Intel has also developed DART [6], a framework for distributed automated regression testing of large-scale network applications. DART supports automated execution of a suite of distributed tests, where each test consists of an XML script as well as the test code and data. Regarding HPC application testing, though, it is not clear whether DART is aware of job schedulers which are mainly used for job submission in HPC systems.

7   Conclusions and Future Directions

In this paper, we presented ReFrame, a framework for writing regression tests for HPC systems and scientific applications. It was designed from ground up to allow users to easily write regression tests for their systems or software, focusing only on the logic of their tests and not mixing up the low-level system-specific details. At the same time, it does not restrict the tests' capabilities, by allowing its users to write their regression tests in a high-level modern programming language, such as Python. ReFrame's frontend allows the efficient management and execution of tests on any system (from a local desktop to a supercomputer) and enables its easy integration with well established continuous integration tools. We have also presented the concrete use cases from three supercomputing centers, namely CSCS, NERSC and OSC, that have deployed ReFrame for testing, benchmarking and monitoring their systems. Due its clean and simple interfaces, ReFrame was able to be integrated seamlessly with other tools for monitoring and continuous integration forming robust system testing workflows.

ReFrame is actively developed and publicly available on Github (https://github.com/eth-cscs/reframe). Some major features that we plan to implement in the future are seamless support for containerized tests, test dependencies and improvements to the high-level test API that would facilitate even more the writing of a test.

Acknowledgements. CSCS would like to thank the members of the User Engagement and Support and the HPC Operations units for their valuable feedback regarding the framework and their contributions in writing regression tests for the system.

This research used resources of the National Energy Research Scientific Computing Center (NERSC), a U.S. Department of Energy Office of Science User Facility operated under Contract No. DE-AC02-05CH11231.

References

1. OpenHPC: Community building blocks for HPC systems. https://github.com/openhpc/ohpc
2. Pavilion2. https://github.com/lanl-preteam/pavilion2
3. Cray Lightweight Log Manager (LLM) (2019). https://pubs.cray.com/content/S-2393/CLE%207.0.UP00/xctm-series-system-administration-guide/cray-lightweight-log-manager-llm
4. Adams, M., Brown, J., Shalf, J., Straalen, B.V., Strohmaier, E., Williams, S.: HPGMG 1.0: a benchmark for ranking high performance computing systems. Technical report, LBNL-6630E, Lawrence Berkeley National Laboratory, May 2014. http://escholarship.org/uc/item/00r9w79m

5. Checconi, F., Petrini, F., Willcock, J., Lumsdaine, A., Choudhury, A.R., Sabharwal, Y.: Breaking the speed and scalability Barriers for Graph exploration on distributed-memory machines. In: SC 2012: Proceedings of the International Conference on High Performance Computing, Networking, Storage and Analysis, pp. 1–12, November 2012. https://doi.org/10.1109/SC.2012.25

6. Chun, B.N.: DART: distributed automated regression testing for large-scale network applications. In: Higashino, T. (ed.) OPODIS 2004. LNCS, vol. 3544, pp. 20–36. Springer, Heidelberg (2005). https://doi.org/10.1007/11516798_2

7. Colby, K., Maji, A.K., Rahman, J., Bottum, J.: Testpilot: A flexible framework for user-centric testing of HPC clusters. In: Proceedings of the Fourth International Workshop on HPC User Support Tools, HUST 2017, pp. 5:1–5:10. ACM, New York (2017). https://doi.org/10.1145/3152493.3152555. http://doi.acm.org/10.1145/3152493.3152555

8. Dongarra, J., Heroux, M.A., Luszczek, P.: HPCG benchmark: a new metric for ranking high performance computing systems. Technical report, UT-EECS-15-736, Electrical Engineering and Compute Science Department, University of Tennessee, Knoxville, November 2015. https://library.eecs.utk.edu/storage/594phpwDhjVNut-eecs-15-736.pdf

9. Dubois, P.F.: Testing scientific programs. Comput. Sci. Eng. **14**(4), 69–73 (2012). https://doi.org/10.1109/MCSE.2012.84

10. Furlani, J.L., Osel, P.W.: Abstract yourself with modules. In: Proceedings of the 10th USENIX Conference on System Administration, LISA 1996, pp. 193–204. USENIX Association, Berkeley (1996). http://dl.acm.org/citation.cfm?id=1029824.1029858

11. Gamblin, T., et al.: The Spack package manager: bringing order to HPC software chaos. In: Proceedings of the International Conference for High Performance Computing, Networking, Storage and Analysis, SC 2015, pp. 40:1–40:12. ACM, New York (2015). https://doi.org/10.1145/2807591.2807623. http://doi.acm.org/10.1145/2807591.2807623

12. GrafanaLabs: Grafana: The open platform for beautiful analytics and monitoring. https://grafana.com/

13. Graylog Community: Enterprise Log Management for All. https://www.graylog.org/

14. Horenko, I.: Finite element approach to clustering of multidimensional time series. SIAM J. Sci. Comput. **32**(1), 62–83 (2010). https://doi.org/10.1137/080715962

15. Hoste, K., Timmerman, J., Georges, A., Weirdt, S.D.: Easybuild: building software with ease. In: 2012 IEEE International Conference on Services Computing (SCC), pp. 572–582, November 2013. https://doi.org/10.1109/SC.Companion.2012.81. doi.ieeecomputersociety.org/10.1109/SC.Companion.2012.81

16. Jülich Supercomputing Centre: JUBE Benchmarking Environment. https://apps.fz-juelich.de/jsc/jube/jube2/docu/index.html

17. Khuvis, S., et al.: A continuous integration-based framework for software management. In: Proceedings of the Practice and Experience in Advanced Research Computing on Rise of the Machines (Learning), PEARC 2019, pp. 28:1–28:7. ACM, New York (2019). https://doi.org/10.1145/3332186.3332219. http://doi.acm.org/10.1145/3332186.3332219

18. Kurth, T., et al.: Analyzing performance of selected NESAP applications on the Cori HPC system. In: Kunkel, J.M., Yokota, R., Taufer, M., Shalf, J. (eds.) ISC High Performance 2017. LNCS, vol. 10524, pp. 334–347. Springer, Cham (2017). https://doi.org/10.1007/978-3-319-67630-2_25

19. Lockwood, G.: IOR and mdtest (2019). https://github.com/hpc/ior
20. Ma, Wenjing, Ao, Yulong, Yang, Chao, Williams, Samuel: Solving a trillion unknowns per second with HPGMG on Sunway TaihuLight. Cluster Comput. 1–15 (2019). https://doi.org/10.1007/s10586-019-02938-w
21. McLay, R.: Lmod: A New Environment Module System. https://lmod.readthedocs.io/
22. Merchant, S., Prabhakar, G.: Tool for performance tuning and regression analyses of HPC systems and applications. In: 2012 19th International Conference on High Performance Computing, pp. 1–6, December 2012. https://doi.org/10.1109/HiPC.2012.6507528
23. Open Source: Environment Modules. http://modules.sourceforge.net/
24. Sauers, J.: Onyx Point works with Exascale Computing Project to bring CI to supercomputing centers (2018). https://www.onyxpoint.com/onyxpoint-works-with-ecp-to-bring-ci-to-supercomputers/
25. Shan, H., Williams, S., Zheng, Y., Kamil, A., Yelick, K.: Implementing high-performance geometric multigrid solver with naturally grained messages. In: 2015 9th International Conference on Partitioned Global Address Space Programming Models, pp. 38–46, September 2015. https://doi.org/10.1109/PGAS.2015.12
26. Siddiqui, S.: Buildtest: A HPC Application Testing Framework. https://github.com/HPC-buildtest/buildtest
27. Whitney, C., Bautista, E., Davis, T.: The NERSC Data Collect Environment. In: Cray User Group 2016. CUG16 (2016). https://cug.org/proceedings/cug2016_proceedings/includes/files/pap101s2-file1.pdf
28. Yoo, A.B., Jette, M.A., Grondona, M.: SLURM: simple Linux utility for resource management. In: Feitelson, D., Rudolph, L., Schwiegelshohn, U. (eds.) JSSPP 2003. LNCS, vol. 2862, pp. 44–60. Springer, Heidelberg (2003). https://doi.org/10.1007/10968987_3. https://slurm.schedmd.com/

Tools for Monitoring CPU Usage and Affinity in Multicore Supercomputers

Lei Huang, Kent Milfeld, and Si Liu$^{(\boxtimes)}$

Texas Advanced Computing Center, The University of Texas at Austin,
10100 Burnet Road, Austin, TX 78758, USA
{huang,milfeld,siliu}@tacc.utexas.edu
https://www.tacc.utexas.edu/

Abstract. Performance boosts in HPC nodes have come from making SIMD units wider and aggressively packing more and more cores in each processor. With multiple processors and so many cores it has become necessary to understand and manage process and thread affinity and pinning. However, affinity tools have not been designed specifically for HPC users to quickly evaluate process affinity and execution location. To fill in the gap, three HPC user-friendly tools, *core_usage*, *show_affinity*, and *amask*, have been designed to eliminate barriers that frustrate users and impede users from evaluating and analyzing affinity for applications. These tools focus on providing convenient methods, easy-to-understand affinity representations for large process counts, process locality, and run-time core load with socket aggregation. These tools will significantly help HPC users, developers and site administrators easily monitor processor utilization from an affinity perspective.

Keywords: Supercomputers · User support tool · Multicore system · Affinity · Resource utilization · Core binding · Real-time monitoring · Debugging

1   Introduction

Up to the millennium, the processor frequency of commodity CPUs increased exponentially year after year. High CPU frequency had been one of the major driving forces to boost CPU performance, other than the introduction of vector processor units. However, it ceased to grow significantly in recent years due to both technical reasons and market forces. To accommodate the high demand of computing power in HPC, significantly more cores are being packed into a single compute node [12].

The needs of HPC and the use of core-rich processors are exemplified in the extraordinary large-scale supercomputers found throughout the world. The Sierra supercomputer [16] at the Lawrence Livermore National Laboratory and the Summit supercomputer [19] at the Oak Ridge National Lab have 44 processing cores per compute node with two IBM Power9 CPUs [13]. The Sunway TaihuLight supercomputer [18] at the National Supercomputing Center in

© Springer Nature Switzerland AG 2020
G. Juckeland and S. Chandrasekaran (Eds.): HUST 2019/SE-HER 2019/WIHPC 2019,
CCIS 1190, pp. 69–86, 2020.
https://doi.org/10.1007/978-3-030-44728-1_4

Wuxi deploys Sunway SW26010 manycore processors, containing 256 processing cores and additional 4 auxiliary cores for system management [32] per node. The Stampede2 supercomputer [28] at the Texas Advanced Computing Center (TACC) provides Intel Knights Landing (KNL) nodes with 68 cores per node. The Stampede2 [28] and Frontera [27] supercomputers at TACC provide 48 and 56 processing cores per node with Intel's Skylake (SKX) and Cascade Lake (CLX) processors [31], respectively. These, and other HPC processors, also support Simultaneous Multi-Threading (SMT) to a level of 2 to 4 per core. Consequently, there could be 2x to 4x more logical processors than physical processors on a node.

When working with nodes of such large core counts, the performance of HPC applications is not only dependent upon the number and speed of the cores, but also upon proper scheduling of processes and threads. HPC application runs with proper affinity settings will take full advantage of resources like local memory, reusable caches, etc., and will obtain a distinct benefit in performance.

2   Background

2.1   Process and Thread Affinity

A modern computer often has more than one socket per node and therefore HPC applications may have non-uniform access to memory. Ideally, an application process should be placed on a processor that is close to the data in memory it accesses, to get the best performance. Process and thread affinity/pinning allows a process or a thread to bind to a single processor or a set of (logical) processors. The processes or threads with specific affinity settings will then only run on the designated processor(s). For Single-Program Multiple-Data (SPMD) applications, managing this affinity can be difficult. Moreover, the present-day workflows on modern supercomputers have moved beyond the SPMD approach and now include hierarchical levels of Multiple-Program Multiple-Data (MPMD), demanding even more attention to affinity.

MPI affinity for Intel MPI (IMPI), MVAPICH2 (MV2), Open MPI (OMPI), and IBM Spectrum MPI (SMPI) have a variety of mechanisms for setting affinity. IMPI relies solely on "I_MPI_x" environment variables; MV2 relies on environment variables "MV2_CPU/HYBRID_BINDING_x", "MV2_CPU_MAPPING_x", etc. SMPI uses both environment variables (MP_TASK/CPU_x) and mpirun command-line options (-map-by, -bind-to, -aff shortcuts, etc.). Similarly, OMPI uses mpirun options (-bind-to-core, –cpus-per-proc, etc.) and also accepts a rankfile file with a map (slot-list) for each rank.

When no affinity is specified, these MPIs evaluate a node's hardware configuration (for example with hwloc for MV2 and OMPI) and make appropriate default affinity settings. OpenMP affinity for hybrid runs can be specified by various "vendor" methods. However, since all of these MPIs accept OpenMP's OMP_PLACES/OMP_PROC_BIND specifications, it is best to use the standard's mechanism. Hence, for portable hybrid computing a user must deal with many ways of setting each rank's affinity. (When a master thread encounters a parallel region it inherits the MPI rank's mask, and OpenMP Affinity specifications take over).

Figure 1 shows a schematic of the affinity process. A mask is maintained for each process by the kernel that describes which processor(s) the process can run on. The mask consists of a bit for each processor, and the process can execute on any processor where a mask bit is set. There are a myriad of ways to set and alter the affinity mask for processes of a parallel application. For instance, vendors have their own way to set affinities for MPI and OpenMP, usually through environment variables. Only recently has OpenMP 4.5 [20, 21] provided a standard way to set affinity for threads, and MPI has yet to do this for MPI tasks. As shown in Fig. 1 the affinity can not only be affected before an application is launched but also while it is running. There are utilities such as *numactl* [2] and util-linux *taskset* [7] to do this. Furthermore, the affinity can even be changed within a program with the *sched_setaffinity* [6] function.

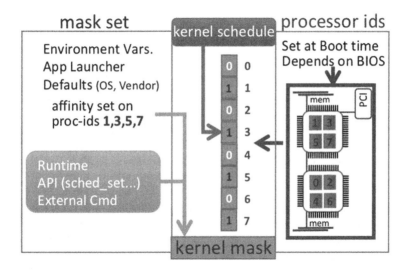

Fig. 1. The left box indicates mechanisms for setting the affinity mask. The right box illustrates how a BIOS setting has designated the processor ids for the hardware (cores). The center section shows a mask with bits set for execution on cores 1, 3, 5, and 7.

Understanding the "vernaculars" of all these methods can be challenging. Even the default settings are sometimes unknown to users. In addition, users are commonly uncertain of their attempts to set the affinity for processes of their parallel applications. Other factors (see Fig. 1), such as user environment variables, the MPI launcher, etc., also create a lack of confidence in a user's attempt to control affinity. Incorrect core binding for processes and/or threads can have adverse effects on performance, even reducing the program performance by single or multi-digit factors.

2.2   Related Work

There are many ways to view CPU loads and the affinity mask of a process. Moreover, some methods are not well-known or only available through unexpected means.

The Linux command-line tool *top* [8] and its more recent counterparts (*htop* or *atop*) can be used to monitor CPU loads, and manage process and thread affinity in real time. The Linux command *ps* [3] can report which core a process is running on. However, it does not report the affinity mask explicitly. It only reports the core the process is presently running on. The *taskset* [7] command-line utility is normally more helpful since it can query and modify the binding affinity of a given thread or process. Linux also provides API functions *sched_getaffinity* [5] and *pthread_setaffinity_np* [4] for a process or thread to query and set the affinity (kernel mask) of itself.

While these tools are pervasive and do provide the information needed, they are sometimes cumbersome to use, particularly for supercomputer users working with large core counts.

For HPC users, these tools may provide too much administrative information, and it may not be apparent how to get HPC-relevant information for their applications. Users need to remember extra options or give extra instructions to obtain relevant CPU information. For instance, *top* does not show the loads of individual processors by default. For example, pressing "1" within a *top* session is required to display the performance data of individual CPUs; and pressing "z" is needed to display running process in color. The *htop* utility does show usage information for all logical processors and the load on each individual core is represented by a progress bar in text mode. It works up to about one hundred sixty cores. However, the progress bar is distracting on a computer with many cores.

Furthermore, such tools were originally designed for administrators to display multi-user information, not for a single-user screen display of HPC information. Therefore, there is a real need for convenient HPC tools to readily display each CPU utilization and affinity information for multicore compute nodes.

The MPI libraries and OpenMP 5.0 [20] implementations themselves can present affinity mask information on the processes or threads they instantiate. For instance, by setting the I_MPI_DEBUG environment to 4 or above, the Intel MPI runtime will print a list of processor ids (mask bits set) for each process (rank) at launch time. Likewise for OpenMP 5.0 implementations, setting OMP_AFFINITY_DISPLAY to TRUE will have the runtime print a line for each thread (number) reporting the processor ids associated with its binding, at the beginning of the first parallel region. However, it is difficult to make sense of these lists for multicore or manycore compute nodes.

There are other comprehensive tools that can be used to collect the CPU loads and the affinity information. TACC Stats [10] is a well-established one. It monitors parallel jobs on supercomputers and collects a series of system statistics and hardware performance count including the CPU usage of each core. But the data processing and display is not real-time and this tools is mainly designed for system administrators. Another practical tool suite is Likwid [23,30]. It consists of many convenient command-line applications. Particularly, *likwid-topology* is used to print thread, cache, and NUMA information. *likwid-pin* can be used to pin threaded applications.

Based on years of experience administrating multiple supercomputer systems and supporting thousands of HPC users, the following questions are always asked by users and administrators when monitoring a program running on an HPC system: Does my application use the maximum capacity of CPU? How many physical or logical processors are practical for a running application? What is the currently used process and thread affinity pattern based on my current settings? To help HPC users and administrators answer these questions easily, three innovative tools *core_usage*, *show_affinity*, and *amask* were designed and developed. They are now serving the HPC communities by presenting real-time CPU usage and affinity information on systems with large core counts.

3   Three Innovative Tools

3.1   *core_usage*

Implementation. The first tool we designed and developed to quickly and efficiently show processor loads is *core_usage* [25]. It employs the logical processor (core) usage information directly from /proc/stat on Linux systems. Specifically, non-idle time ($t\_NonIdle$) has six components: user, nice, system, irq, softirq, and steal columns. Idle time (t_Idle) is calculated as the sum of idle and iowait columns. *core_usage* regularly reads kernel activity information of every logical processor on a node, then calculates core utilization with the two most-recent core status data points according to the following equation.

$$utilization = \frac{t_{NonIdle\_new} - t_{NonIdle\_old}}{(t_{NonIdle\_new} + t_{Idle\_new}) - (t_{NonIdle\_old} + t_{Idle\_old})} \tag{1}$$

core_usage then displays CPU load for all logical processors. The data are grouped by socket id and the first core of every socket is highlighted to make it easy to determine if the processes/threads are evenly distributed across sockets.

Commands and Reports. The syntax to run *core_usage* is:

```
core_usage [<int>] [txt]
```

where <int> is the update interval and must be an integer or float (unit is second, default is 1). For example, "core_usage 3" will provide an update every three seconds. Users can also add "txt" as a parameter to force the text mode.

The *core_usage* command can present a graphical-user-interface (GUI) or a command-line-interface (CLI). When X Forwarding is supported in the current environment, the GUI version is presented. In the GUI, the size of the plot area is automatically set according to the number of cores on the running computer.

The usage percentage of each individual logical processor is represented by the height of a blue bar, as shown in Fig. 2, for a hybrid job run on the Stampede2 system. The GUI version is an ideal way to visualize core usage information and can easily be extended to support thousands of cores per node in the future by adding more rows in the bar chart.

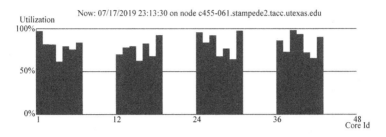

Fig. 2. Snapshot of *core_usage* (GUI) display for a hybrid application run with 4 MPI and 8 threads per MPI task on a Stampede2 Intel Xeon Skylake compute node. Colors and format are slightly modified for presentation.

If X Forwarding is not detected, the CLI version automatically launches the reports in text mode as shown in Fig. 3. A floating point number between 0.0 and 1.0 is calculated and displayed for each logical processor to represent the current core usage. The text is monochrome if the core is idle (usage less than 2%), otherwise it is green to highlight the cores in use.

From these figures, it can be seen that *core_usage* presents in logical order the current usage of each individual processor in real time. The results are collected and displayed in a socket-aware manner so that users can easily track processor status by socket. In the latest version, *core_usage* explicitly displays the name of the application that keeps the individual core busy as shown in Fig. 3. To make the results clear and concise, *core_usage* only shows the application with the top usage for each individual logical processor in this version.

As mentioned above, it is also possible to run *core_usage* manually in terminal mode with an argument "txt", even if X11 environment is available and GUI is the default starting mode.

3.2 *show_affinity*

Background and Implementation. Though *core_usage* is valuable for monitoring individual CPU core usage and detecting under utilization issues, it doesn't report the process and thread binding (affinity) that may be needed to adjust the resource usage.

Normally, the Linux tool *taskset* [7] can be used to retrieve the CPU binding affinity of individual threads or processes with commands like "taskset -p pid". However, users need to compile a full list of pid/tid's for all processes/threads, and this would require running *taskset* for each process. This would be tedious

Now: 06/30/2019 12:01:53 on node c426-052.stampede2.tacc.utexas.edu

	T0	T1	T2	T3		T0	T1	T2	T3
CORE 0:	1.00 (wrf.exe)	1.00 (wrf.exe)	1.00 (wrf.exe)	1.00 (wrf.exe)	CORE 34:	1.00 (wrf.exe)	1.00 (wrf.exe)	1.00 (wrf.exe)	1.00 (wrf.exe)
CORE 1:	1.00 (wrf.exe)	1.00 (wrf.exe)	1.00 (wrf.exe)	1.00 (wrf.exe)	CORE 35:	1.00 (wrf.exe)	1.00 (wrf.exe)	1.00 (wrf.exe)	1.00 (wrf.exe)
CORE 2:	1.00 (wrf.exe)	1.00 (wrf.exe)	1.00 (wrf.exe)	1.00 (wrf.exe)	CORE 36:	1.00 (wrf.exe)	1.00 (wrf.exe)	1.00 (wrf.exe)	1.00 (wrf.exe)
CORE 3:	1.00 (wrf.exe)	1.00 (wrf.exe)	1.00 (wrf.exe)	1.00 (wrf.exe)	CORE 37:	1.00 (wrf.exe)	1.00 (wrf.exe)	1.00 (wrf.exe)	1.00 (wrf.exe)
CORE 4:	1.00 (wrf.exe)	1.00 (wrf.exe)	1.00 (wrf.exe)	1.00 (wrf.exe)	CORE 38:	1.00 (wrf.exe)	1.00 (wrf.exe)	1.00 (wrf.exe)	1.00 (wrf.exe)
CORE 5:	1.00 (wrf.exe)	1.00 (wrf.exe)	1.00 (wrf.exe)	1.00 (wrf.exe)	CORE 39:	1.00 (wrf.exe)	1.00 (wrf.exe)	1.00 (wrf.exe)	1.00 (wrf.exe)

... ...

CORE 28:	1.00 (wrf.exe)	1.00 (wrf.exe)	1.00 (wrf.exe)	1.00 (wrf.exe)	CORE 62:	1.00 (wrf.exe)	1.00 (wrf.exe)	1.00 (wrf.exe)	1.00 (wrf.exe)
CORE 29:	1.00 (wrf.exe)	1.00 (wrf.exe)	1.00 (wrf.exe)	1.00 (wrf.exe)	CORE 63:	1.00 (wrf.exe)	1.00 (wrf.exe)	1.00 (wrf.exe)	1.00 (wrf.exe)
CORE 30:	1.00 (wrf.exe)	1.00 (wrf.exe)	1.00 (wrf.exe)	1.00 (wrf.exe)	CORE 64:	0.00	0.00	0.00	0.00
CORE 31:	1.00 (wrf.exe)	1.00 (wrf.exe)	1.00 (wrf.exe)	1.00 (wrf.exe)	CORE 65:	0.00	0.00	0.00	0.00
CORE 32:	1.00 (wrf.exe)	1.00 (wrf.exe)	1.00 (wrf.exe)	1.00 (wrf.exe)	CORE 66:	0.00	0.00	0.00	0.00
CORE 33:	1.00 (wrf.exe)	1.00 (wrf.exe)	1.00 (wrf.exe)	1.00 (wrf.exe)	CORE 67:	0.00	0.00	0.00	0.00

Use Ctrl+c to quit.

Fig. 3. Snapshot of *core_usage* CLI text report for a Weather Research and Forecasting (WRF) run with 16 MPI tasks and 4 OpenMP threads per MPI task on one Stampede2 KNL compute node. Colors and format are slightly modified for presentation.

and error-prone, and "simple" command-line expressions or scripts may require Unix skills unfamiliar to inexperienced HPC users.

To report this type of affinity information automatically and clearly, the *show_affinity* [26] tool was developed. This tool was also designed to be intuitive and simple to use. When executing *show_affinity*, all running processes/threads on a computer node are enumerated by inspecting the directories under /proc and their owners. To avoid unnecessary information, *show_affinity* only queries and reports binding affinity for the processes owned by the current user (on a compute node). Application names are then extracted from /proc/pid/exe. For each process the threads are enumerated and the core binding affinity of each individual process/thread is queried and displayed.

Commands and Reports. There are two modes of operation for *show_affinity*. The syntax is:

```
show_affinity [all]
```

In the first and default mode, the tool shows the processes/threads launched by the current user that keeps CPUs busy as demonstrated in Fig. 4. To make the results more concise and clear, the outputs are organized in four columns: process id (pid), executable name, thread id (tid), and binding affinity respectively. They are grouped with pid. The second mode is invoked with the "all" argument, and *show_affinity* displays all running processes and threads on the current compute node owned by the current user as demonstrated in Fig. 5.

pid	Exe_Name	tid	Affinity
91884	namd2_skx	91884	0
		91910	2
		91915	4
		. . .	
		91942	20
		91945	22
91885	namd2_skx	91885	24
		91911	26
		91914	28
		. . .	
		91941	44
		91944	46
91886	namd2_skx	91886	1
		91909	3
		91913	5
		. . .	
		91943	21
		91946	23
91887	namd2_skx	91887	25
		91908	27
		91912	29
		. . .	
		91950	45
		91951	47

Fig. 4. Snapshot of *show_affinity* showing the running processes and threads that keep CPU busy for a NAMD [22] run with 4 MPI tasks and 12 threads per MPI task on one Stampede2 Skylake compute node. The output contains four columns: process id (pid), executable name, thread id (tid), and core binding affinity. Format is slightly modified for presentation.

3.3 *amask*

Background and Implementation. The initial *amask* utility [24] was designed [1] as an analysis tool to confirm affinity settings for the OpenMP 4.0 Affinity implementation on the manycore Intel Xeon Phi system (68 cores, 272 processor ids). It consisted of a single, argumentless library function called within an application. However, it was found that users were more interested in executing a command immediately before their application (and after setting the affinity environment) to report the affinity of a "generic" parallel region, rather than instrumenting an application with a library call. Therefore, standalone external commands were created. *amask* was soon adapted for MPI, and the external commands (and library calls) became *amask_omp*, *amask_mpi*, and *amask_hybrid* for pure OpenMP, pure MPI, and hybrid OpenMP-MPI applications, respectively.

The OpenMP component works for any version of OpenMP. The commands with MPI components must be compiled/used with the same flavor (OpenMPI,

pid	Exe_Name	tid	Affinity
91544	slurm_script	91544	0-95
91551	sleep	91551	0-95
91649	sshd	91649	0-95
91650	bash	91650	0-95
91829	ibrun	91829	0-95
91879	mpiexec.hydra	91879	0-95
91880	pmi_proxy	91880	0-95
91884	namd2_skx	91884	0
		91905	0,2,4,...
		91910	2
		...	
		91942	20
		91945	22
91885	namd2_skx	91885	24
		91904	24,26,...
		91911	26
		...	
		91941	44
		91944	46
91886	namd2_skx	91886	1
		91906	1,3,5,...
		91909	3
		...	
		91943	21
		91946	23
91887	namd2_skx	91887	25
		91907	25,27,...
		91908	27
		...	
		91950	45
		91951	47
91975	tee	91975	0-95

Fig. 5. Snapshot of *show_affinity* with "all" argument showing all running processes and threads for a NAMD run with 4 MPI tasks and 12 threads per MPI task on one Stampede2 Skylake compute node. Format is slightly modified for presentation.

IMPI, MVAPICH2, etc.) used by the application, so that the same runtimes are invoked. It is worth mentioning that the *amask* code does not rely on any vendor-specific features or APIs. The library (and other utilities) remain available for developers or power-users who want in-situ reporting.

Commands and API. All three *amask* commands accept the same options. The syntax is:

```
amask_[omp|mpi|hybrid] -h -vk -w#  -pf
```

Commands ***amask_omp*** or ***amask_mpi*** are for reporting masks for a pure OpenMP or pure-MPI run. The ***amask_hybrid*** command is used for reporting the (parent) MPI masks followed by the OpenMP thread masks for each MPI task. The $-h$ option provides help. The $-vk$ option overrides the automatic core view, forcing a kernel (k) view (mask of processor ids). ***amask*** will load each process for # seconds when the $-w$ (wait) option is invoked (default is 10). This is helpful when used in combination with monitoring tools like ***core_usage*** and ***htop***. A slight pause after printing each row (mask) was found to give the viewer time to start comprehending the content of each mask, and then allow analysis of the pattern as more rows are reported. This slow-mode can be turned off by requesting the fast printing mode with $-pf$.

The library has function names corresponding to the commands:

```
C/C++                  Fortran
amask_omp();           call amask_omp()
amask_mpi();           call amask_mpi()
amask_hybrid();        call amask_hybrid()
```

These can be inserted in a pure OpenMP parallel region, after an MPI_Init of a pure MPI code, or within an OpenMP parallel region of a hybrid code (calls within a loop structure should be conditionally executed for only one iteration).

Reports. The important feature that makes ***amask*** more useful is that it reports a mask for each process of a parallel execution in a matrix format (process number vs. processor id), so that the user can quickly visualize relevant patterns of the affinity (such as socket, NUMA nodes, tile, core, and single hardware-thread assignments).

In the reports shown in Fig. 6, each row represents a "kernel" mask for the process number labeled at the left. Each label (process) is followed by N characters, one for each bit of the kernel's affinity mask. A dash (-) represents an unset bit, while a digit (0–9) represents a set bit. In order to easily evaluate the process id of a set bit, the single digit (0–9) of the set bit is added to the header group process id label at the top (labels represent groups of 10s).

For instance, the mask of process 1 in Fig. 6(a) has mask bit 12 (proc-id 12) set (proc-id = "2" + "10" from group value). This single-character bit mask representation is ideal for working with systems with hundreds of logical processors.

Figure 6(a) and (b) show processes bound to single cores and sockets, respectively (where proc-ids sets 0–11 and 12–23 are on different sockets). In the latter case each process can "float" on any core in the socket. Figure 6(c) illustrates a socket affinity, just as in Fig. 6(b), but for a system with even and odd proc-id sets for each socket. While the sequential or even-odd assignments could have been determined from hwloc [9], or /proc/cpuinfo on certain Linux systems, the ***amask*** report identifies the proc-id assignment pattern. The last report, Fig. 6(d), shows a scenario where each process is allowed to execute on any core of the system.

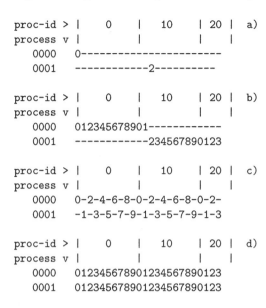

```
proc-id > |    0    |    10    | 20 |  a)
process v |         |          |    |
   0000     0-----------------------
   0001       ------------2----------

proc-id > |    0    |    10    | 20 |  b)
process v |         |          |    |
   0000     012345678901------------
   0001       ------------234567890123

proc-id > |    0    |    10    | 20 |  c)
process v |         |          |    |
   0000     0-2-4-6-8-0-2-4-6-8-0-2-
   0001     -1-3-5-7-9-1-3-5-7-9-1-3

proc-id > |    0    |    10    | 20 |  d)
process v |         |          |    |
   0000     012345678901234567890123
   0001     012345678901234567890123
```

Fig. 6. Masks for 2 processes on a 2-socket, 24 core platform. Dash (-) represents unset bit, while a single digit represents a set bit. Add digit to column group value to obtain processor id (core number) value. (a) Process 0 can only execute on core 0; process 1 can only execute on core 12. (b) Process 0 can execute on cores 0–11; process 1 can execute on cores 12–23. (c) Process 0 can execute on even-numbered cores; process 1 can execute on odd-numbered cores. (d) Processes 0 and 1 can execute on any cores

With simultaneous multithreading (SMT), available on IBM, Intel, AMD, and other processors, the OS assigns multiple (virtual) processors to a core. Hence each core has multiple processor ids, also called hardware threads (HWT) - the term used here.

When **amask** detects hardware threading, it reports a "core" view, showing a column for each core id, and each process reporting a row (mask) for each hardware thread. Hence, core group numbers appear in the header instead of processor-id group numbers.

For a 2-socket system with sequential process id numbering Fig. 7(a) shows the affinity mask for process 0 execution on either HWT of core 0, and process 1 execution on either HWT on core 12; while Fig. 7(b) shows executions are available only on the 1st hardware thread of two adjacent cores. Figure 7(c) shows 68 threads executing with "cores" affinity (execution available on all hardware threads of a core) for a 4-SMT, 68-core Intel Xeon Phi system. It is easy to see that each process is assigned to all HWTs of a core. A process id list for core number 67 is the set {67, 135, 203, 271}, and determining that these represent a single core in the **amask** kernel (processor id) view would be difficult, and checking the assignment with just a process id listing would be tedious.

For multi-node executions, **amask** reports the masks on each node, and labels each process (row) with a node name and rank number as shown in

Fig. 8(a). Masks for Hybrid (OpenMP/MPI) executions are reported by the **amask_hybrid** command. The report consists of two parts. The first part contains the masks of the MPI task (just as the **amask_mpi** would report). It is important to show these masks, because the OpenMP runtime inherits the task's map for the parallel region, and can only assign thread masks as subsets (or the full set) of the set bits in the MPI task mask. Figure 8(b) shows the MPI (parent) masks and thread masks for a hybrid run of 4 MPI tasks with 6 OpenMP threads per task. Each thread is bound to a single core, as would be desired for a 4×6 (task × thread) run on a 24-core system.

4   Case Study

4.1   Unexpected Slow VASP Runs

In 2018, one of our experienced Vienna Ab Initio Simulation Package (VASP) [11] users reported unexpected performance drop in his jobs and he needed help to debug this issue on TACC's Stampede2 system. The user had created a top-level script in Python to manage the overall workflow, and invoked numpy [29] in this script for scientific computing work. Numpy then invoked Intel Math Kernel Library (MKL) [14] for threaded and vectorized function calls. Executions of VASP were employed later by the Python scripts for material modeling simulations.

We could reproduce the user's issue and we employed our new tools on the user's workflow. **core_usage** demonstrated that all cores were allocated and used at the beginning of the job. However, after a while only a single core was busy when the VASP runs finally started. **show_affinity** also showed that all running threads on a compute node were bound to a single core (0) instead of separate cores. A more in-depth investigation revealed that the Intel MKL functions called Intel OpenMP function "omp_get_num_procs" from the Intel OpenMP library. This function was directly binding the parent process (where the python script was calling numpy) to only core 0. This is an Intel default setting when the environment variable "OMP_PROC_BIND" is not set. Consequently, all child processes of the python script including the following VASP runs inherited this binding affinity unexpectedly. Hence only a single core was used by all new processes/threads for the VASP runs, though they were designed to run in parallel on all the available cores.

Due to this incorrect binding, the job ran a hundred times slower. With the **core_usage** and **show_affinity** tools, the source of the problem was quickly and efficiently determined. The fix was easy: "OMP_PROC_BIND" was set to TRUE in the user's default environment, forcing each parallel region to obey OpenMP's affinity policy.

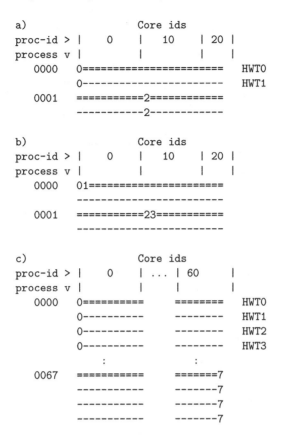

Fig. 7. Core view of masks for SMT systems: Equals (=) represent unset bits and distinguishes the first HWT. Dashes (-) represent unset bits for the other HWTs. (a) Process 0 can execute on either HWT of core 0. Process 1 can execute on either HWT of core 12. (b) Process 0 can execute only on HWT 0 of cores 0 and 1. Process 1 can execute only on HWT 0 of cores 12 and 13. (c) Process i can execute on any HWT of core i. (for a 68-core 4-SMT system)

4.2 MPI Library Evaluation on a New System

When building and deploying the new Frontera system [27] at TACC in 2019, several different MPI Stacks were tested and evaluated, including the Intel MPI library [15], the MVAPICH2 library [17], etc. The objective was to determine configurations and settings for optimal performance of the system. In the evaluation process, two significant issues related to process/thread affinity were discovered for hybrid (MPI + OpenMP) application runs.

The first problem was an unbalanced work distribution when all cores on a compute node were not fully used (due to memory or other limitations). On Frontera CLX nodes there are 56 physical cores on two sockets (28 cores/socket). The initial MVAPICH2 "MV2_HYBRID_BINDING_POLICY" was set to "linear" at TACC

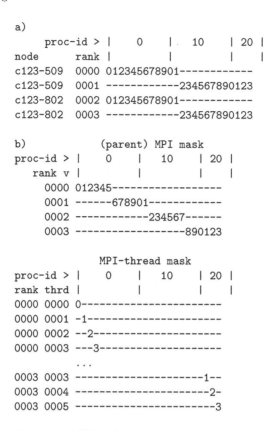

```
a)
      proc-id > |    0    | . 10    | 20 |
node      rank |         |         |    |
c123-509  0000 012345678901------------
c123-509  0001 ------------234567890123
c123-802  0002 012345678901------------
c123-802  0003 ------------234567890123


b)              (parent) MPI mask
proc-id > |    0    |   10    | 20 |
   rank v |         |         |    |
     0000 012345------------------
     0001 ------678901------------
     0002 ------------234567------
     0003 ------------------890123


              MPI-thread mask
proc-id > |    0    |   10    | 20 |
rank thrd |         |         |    |
0000 0000 0----------------------
0000 0001 -1---------------------
0000 0002 --2--------------------
0000 0003 ---3-------------------
          . . .
0003 0003 ---------------------1--
0003 0004 ----------------------2-
0003 0005 -----------------------3
```

Fig. 8. (a) Affinity for a pure MPI multi-node execution, 4 MPI tasks on two separate nodes. (b) Affinity for an OpenMP/MPI hybrid (*amask_hybrid*) execution with parent MPI and hybrid (rank/thread) reports.

as the default and recommended value. By evaluating application executions with our tools, it was soon discovered that this was not an appropriate setting for hybrid applications that did not use all the cores of a node. For instance for application requiring 2^n cores/node, an application execution with 2 tasks per node and 16 threads per task was assigning 28 cores on the first socket and 4 cores on the second, while ideally one would want 16 cores assigned to each socket. The default setting was changed to "spread", which generally works well for all cases.

The second problem was with the different thread binding behavior of Intel MPI and MVAPICH2. The default/recommended setting of Intel MPI binds each process to a single core throughout a run. The bind-to-one-core affinity assumes that cache/memory locality will normally provide optimal performance. However, with MVAPICH2, every bit in a process mask is set to 1 by default, and therefore each process can run on any core. Explicitly setting core binding for certain hybrid applications compiled with MVAPICH2 has been found to increase performance slightly.

4.3 Affinity Discovery

While **amask** has benefited many in discovering the affinity for their HPC applications, another potential feature is learning how to correctly interpret the complicated syntax of certain MPI implementations. That is, a concise report of
affinity can help users when experimenting with unfamiliar options and syntax.
While the syntax for OpenMP Affinity is standard, the implementation of certain features is implementation defined – **amask** can quickly show the effects of
an implementation-defined affinity setting in its report.

Discovering the affinity for a pure MPI application can be complicated even
if the number of processes does evenly divide the number of processors. For
instance, on Intel KNL with 68 cores (4 SMT threads per core), users might
want to use 16 MPI tasks. The default setting will mask 17 sequential bits (in
proc-id space, from 0 to 271) for each task. However, this mask allows tasks
(processes) to overlap on a single core as shown in Fig. 9. Using 17 MPI tasks
produces 16 sequential bits (4 cores) for each mask and makes for a more balanced distribution without core sharing.

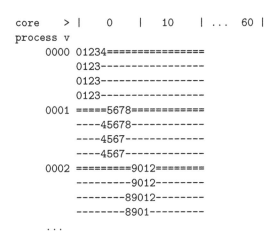

```
core    > |   0   |   10   | ... 60 |
process v
   0000 01234================
        0123-----------------
        0123-----------------
        0123-----------------
   0001 =====5678============
        ----45678------------
        ----4567-------------
        ----4567-------------
   0002 =========9012========
        ---------9012--------
        --------89012--------
        --------8901---------
   ...
```

Fig. 9. *amask* shows process 0 and 1 masks overlapping on core 4; likewise process 1
and 2 overlap on core 8.

4.4 General

These cases demonstrate that with our affinity tools, process/thread kernel
masks can be determined easily and process execution location can be easily
monitored in real time. This can be particularly important when one begins to
work on a new system and/or in an unfamiliar environment. These tools also
help users and site staff discover issues that can be immediately reported back
to developers and site administrators so that parallel applications can achieve
higher performance.

5   Best Practice

The *core_usage* and *show_affinity* tools are simple and convenient. They are recommended for daily use, especially when a workflow is changed or any environment variables related to process/thread binding are introduced or modified. Neither the source code nor the workflow needs to be changed. A user or a system administrator can easily ssh to the compute node that is running an application and then run *core_usage* and *show_affinity* at any time. *core_usage* shows how many cores are being used by an application so that a user can validate that it is the expected number. If the core occupation count is smaller than the number of tasks/threads set by the user, *show_affinity* should be run to check whether multiple processes/threads are bound to a core. Whenever users observe a drastic drop in application performance, *show_affinity* should be executed with the job to make sure that the number of worker threads/processes is correct and they have expected binding affinities.

It should be noted that it may take some time, e.g. up to several minutes, for a large job to complete MPI initialization or read large input files before all working threads execute. Complicated model design and workflow may also alter the process/thread binding status through the job, and different process/thread binding patterns are likely present during the run of these jobs. Users can try Linux commands *watch* and *show_affinity* to monitor thread affinity in real time for very complicated workflows. If a test application finishes in less than a few milliseconds, *show_affinity* may not have enough time to determine the binding affinity.

The *amask* tool allows users to quickly see the kernel mask of all processes/threads in a "matrix" format that facilitates analysis of the interaction between processes/threads. It can also be used to evaluate the effects of changing affinity settings that may not be familiar to the user.

6   Conclusion

Working with modern supercomputers with large core counts is not trivial. To help supercomputer users run parallel applications efficiently with the hardware, three convenient tools *core_usage*, *show_affinity*, and *amask* were designed and developed to monitor how computing resources are utilized in practice. These tools have helped many HPC users and administrators detect, understand, and resolve issues related to process and thread affinity. Consequently, they help user jobs to run faster and supercomputers to be used more efficiently.

Acknowledgments. We would like to thank all our users who worked with these new tools and provided us with constructive feedback and suggestions to make improvements. We would also like to thank our colleagues in the High-Performance Computing group and Advanced Computing Systems group who provided expertise and insight that significantly assisted this work. Particularly, we would like to show our gratitude to Hang Liu, Albert Lu, John Cazes, Robert McLay, Victor Eijkhout, and Bill Barth who helped us design, test, and debug the early versions of these products. We also appreciate the technical writing assistance from Bob Garza.

All these tools are mainly developed and tested on TACC's supercomputer systems, including Stampede, Stampede2, Lonestar5, Wrangler, Maverick2, and Frontera. The computation of all experiments was supported by the National Science Foundation, through the Frontera (OAC-1818253), Stampede2 (OAC-1540931) and XSEDE (ACI-1953575) awards.

References

1. 2017 IXPUG US Annual Meeting, Austin, TX, USA (2017). https://www.ixpug. org/events/ixpug-2017-us. Accessed 27 Aug 2019
2. Linux Documentation: numactl(8): Linux man page (2019). https://linux.die.net/ man/8/numactl. Accessed 27 Aug 2019
3. Linux Documentation: ps(1): Linux man page (2019). https://linux.die.net/man/ 1/ps. Accessed 27 Aug 2019
4. Linux Documentation: pthread_setaffinity_np(3) - Linux man page (2019). https:// man7.org/linux/man-pages/man3/pthread_setaffinity_np.3.html. Accessed 27 Aug 2019
5. Linux Documentation: sched_getaffinity(2): Linux man page (2019). https://linux. die.net/man/2/sched_getaffinity. Accessed 27 Aug 2019
6. Linux Documentation: sched_setaffinity(2): Linux man page (2019). https://linux. die.net/man/2/sched_setaffinity. Accessed 27 Aug 2019
7. Linux Documentation: taskset(1): Linux man page (2019). https://linux.die.net/ man/1/taskset. Accessed 27 Aug 2019
8. Linux Documentation: top(1) - Linux man page (2019). https://linux.die.net/man/ 1/top. Accessed 27 Aug 2019
9. Broquedis, F., et al.: hwloc: A generic framework for managing hardware affinities in HPC applications. In: PDP 2010 - The 18th Euromicro International Conference on Parallel, Distributed and Network- Based Computing (2010)
10. Evans, T., et al.: Comprehensive resource use monitoring for HPC systems with TACC stats. In: 2014 First International Workshop on HPC User Support Tools, pp. 13–21, November 2014. https://doi.org/10.1109/HUST.2014.7
11. Hafner, J., Kresse, G.: The Vienna AB-initio simulation program VASP: an efficient and versatile tool for studying the structural, dynamic, and electronic properties of materials. In: Gonis, A., Meike, A., Turchi, P.E.A. (eds.) Properties of Complex Inorganic Solids, pp. 69–82. Springer, Boston (1997). https://doi.org/10.1007/978-1-4615-5943-6_10
12. Hennessy, J., Patterson, D.: Computer Architecture: A Quantitative Approach. The Morgan Kaufmann Series in Computer Architecture and Design, 6th edn. Elsevier, Amsterdam (2017)
13. IBM: POWER9 Servers Overview, Scalable servers to meet the business needs of tomorrow (2019). https://www.ibm.com/downloads/cas/KDQRVQRR. Accessed 27 Aug 2019
14. Intel: Intel Math Kernel Library Developer Reference (2019). https://software. intel.com/en-us/articles/mkl-reference-manual. Accessed 27 Aug 2019
15. Intel-developers (2019). https://software.intel.com/en-us/mpi-library. Accessed 27 Aug 2019
16. Lawrence Livermore National Laboratory: Sierra supercomputer (2019). https:// computation.llnl.gov/computers/sierra. Accessed 27 Aug 2019

17. Mvapich-developers (2019). http://mvapich.cse.ohio-state.edu/. Accessed 27 Aug 2019
18. National Supercomputer Center in Wuxi: The Sunway TaihuLight system (2019). http://www.nsccwx.cn/wxcyw/soft1.php?word=soft&i=46. Accessed 27 Aug 2019
19. Oak Ridge National Lab: Summit: Oak Ridge National Laboratory's 200 petaflop supercomputer (2019). https://www.olcf.ornl.gov/olcf-resources/compute-systems/summit/. Accessed 27 Aug 2019
20. OpenMP Architecture Review Board: OpenMP Application Programming Interface, Version 4.5, November 2015 (2015)
21. OpenMP Architecture Review Board: OpenMP Application Programming Interface, Version 5.0, November 2018 (2018)
22. Phillips, J.C., et al.: Scalable molecular dynamics with NAMD. J. Comput. Chem. **26**, 1781–1802 (2005)
23. Roehl, T., Treibig, J., Hager, G., Wellein, G.: Overhead analysis of performance counter measurements. In: 43rd International Conference on Parallel Processing Workshops (ICCPW), pp. 176–185, September 2014. https://doi.org/10.1109/ICPPW.2014.34
24. TACC Staff: TACC: amask project page (2019). https://github.com/TACC/amask/. Accessed 27 Aug 2019
25. TACC Staff: TACC core_usage project page (2019). https://github.com/TACC/core_usage/. Accessed 27 Aug 2019
26. TACC Staff: TACC show_affinity project page (2019). https://github.com/TACC/show_affinity/. Accessed 27 Aug 2019
27. Texas Advanced Computing Center: Frontera User Guide (2019). https://portal.tacc.utexas.edu/user-guides/frontera. Accessed 27 Aug 2019
28. Texas Advanced Computing Center: Stampede2 User Guide (2019). https://portal.tacc.utexas.edu/user-guides/stampede2. Accessed 27 Aug 2019
29. Travis, O.: NumPy: A Guide to NumPy. Trelgol Publishing, USA (2006). http://www.numpy.org/. Accessed 27 Aug 2019
30. Treibig, J., Hager, G., Wellein, G.: LIKWID: a lightweight performance-oriented tool suite for x86 multicore environments. In: Proceedings of PSTI2010, the First International Workshop on Parallel Software Tools and Tool Infrastructures, San Diego, CA (2010)
31. Wikipedia contributors: List of Intel CPU microarchitectures (2019). https://en.wikipedia.org/wiki/List_of_Intel_CPU_microarchitectures. Accessed 27 Aug 2019
32. Wikipedia contributors: The Sunway TaihuLight Supercomputer (2019). https://en.wikipedia.org/wiki/Sunway_TaihuLight. Accessed 27 Aug 2019

SE-HER - International Workshop on Software Engineering for HPC-Enabled Research

A Study of Hydrodynamics Based Community Codes in Astrophysics

A. Dubey[✉][iD]

Argonne National Laboratory, Lemont, IL, USA
adubey@anl.gov

Abstract. Advances in mathematical models and numerical algorithms for understanding multiphysics and multiscale phenomena have made software development for simulations a large and complex task. Development and adoption of community codes is one way to address this challenge. The astrophysics community has been ahead of many other science communities in making research codes publicly available and therefore has led the development and adoption of community codes. A study of publicly available software and their penetration in the research conducted by the community can provide important insight for other communities that are facing similar issues. In this paper we analyze software available in Astrophysics Source Code Library, focusing on simulations that include hydrodynamics. We use the citation history of these codes to gauge their impact on the community.

Keywords: Computational software · Community code · Software engineering · Software productivity

1 Introduction

Advances in mathematical models and numerical algorithms, combined with increasing reliance on simulations for understanding the world around us, have made software development for simulations a large and complex task. The model of small groups developing their own software still applies to specific limited-phenomena research, but increasingly the research problems being pursued through simulations are multiphysics and multiscale in nature. Such problems typically require several independent or interdependent solvers to properly model all phenomena of interest, and they need high performance computing (HPC) resources. The solvers often have divergent requirements of data management and place different demands on the computing platforms. For integrated simulations, however, several included solvers may need to interoperate with one another. When we take into account the diversity of computing platforms and their typical shelf life, and compare these with the number of person-years needed to build a reliable and efficient multiphysics software for one platform, we can clearly see that the task of building highly capable multiphysics scientific research software has gone beyond the resources of individual, or even small

© Springer Nature Switzerland AG 2020
G. Juckeland and S. Chandrasekaran (Eds.): HUST 2019/SE-HER 2019/WIHPC 2019,
CCIS 1190, pp. 89–97, 2020.
https://doi.org/10.1007/978-3-030-44728-1_5

groups of researchers. Development and adoption of community codes is one way to address this challenge.

The astrophysics community has been among the leaders in science communities that have embraced the practice of making their software publicly available. ZEUS-2D [27] was one of the earliest codes to become public; and it has been followed by several others, many of which are considered in this paper. That this domain takes community development seriously is also reflected by a comprehensive list of freely available software compiled in The Astrophysics Source Code Library (ASCL) [2]. A study of publicly available software and their penetration in the research conducted by the community can provide important insight for other communities that are facing similar issues. Astrophysics is the ideal community to begin such analysis because of the number of open source codes and resources such as ASCL. In this paper we analyze a subset of astrophysics software used for simulations involving hydrodynamics or magnetohydrodynamics. We note that the presence of hydrodynamics does not preclude inclusion of other physics models in the simulations, it implies only a necessary condition.

The objective of this paper is not to study the codes themselves or to discuss processes and practices that might help individual code projects. Instead, the objective is to understand whether any correlation exists between the capabilities and features of the codes and their adoption by its target community. We assume that the usage of the code is roughly captured by the citation history of the paper describing the code. The paper is organized as follows. In Sect. 2 we summarize the growth of scientific simulations over the previous two decades and the motivation for this study. In Sect. 3 we describe the methodology for our selection of codes and their analysis. Section 4 provides a detailed analysis of collected information and our inferences, and in Sect. 5 we present our conclusions and discuss future directions.

2   Background

The most common mode of development in computational science has historically been "heroic," where individual researchers and small teams were able to make significant progress through highly simplified models. Such models were often first glimpses into the phenomena of interest, and therefore approximations were necessary in order to avoid having too many degrees of freedom in the models. Some projects can still successfully operate in that mode, especially in new fields of scientific enquiry. As understanding grows and models become more complex, however, the heroic programmer model becomes problematic.

As an example, consider the case of Type Ia supernova simulations in astrophysics. As with most sciences the simulations started with 1D and 2D models [10, 18] which gave some insight into the workings of their causes. Early 3D simulations assumed symmetry and modeled only an octant of the star, because of computational resource limitations. While all those simulations advanced the state of scientific knowledge, the real scientific gains from those simulations were the insights about where to use approximate models and where to do direct numerical simulations. Not until the symmetry imposed by the octant was elim-inated did scientists obtain the first insight into the cause of the star going supernova [17]. The software used for the full-star 3D simulation had enough complexity that it could not have been done in the heroic programmer mode. FLASH [12,13], the software used for the simulations, had been in development by a team for nearly a decade by that time. It had undergone three revisions to incorporate extensible and composable software design, and t had evolved a well-defined software process, both of which were critical to the series of simulations that led to the scientific insight.

Similar to FLASH's experience, in the late 1990s - for various reasons includ-ing greater understanding of the underlying phenomena - models began to become more refined and started to acquire a multiphysics aspect [3,9]. Invest-ment was made in developing software frameworks for such multiphysics simu-lations, [4,8]. Not all frameworks survived; however, a sufficient fraction of the frameworks developed during that time have evolved into ongoing community codes.

In an earlier study we analyzed the community impact of three codes in the astrophysics community. The authors of the study were also members of one or more of corresponding software development teams [14]. The study was therefore based on internal knowledge and direct experience with the user com-munity. Community growth had been important to all three projects, where an active user and developer community served to reduce the barrier to entry for new researchers using HPC resources for scientific simulations. The impact was found to have been most marked on the younger members of the commu-nity - graduate students and postdoctoral researchers- who instead of expending tremendous amount of effort in developing codes from scratch, were able to focus on advancing their research. An added advantage was using tools that had been vetted by multiple researchers and were therefore less error-prone than their own necessarily less-tested code would have been.

Another in-depth study focused on a single code, FLASH, for which data about user community was available through multiple surveys [15]. The code team had adopted version control from the beginning, and therefore the history of the team members participation could be derived. Additionally, the code team had compiled a database of publications that used the code for obtaining their results, which also became a rich source of data. The publications database could be used to trace the timeline of capability additions and could be correlated with the expansion of the code's reach. This study was instrumental in highlighting the synergies that exist among scientific communities. Capabilities added by one science community often benefited several other science communities.

Here we study a broader collection of software. However, since we do not have access to internal information about all the projects or direct user experience about them, we rely on literature and resources available from the web for our analysis. We primarily use ASCL to search for codes and the astrophysics data system [1], to access the citation history, which is the basis of most of the analysis in this paper. We assume that the citation history of the paper describing the code also reflects its use by the community in conducting their own research.

3   Methodology

For selecting the codes to study we started with ASCL, which catalogs 2030 codes. Because the library is too large for all codes to be analyzed, we narrowed our focus to those codes that have some form of hydrodynamics solver. This step reduced the number of codes to roughly 80. In the next iteration we eliminated codes that appear to have not been updated for five years or more, since that suggests that there may be no ongoing development. Several codes are present in the library exclusively for reproducibility purposes; those also were eliminated from the list. One code was removed because it was explicitly stated that it was not meant to be used for production.

The next iteration eliminated codes that did not have a paper describing them, because we use paper citation history for our analysis. Although one can argue that doing so could skew the results, such codes turned out to be too few to make much difference. We also removed codes whose papers had too few citations, especially if they have been around for some time, because we took that to indicate a lack of interest by the community. Because the citation counts varied greatly, we further binned the codes based on their counts. To do the binning, we computed the annual average citations for the paper describing the corresponding code. Several codes have had upgrades over the years, and newer papers describing the upgraded code have been published. In such instances, where we found newer papers, we cumulated the counts for all papers. Nine of the codes that have been around for more than seven years had an average citation rate of around 10. Following our earlier logic, we assumed that these papers also do not play an important role in the community research. We therefore eliminated these codes, bringing the number down to 16 for our analysis.

Our parameters of analysis were the following:

1. Method used for hydrodynamics calculations.
2. Whether the code has multiphysics capabilities.
3. Citation history related to the code lifetime.

Of the codes analyzed in this study, ones that have been in existence for longer than 5 years, are tabulated with their characteristics in Table 1, while the newer codes that have been around for less than five years are listed in Table 2. This distinction was made because it takes roughly 2–4 years for a code to become known in the community. Therefore, inferences drawn from their usage data have be treated differently from inferences drawn from usage data of longer-lived codes. Additionally, binning the codes in these two groups can help determine what, if any, new methods are gaining acceptance and prominence for solving similar problems and whether any fundamental difference has emerged in the computing paradigm.

In a second categorization, the codes that use smooth particle hydrodynamics [21] (Lagrangian formulation) are listed as *SPH*, and those that use grids (Eulerian formulation) [11] are listed as *Grid*. Among the newer codes some do not fit into either category, they are listed more explicitly. Many codes include gravity solvers in addition to hydrodynamics, and a few have several other solvers.

A "yes" in the column "Other physics" indicates that the code includes at least one solver in addition to hydrodynamics that is not gravity.

Table 1. Features of astrophysics simulation codes that have been in existence for more than five years.

Code	Hydrodynamics	Gravity	Other physics	Year
CoCoNut	Grid	Yes	Yes	2012
Castro	Grid	Yes	Yes	2010
Gr1D	Grid	Yes	Yes	2010
Pluto	Grid	No	No	2007
Athena	Grid	No	No	2006
Enzo	Grid	Yes	Yes	2004
WhiskyMHD	Grid	Yes	Yes	2005
Gasoline	SPH	Yes	No	2004
RAMSES	SPH	Yes	Yes	2002
FLASH	Grid	Yes	Yes	2000
Gadget-2	SPH	Yes	No	2000

Table 2. Features of newer astrophysics simulation codes that have been in existence for less than five years.

Code	Hydrodynamics	Gravity	Other physics	Year
ChaNGa	SPH	Yes	No	2015
SNEC	Rad-Hydro	No	Yes	2015
Gizmo	Lagrangian Godunov	Yes	No	2015
Fargo3d	Grid	No	No	2016
Phantom	SPH	Yes	Yes	2018

4   Analysis and Inferences

Our initial inspection of data quickly revealed a shift in the algorithmic preference in the last five years. Therefore, the analysis was split into two sections. We begin by discussing older codes and their history. Figures 1 and 2 plot citations per year for codes that have been in existence for more than five years. We have split the figure into two for clarity; all plots in one figure would have been difficult to read and discuss.

As expected, the majority of codes show an upward trend in citations in their first few years, beyond which the trends vary. Note that the last data point in all the figures is incomplete because the data was collected in the middle of

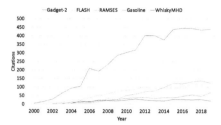

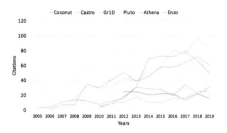

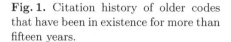

Fig. 1. Citation history of older codes that have been in existence for more than fifteen years.

Fig. 2. Citation history of older codes that have been in existence for five to fifteen years.

2019. Some codes have a downward trend either because the codes are no longer in use at the same level as before, or because the code may have undergone a new incarnation. Wherever we were able to find a link between old and new versions of the code, and accompanying papers describing the newer versions, we cumulated citations of all papers. For example, Athena and Enzo have had new versions, and papers exist about the upgraded versions. On the other side, codes like FLASH have had version upgrades but not paper upgrade, so the original paper still continues to be the one cited. However, we cannot claim to have conducted a comprehensive search, and therefore some of the codes may have more citations than we count. This may make some quantitative difference in the plots, but we do nor believe that there is likely to be significant qualitative difference in the inferences.

An observation that stands out is that the Gadget-2 [26] code has dominated in the user community throughout its existence. Its citations stand far above all the rest of the codes. Since having a plot for Gadget clusters all the remaining codes too closely to follow their trend, we split the plots in a different way. Figures 3 shows citation histories of codes that have grid-based hydrodynamics methods while Fig. 4 plots them for codes with the SPH method. Among the grid-based codes, FLASH and RAMSES [28] have dominated the user community, and have been in existence for the longest time. The two codes have different flavors of mesh adaptivity; although they are both multiphysics. Pluto [20], although not multiphysics in the same way as FLASH and RAMSES are, also shows a steep upward trend and has almost caught up with those two codes. Part of the reason may have been that it was ready to use accelerators long before the other larger codes were. A cluster of codes including Castro [5], Gasolinegasoline, CoCoNut [23], Gr1D [24], and WhiskyMHD [6], have remained on the lower side of citations throughout their history, indicating a relatively small user group. They all came into existence after FLASH and RAMSES had been around for a while and had become community codes. Newer codes appear not to have had much success in matching the impact of these two codes, let alone replacing them in the user community.

An interesting observation is that among the older codes only two codes use SPH methods, and Gadget-2 clearly dominates that space. Historically the SPH methods were not able to capture all features of turbulent flows and were therefore not considered suitable for all astrophysical flows. However, they had the advantage of being simpler than grid-based codes, and so were preferred where the regime did not demand grid-based method. Gadget-2 specifically targeted such applications, and that could be the strongest reason why it dominated among users interested in that class of problems.

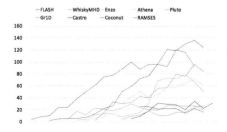

Fig. 3. Comparison of code citation history of older codes that have Grid based hydrodynamics.

Fig. 4. Comparison of code citation history of older codes that have SPH based hydrodynamics.

In contrast, the hydrodynamics implementations in the newer codes are quite diverse. Only one, FARGO3D [7], has a grid-based implementation, while ChaNGa [19] and PHANTOM [25] have SPH methods. SNEC [22] implements a radiation-hydrodynamics method, while GIZMO [16] has a completely new method that is Lagrangian but with a Godunov type scheme. In recent years many of the shortcomings of SPH methods have been eliminated, and several scientists in the

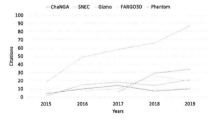

Fig. 5. Citation history of codes that have been in existence for less than five years.

community argue that these methods can provide the same fidelity in most regimes that grid-based methods can. The trend toward newer codes preferring SPH methods or other Lagrangian formulations certainly seems to substantiate those claims. It is difficult to predict which, if any, of these codes will persist in future, or come to replace any of the old codes. With the exception of Phantom, being younger, they offer fewer capabilities to the users than the older codes. However, this situation is likely to change with time. If a code gains acceptance in the community, newer ways of using the code are likely to cause capability addition, as has occurred in the older codes. Figure 5 plots the citation histories of these five relatively young codes. The GIZMO and PHANTOM plots have a similar slope, although PHANTOM is still too new to predict whether this trend will persist. Because GIZMO has a new method, it is perhaps not surprising that it is showing signs of strong adoption by the community.

5   Conclusions

Ad the general analysis of the codes in existence and their citation histories indicates, community codes continue to thrive in the astrophysics community. Several of the old codes are holding steady, while newer codes are coming into being. Additionally, several of the older codes have been regularly upgraded, either to include newer solvers or to be able to compute on newer platforms. Furthermore, in any category of codes there appear to be good alternative to choose from. Thus the astrophysics community continues to provide a good model for growth of computational research through open and cooperative practices. It would be interesting to do similar studies of other major communities where open software is the norm, as also a more in-depth study of the code history similar to [15]. Even more interesting would be to do a study comparing the astrophysics community with those communities that do not have such norms and do not share their software.

Acknowledgements. This material was based upon supported by the U.S. Department of Energy Office of Science, Office of Advanced Scientific Computing Research under Contract No. DE-AC02-06CH11357.

References

1. Astrophysics data system. https://ui.adsabs.harvard.edu/
2. Astrophysics source code library. https://ascl.net/
3. The GENE Code. http://genecode.org/
4. SAMRAI structured adaptive mesh refinement application infrastructure. Lawrence Livermore National Laboratory, December 2007. https://computation.llnl.gov/casc/SAMRAI/
5. Almgren, A.S., et al.: CASTRO: a new compressible astrophysical solver, I: hydrodynamics and self-gravity. Astrophys. J. **715**, 1221–1238 (2010). https://doi.org/10.1088/0004-637X/715/2/1221
6. Baiotti, L., et al.: Three-dimensional relativistic simulations of rotating neutron-star collapse to a Kerr black hole. Phys. Rev. D **71**(2), 024035 (2005). https://doi.org/10.1103/PhysRevD.71.024035
7. Benítez-Llambay, P., Masset, F.S.: FARGO3D: a new GPU-oriented MHD code. Astrophys. J. Suppl. Ser. **223**, 11 (2016). https://doi.org/10.3847/0067-0049/223/1/11
8. Blazewicz, M., et al.: From physics model to results: an optimizing framework for cross-architecture code generation. Sci. Program. **21**(1–2), 1–16 (2013)
9. Bryan, G.L., et al.: ENZO: an adaptive mesh refinement code for astrophysics. Astrophys. J. Suppl. Ser. **211**(2), 19 (2014). http://stacks.iop.org/0067-0049/211/i=2/a=19
10. Burrows, A., Fryxell, B.A.: A convective trigger for supernova explosions. APJ **418**, L33 (1993). https://doi.org/10.1086/187109
11. Colella, P., Woodward, P.R.: The Piecewise Parabolic Method (PPM) for gas-dynamical simulations. J. Comput. Phys. **54**(1), 174–201 (1984). https://doi.org/10.1016/0021-9991(84)90143-8. http://www.sciencedirect.com/science/article/pii/0021999184901438

12. Dubey, A., et al.: Evolution of FLASH, a multiphysics scientific simulation code for high performance computing. Int. J. High Perform. Comput. Appl. **28**(2), 225–237 (2013). https://doi.org/10.1177/1094342013505656

13. Dubey, A., et al.: Extensible component based architecture for FLASH, a massively parallel, multiphysics simulation code. Parallel Comput. **35**, 512–522 (2009). https://doi.org/10.1016/j.parco.2009.08.001.   http://www.sciencedirect.com/ science/article/B6V12-4X54JHJ-1/2/b261a63ad1957b89222e859101236ca7

14. Dubey, A., Turk, M., O'shea, B.: The impact of community software in astrophysics. In: Onate, E., Olivier, J., Huerta, A. (eds.) Proceedings of WCCM-XI;ECCM-V;ECFD-VI (2014)

15. Dubey, A., Tzeferacos, P., Lamb, D.: The dividends of investing in computational software design: a case study. Int. J. High Perform. Comput. Appl. (2018). https:// doi.org/10.1177/1094342017747692

16. Hopkins, P.F.: A new class of accurate, mesh-free hydrodynamic simulation methods. MNRAS **450**, 53–110 (2015). https://doi.org/10.1093/mnras/stv195

17. Jordan IV, G.C., et al.: Three-dimensional simulations of the deflagration phase of the gravitationally confined detonation model of type la supernovae. Astrophys. J. **681**(2), 1448 (2008). http://stacks.iop.org/0004-637X/681/i=2/a=1448

18. Janka, H.T., Müller, E.: The first second of a type II supernova: convection, accretion, and shock propagation. Astrophys. J. **448**(2) (1995). https://doi.org/10.1086/ 309604

19. Menon, H., et al.: Adaptive techniques for clustered N-body cosmological simulations. Comput. Astrophys. Cosmol. **2**(1), 1–16 (2015). https://doi.org/10.1186/ s40668-015-0007-9

20. Mignone, A., et al.: PLUTO: a numerical code for computational astrophysics. Astrophys. J. Suppl. Ser. **170**, 228–242 (2007). https://doi.org/10.1086/513316

21. Monaghan, J.J.: Smoothed particle hydrodynamics. Ann. Rev. Astron. Astrophys. **30**, 543–574 (1992). https://doi.org/10.1146/annurev.aa.30.090192.002551

22. Morozova, V., et al.: Light curves of core-collapse supernovae with substantial mass loss using the new open-source SuperNova Explosion Code (SNEC). Astrophys. J. **814**, 63 (2015). https://doi.org/10.1088/0004-637X/814/1/63

23. Müller, B., Janka, H.T., Marek, A.: A new multi-dimensional general relativistic neutrino hydrodynamics code for core-collapse supernovae. II. Relativistic explosion models of core-collapse supernovae. Astrophys. J. **756**, 84 (2012). https://doi. org/10.1088/0004-637X/756/1/84

24. O'Connor, E.: An open-source neutrino radiation hydrodynamics code for core-collapse supernovae. Astrophys. J. Suppl. Ser. **219**(2), 24 (2015). https://doi.org/ 10.1088/0067-0049/219/2/24

25. Price, D.J., et al.: PHANTOM: a smoothed particle hydrodynamics and magnetohydrodynamics code for astrophysics. Publ. Astron. Soc. Aust. **35**, e031 (2018). https://doi.org/10.1017/pasa.2018.25

26. Springel, V.: The cosmological simulation code GADGET-2. MNRAS **364**, 1105–1134 (2005). https://doi.org/10.1111/j.1365-2966.2005.09655.x

27. Stone, J.M., Norman, M.L.: ZEUS-2D: a radiation magnetohydrodynamics code for astrophysical flows in two space dimensions. I - the hydrodynamic algorithms and tests. Astrophys. J. **80**, 753–790 (1992). https://doi.org/10.1086/191680

28. Teyssier, R.: Cosmological hydrodynamics with adaptive mesh refinement. A new high resolution code called RAMSES. Astron. Astrophys. **385**, 337–364 (2002). https://doi.org/10.1051/0004-6361:20011817

Lightweight Software Process Improvement Using Productivity and Sustainability Improvement Planning (PSIP)

Michael A. Heroux[1], Elsa Gonsiorowski[2], Rinku Gupta[3], Reed Milewicz[1],
J. David Moulton[4], Gregory R. Watson[5], Jim Willenbring[1],
Richard J. Zamora[6], and Elaine M. Raybourn[1(✉)]

[1] Sandia National Laboratories, Albuquerque, NM, USA
emraybo@sandia.gov
[2] Lawrence Livermore National Laboratory, Livermore, CA, USA
[3] Argonne National Laboratory, Lemont, IL, USA
[4] Los Alamos National Laboratory, Los Alamos, NM, USA
[5] Oak Ridge National Laboratory, Oak Ridge, TN, USA
[6] NVIDIA, Santa Clara, CA, USA

Abstract. Productivity and Sustainability Improvement Planning (PSIP) is a lightweight, iterative workflow that allows software development teams to identify development bottlenecks and track progress to overcome them. In this paper, we present an overview of PSIP and how it compares to other software process improvement (SPI) methodologies, and provide two case studies that describe how the use of PSIP led to successful improvements in team effectiveness and efficiency.

Keywords: Software development · Software engineering · Software process improvement

1 Introduction

The Department of Energy (DOE) Exascale Computing Project (ECP) provides an opportunity to advance computational science and engineering (CSE) through high performance computing (HPC). Central to the project is the development of next-generation applications that can fully exploit emerging architectures for optimal performance and provide high-fidelity, multiphysics, and multiscale capabilities. At the heart of the effort is the need to improve developer productivity, positively impacting product quality, development time, staffing

E. Gonsiorowski, R. Gupta, R. Milewicz, J. D. Moulton, G. R. Watson, J. Willenbring, R. J. Zamora, E. M. Raybourn—contributed equally to this work.

R. J. Zamora—work was conducted while employed by Argonne National Laboratory.

G. Juckeland and S. Chandrasekaran (Eds.): HUST 2019/SE-HER 2019/WIHPC 2019,
CCIS 1190, pp. 98–110, 2020.
https://doi.org/10.1007/978-3-030-44728-1_6

resources, and software sustainability, reducing the cost of maintaining, sustaining, and evolving software capabilities in the future.

This paper presents the Productivity and Sustainability Improvement Planning (PSIP) process: a lightweight, iterative workflow where teams identify their most urgent software development and sustainability bottlenecks and track progress on work to overcome them. Through the PSIP process, teams are able to realize process improvements, without a huge disruption to any current development processes.

PSIP is best understood as an instantiation of the Plan-Do-Check-Act management cycle (PDCA, also known as Plan-Do-Study-Adjust), first described by Deming in 1950 [5], which provides the intellectual foundation for much of the modern process literature (including SPI methods and Agile as a philosophy) and is itself a translation of the scientific method to the study of work process. It is both a method to be used by an individual or with a team, and a method to be taught to a team, with the team driving the improvement process. One PSIP process output is the development of Progress Tracking Cards (PTC), brief, shareable documents containing the target, or goal of the planning activity, title of the topic of improvement, and a step-by-step list of activities or outcomes that incrementally lead to improvements in team effectiveness and efficiency. Through the PSIP process, teams are able to realize process improvements, without a huge disruption to any current development processes.

The contributions of this paper are:

- We compare PSIP with other software process improvement (SPI) methodologies.
- We present the PSIP process, a lightweight software process improvement framework.
- We discuss two case studies where a PSIP cycle was implemented by an existing software development team with the help of a facilitator.

2   Background

Techniques for software process improvement (SPI) aim to assess, design, and realize effective development processes. SPI has been the subject of an extensive body of literature, with "classic" SPI frameworks such as CMM(I) or SPICE dating back three decades [4,7,15]; this trend can be traced back even further to the "software crisis" starting in the late 1960s [12] and the realization that an intentional process of creating software was as important to software development as software itself or, as Osterweil put it, "software processes are software too" [14].

Within the context of scientific software research and development, SPI is an undeveloped territory. The most recent notable mention came in 2015; Mesh et al. reported plans to develop a Scientific SPI Framework (SciSPIF) by cataloging common decision factors and project characteristics and their relationships to software engineering practices, ideally realized as an online self-assessment tool [13]. Further work in this area is needed. In 2006, Baxter et al. observed that a lack of basic knowledge about development processes was a significant challenge for the scientific software community [2], but recent studies suggest the situation is now more nuanced. A 2019 survey of scientific software developers by Eisty et al. found that respondents not only saw value in software process, but even "[preferred] using a defined software development process" over ad hoc approaches [6]. This may be a reaction to the increasing importance of software in science: a 2018 survey by Pinto et al. found that 8 out of 10 researchers reported spending "more time" or "much more time" developing software than they did 10 years ago [17]. We argue that the challenge moving forward is to cultivate ways of doing software work that align with the needs of the scientific software community.

Scientific software teams are typically focused on obtaining scientific results from the software they write. Funding is for generating results, not software. This is a competitive process and teams cannot usually expend much time or effort outside of writing the software features that support generating new results. Therefore, any productivity or sustainability improvements must be incremental and integrated into the primary feature development process. Bug fix or refactoring releases are rare.

In our experience, scientific software teams typically have little or modest formal software engineering training. They may be aware of formal terminology such as software lifecycle, requirements elicitation and technical debt, but often have incomplete or incorrect understanding. Furthermore, these teams have an inherent skepticism about formal, heavyweight approaches that might significantly delay their current scientific activities or require large investments before seeing benefits.

In this context, a lightweight, adaptable, iterative and informal approach to improving developer productivity and software sustainability is necessary. A comprehensive review by Kuhrmann et al. found that from 1989 to 2016 an average of 11 new or customized SPI methods were introduced per year [11]. One hypothesis put forward by the authors is that process improvement is a context-specific activity and that methods must be adapted to their context in order to be successful. This trend towards adaptation echoes recent studies that suggest most software companies today use individualized development processes that are hybrids of different methodologies and philosophies [10,20]. Along these lines, PSIP is neither wholly new nor unsupported but is instead a tailored approach that builds upon previous SPI approaches; likewise, it is not all-encompassing but is instead a lightweight toolkit that can be incorporated into existing CSE software development workflows.

3   Methodology

The Interoperable Design of Extreme-scale Application Software (IDEAS-ECP) [8] conducts research on topics of developer productivity and software sustainability in CSE domain. Its PSIP efforts focus on methodologies for improving productivity and sustainability by working with CSE software teams to identify opportunities to iteratively and incrementally improve software team practices and processes.

The objectives of the PSIP process are to capture and convey the practices, processes, policies, and tools of a given software project. The PSIP workflow is intended to be lightweight and fit within a project's planning and development process. It is not meant to be an assessment or evaluation tool. Instead PSIP captures the tacit, more subjective aspects of team collaboration, workflow planning, and progress tracking. Additionally, in the potential absence of planning and development processes, and as scientific software teams scale to larger, more diverse, aggregate teams, unforeseen disruptions or inefficiencies can often impede productivity and innovation [8]. PSIP is designed to bootstrap aggregate team capabilities into best practices, introduce the application of appropriate resources, and encourage teams to adopt a culture of process improvement.

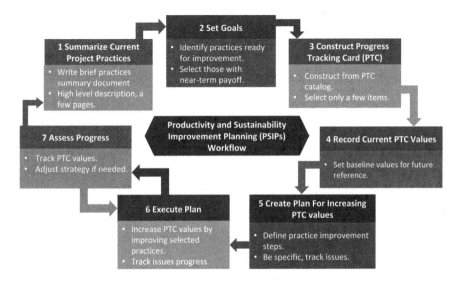

Fig. 1. The Productivity and Sustainability Planning (PSIP) cycle.

At its core, the PSIP framework is an iterative, incremental, repeatable, cyclic process for improvement planning. The cyclic nature of the PSIP process enables software development teams to improve overall project quality and achieve science goals by encouraging frequent iteration and reflection. The multi-step, iterative PSIP Workflow is described below (see Fig. 1). Beginning at the start located at the left of Fig. 1, software teams may work through these steps on their own, or with the assistance of a PSIP facilitator:

1. *Summarize Current Project Practices:* The first phase involves briefly documenting current project practices. It is important to record the original state of the project to both provide a baseline for measuring progress and to help identify areas that are ready for improvement. We find it important to use plain language when defining current project practices to reduce misunderstanding of software engineering terms that might be vaguely or incorrectly

understood by the software team, whose member may not be formally trained in software engineering concepts.

2. *Set Goals:* Completing this step typically brings to light project practices that can benefit from a focused improvement effort. Although any number of goals may be identified in this step, a limited set is selected at any given time to best impact the project and is achievable within a predictable span of time (a few weeks to a few months). Goals not chosen at this time may be tabled for future iterations.

3. *Construct a Progress Tracking Card (PTC):* Recall that a PTC is a brief document containing the target, or goal of the planning activity, title of the topic of improvement, and a step-by-step list of activities or outcomes that incrementally lead to improvements in team effectiveness and efficiency. Each practice will have its own PTC. Teams may select PTCs from the PTC catalog[1]; or define their own PTC or modify PTCs found in the catalog. The purpose of the PTC is to help teams set and achieve improvement goals. The PTC is not a tool for external assessment or comparison with other projects. In fact, since PTCs are custom designed for each project, comparisons are typically not possible.

4. *Record Current PTC Values:* In order to establish baseline capabilities and track progress, teams record the initial values (0–5 are suggested) for each PTC.

5. *Create a Practice Improvement Plan:* In order to increase the values in a PTC (corresponding to improvements in software productivity and sustainability), teams develop a plan to reach a higher value for each PTC.

6. *Execute the Plan:* Team efforts are focused on improving the selected practices described in the PTC. At first, teams may see a slowdown, as they work to start or improve a given practice. It is possible for teams to use complementary SPI methods in executing their plan. The slowdown in most cases is proportional to the amount of change, but ideally teams should see steady progress on a weekly basis after the initial phase and be able to complete execution of a particular practice improvement within a few months.

7. *Assess Progress:* During execution, teams assess, and determine the rate of progress each week. They adjust their strategy for success if needed. If progress is delayed too long, teams usually start the next PSIP iteration.

8. *Repeat:* The PSIP process is iterative. Continual process improvement is a valuable attribute for any software project. The PSIP process may be used to guide improvement planning within software projects and across aggregate projects.

During a PSIP process or at its conclusion, teams may elect to share their PSIP PTCs, best practices, and/or lessons learned with other teams. Teams may share their results with the community in a variety of ways including contributing blog posts on PSIP progress to the Better Scientific Software (BSSw) website[2], presenting lessons learned in the HPC Best Practices for HPC Software

---

[1] https://bssw.io/psip.
[2] https://bssw.io.

Developers webinar series[3], and by modifying, curating, or creating tools such as new PSIP templates, PTCs, or resources for inclusion in the PSIP catalog[4].

4 Related Work

In this section, we situate PSIP in the context of SPI methods. PSIP breaks from classic first wave SPI (such as CMM(I) or SPICE, or non-software methods translated to software like ISO 9000 or Six Sigma), in that it trades comprehensive standards and certification-driven assessment for self-defined, internally-driven goals. It does, however, carry forward first wave ideas such as having staged models of improvement like CMM(I), in the form of progress tracking cards. Additionally, PSIP is more aligned with numerous second wave SPI approaches which incorporate lean and agile thinking into their methods; it adopts their emphasis on iterative improvement and continuous learning.

Recall that PSIP is best understood as an instantiation of the Plan-Do-Check-Act management cycle (PDCA, also known as Plan-Do-Study-Adjust), first described by Deming in 1950 [5]. It is both a method to be used by an individual or with a team, and a method to be taught to a team, with the team driving the improvement process. This situates PSIP within a constellation of bottom-up, inductive SPI methods as characterized by Stojanov 2016 [19]. These include QIP [1], AINSI [3], LMPAF^2 [18], and iFLAP [16]. Each of these methods emphasizes collaborative discovery of goals, tailored improvement solutions, and is designed to be lightweight to support small, resource-constrained organizations. However, they differ in their approaches.

QIP and AINSI (an implementation of QIP) differ from PSIP in that both use a Goal-Questions-Metrics approach to create measures for goals whereas PSIP utilizes progress tracking cards (PTC) that express either quantitatively- or qualitatively-defined goal states. PSIP, like LMPAF^2, may utilize a moderator to conduct interviews in order to construct documentation that captures team's practices, and draw out targets for process improvement. However, LMPAF^2 focuses specifically on maintenance activities and relies on frequent feedback sessions with the moderator to track progress. Finally, iFLAP conducts interviews with individuals drawn from across an organization and triangulates improvement activities by comparing different interview results (as opposed to a group interview), and the assessor(s) are responsible for creating a prioritization scheme for improvement targets (PSIP has no analogous concept).

---

[3] https://bssw.io/events/best-practices-for-hpc-software-developers-webinar-series.
[4] See https://bssw.io/psip for further elaboration.

5   Case Studies

In this section, we present two case studies where an existing software development team collaborated with a facilitator to work through the PSIP process.

5.1   EXAALT

The Exascale Atomistics for Accuracy, Length and Time (EXAALT) project[5] is a part of the Chemistry and Materials Applications area of the Exascale Computing Project. It is a materials modeling framework designed to leverage extreme-scale parallelism to produce accelerated molecular dynamics simulations for fusion and fission energy materials challenges. The official team comprises approximately 10 researchers at Los Alamos National Laboratory (LANL) and Sandia National Laboratories (SNL) working on four sub-projects. While two of these sub-projects are driven by a handful of people, the others are larger open-source efforts with many external contributors.

The EXAALT team was keen to utilize PSIP to improve their software engineering practices, particularly in the area of continuous integration (CI). Since the project integrates four distinct software packages, each with its own list of dependencies, the team frequently struggled with build regressions in the early days of development. After a few informal discussions with the authors, the team agreed that it would be necessary to (1) improve their end-to-end build system, (2) implement a CI pipeline to automatically detect build regressions, and (3) add unit/regression testing to the CI pipeline.

Although the team had not committed to an explicit project-management process at the early stages of the collaboration, the steps taken during these discussions correspond to the first two steps of the PSIP cycle shown in Fig. 1. In order to prioritize their efforts, it was critical to clarify the current project practices and specify both near and long-term goals.

For the initial stage of the implementation of an automated end-to-end build system, the PSIP process was only used implicitly for project planning and execution. For the two remaining goals, however, PSIP was followed explicitly using the PTCs shown in Fig. 2 (in summarized form). During steps 3–4 of the PSIP cycle, these PTCs were both fully annotated, but reflected a "score" of zero. For step 5 of the PSIP cycle, each PTC step was resolved in both Jira and GitLab as distinct stories and issues, respectively. The actual implementation of these Jira/GitLab issues corresponded to step 6 of the PSIP cycle, and the following assessment of the completed work was the final step.

The completion of these cards does not mean that the EXAALT team is finished improving their CI and/or testing infrastructure. Like most aspects of software engineering, PSIP is an iterative process, and the initial plan may need to change if unexpected roadblocks emerge. Whether or not a progress tracking card can be followed to completion, documenting, revising, and repeating the

---

[5] https://www.exascaleproject.org/project/exaalt-molecular-dynamics-at-the-exascale-materials-science.

PSIP Process: Continuous Integration

Target: Implement and document a basic CI pipeline to act as the foundation for automated build and functionality testing.

0	**Initial Status**: No comprehensive CI framework in place.
1	Develop a minimal docker image, with EXAALT dependencies. ✓
2	Implement a minimal 'yml' script for the CI pipeline. ✓
3	Update EXAALT docker image to leverage Cmake, and create a ParSplice-specific image for build testing. ✓
4	Generate step-by-step "how-to" Docker-image documentation. ✓
5	Extend CI to automated build and functionality testing with both Cmake and Boost. ✓

Score (0-5) = **4**

PSIP Process: Testing

Target: Implement and document practical testing examples for ongoing EXAALT development.

0	**Initial Status**: No comprehensive testing framework in place.
1	Add 1-3 example tests using the existing CMake infrastructure (CTest). ✓
2	Add 1-3 example tests using the 'Boost Test' library ✓
3	Integrate the CTest infrastructure with the new Boost tests. ✓
4	Integrate the Boost-enabled CTest framework into the CI pipeline ✓
5	Bonus: Work with EXAALT team to add more advanced tests to improve code coverage. ☐

Score (0-5) = **3**

Fig. 2. Summarized versions of PSIP PTCs used for the EXAALT-IDEAS collaboration. The specific scores in the figure correspond to the state of the project. Note that some details about dependencies and timeline are excluded from the PSIP cards for clarity.

process makes sense when a natural finishing point is reached. The PTC used in this effort (see Fig. 2) is available in the PSIP PTC catalog.

At this stage, the EXAALT team members have successfully adopted a minimal CI framework and are ready to apply the PSIP process to improve their CI pipeline further. The current plan is to modify the existing infrastructure to interface with ECP-supported facilities (e.g., Argonne Leadership Computing Facility and Oak Ridge Leadership Computing Facility). In addition, they are applying the PSIP process to further improve test coverage, specifically in the area of statistical tests for non-deterministic components and task management.

5.2   Exascale MPI

The Exascale MPI (Message Passing Interface) project consists of team members from Argonne National Laboratory. The project focuses on developing a production-ready, high-performance MPI implementation that scales to the largest supercomputers in the world. One particular challenge for the Exascale MPI project is a continuous influx of new contributors within the project. These new contributors are expected to already have technical expertise with MPI or learn these skills on-the-fly as needed by the job. While the team does provide some mentoring to new members, limited resources require that newcomers be fairly independent and proactive when it comes to learning the basic technical aspects of MPI.

The Exascale MPI team worked with a facilitator to implement the PSIP process. Through the documentation of current practices, the need to improve the project's onboarding processes was identified. Both the Exascale MPI team and the facilitator agreed to work on a PSIP cycle focused around improving the training for team contributors. This would take the form of a single destination resource containing all the required training material that could be provided to new team members during the onboarding process.

Once the overall goal was identified, the Exascale MPI team, together with the facilitator, identified key aspects of a satisfactory solution. These aspects included the need for:

- A central "repository" for all training material, relevant to the Exascale MPI team.
- Visually interesting, and easy navigation across all topics.
- Easy administration and ability to update the "repository" sustainably.
- Open collaboration to allow external contributors to contribute new technical topics and resources.

With the overall goal and desired outcome defined, the Exascale MPI team worked with the facilitator to create a timeline based on the resources available, followed by the creation of a PTC. Figure 3 shows a snapshot of the PTC created for this PSIP activity. Each step in the PTC, in this case, serves as an important checklist step to move towards the desired goal. As mentioned, these PTC cards are live entities and they may change depending on unexpected progress or bottlenecks.

Once the PTC was created, the team focused on the execution aspect of the PTC. The PSIP process aims to engage a full team through the execution of PTC steps. Each step is approachable, yet builds towards a larger goal. Throughout the PSIP process, the Exascale MPI team, with help from the facilitator, continually evaluated their progress on the path to building a resource for improving onboarding and training.

For improving the training process, the teams identified what categories of topics needed to be covered in the onboarding training. For each category, the team worked and solicited resources (based on the potential expertise level of new onboarding members), reviewed the material for accuracy and applicability,

PSIP Process: Onboarding

Target: Implement a technical onboarding process to
facilitate integration of new team members.

0	**Initial Status**: No training process in place.	
1	Understand MPICH current onboarding training practices and define training categories	✓
2	Review and gather resources for training in at least two categories	✓
3	Design website and integrate content for two categories	✓
4	Solicit feedback, improve content, design processes for external contributions and updating of website	✓

Score (0-4) = **3**

Fig. 3. Progress Tracking Card snapshot for Exascale MPI team, including date of completion. Row 0 indicates the team's status at the beginning of implementing the PSIP process.

and worked on the design to integrate them into the training website/portal[6]. The Exascale MPI team, with help from the facilitator, explored the viability of using existing cloud repository services (e.g., Google Drive). In the end, the team decided to design a custom stand-alone website to serve as a training portal, based on their needs and input from the team members. The training-base portal is a continual work-in-progress by the Exascale MPI team and can be a resource for the entire HPC community. At this stage, the Exascale MPI team is testing the training portal with their new hires and soliciting feedback. The next step for this PSIP is to create a plan to improve the training portal, which will focus on adding new content categories and establishing processes to sustain the content and its validity.

6   Discussion and Future Work

With the Exascale MPI PSIP process, we learned that PSIP topics developed for a particular team may sometimes be generalizable enough to be relevant and important to several teams in an organization or across multiple organizations. The topic of technical onboarding training for new hires may sometimes be team-specific, however most teams working in the HPC field need to train people in the common practices of the community. Thus, a PTC created for one team (as in the case of the Exascale MPI team) can be used by many other teams as a starting point. We also realized that not only the PTC, but also the resulting output (as in the case of the training portal) could end up being immensely

---

[6] Exascale Onboarding training portal: https://sites.google.com/view/hpc-training-base/home.

useful across many other teams as well. The PTC used in this effort (see Fig. 3) is available in the PSIP PTC catalog.

For EXAALT, we learned that one significant advantage of the PSIP management approach is that it forces the team to specify the 4–6 steps needed to reach a given goal. In this case, the process helped formulate the actionable items needed to lay the foundation for CI within the existing EXAALT software repository. Although PSIP can be used to manage the goals of any software project, the specific details of each step are highly dependent on the project. For example, different projects will most likely need to work with slightly different technologies to build a practical CI pipeline. Specific details will depend on where and how the source code repository is organized, as well as the limitations/capabilities of the existing library dependencies. For EXAALT, this process required careful discussion between teams in order to determine the key technologies to use.

In summary, PSIP is a lightweight adaptable framework for iterative and incremental improvement, applicable to any CSE software project, regardless of how software is developed and used. PSIP is easy to learn, especially for scientists who cannot dedicate time and resources to more formal or heavyweight approaches.

PSIP is meant to provide a mechanism to set goals collaboratively, get team buy-in, and enable periodic status checks to ensure the goals and execution are aligned. In some cases, teams may want to utilize a facilitator. This person may augment the PSIP by bringing process experience and objectivity to the effort, coaching the team on improving effectiveness and efficiency.

PSIP does have limitations. It is not as quantitative as other tools (not designed that way) and will possibly seem trivial to professional software engineering teams. It is presently best applied in research software settings and untested in large enterprises with product deliverables. Finally, no empirical research on PSIP is available currently, only a few case studies.

Presently, PSIP improvements will likely come from further experience using it. We already know that one of the challenges of PSIP is making sure that progress on the topic of a PTC is not blocked by some prerequisite impediment that must be addressed first. Other needs include more documentation to support conducting PSIP without a facilitator to improve scalable application of PSIP. We also need to grow our PTC catalog and conduct more research on the use of PSIP with open source software teams, and large enterprises. Finally, PSIP does not address the issue of teams not being rewarded for efforts to improve developer productivity and software sustainability. In order for PSIP to be broadly effective, the CSE community must prioritize the value of these improvements, something that we observe is happening slowly.

7   Conclusion

In this work we introduced PSIP, a lightweight, iterative SPI framework and method best understood as a Plan-Do-Check-Act management cycle. Drawing upon a well-supported foundation of software improvement theory and practice,

PSIP was developed to help CSE software teams, and specifically HPC teams achieve software process maturity, an answer to the call by the National Strategic Computing Initiative for "a portfolio of new approaches to dramatically increase productivity in the development and use of parallel HPC applications" [9]. We provided two case studies where the PSIP cycle was implemented by existing scientific software development teams with the help of a facilitator. Beyond scientific computing, we hope that our study of SPI methods and their use outside of conventional software development environments will inform and drive further innovation in the domain of software processes and methodologies.

Acknowledgements. Special thanks to Lois McInnes (ANL) and the members of IDEAS-ECP. Thanks to PSIP partners Danny Perez (LANL), Art Voter (LANL), Christoph Junhans (LANL), and Pavan Balaji (ANL). Images used by permission.

This work was supported by the U.S. Department of Energy Office of Science, Office of Advanced Scientific Computing Research (ASCR), Office of Biological and Environmental Research (BER), and by the Exascale Computing Project (17-SC-20-SC), a collaborative effort of the U.S. Department of Energy Office of Science and the National Nuclear Security Administration.

This work was performed under the auspices of the U.S. Department of Energy by Lawrence Livermore National Laboratory under Contract DE-AC52-07NA27344.

Sandia National Laboratories is a multimission laboratory managed and operated by National Technology & Engineering Solutions of Sandia, LLC, a wholly owned subsidiary of Honeywell International Inc., for the U.S. Department of Energy's National Nuclear Security Administration under contract DE-NA0003525. SAND2019-9693 C.

References

1. Basili, V.R., Caldiera, G.: Improve soft-ware quality by reusing knowledge and experience. Sloan Manag. Rev. **37**, 55 (1995)
2. Baxter, S.M., Day, S.W., Fetrow, J.S., Reisinger, S.J.: Scientific software development is not an oxymoron. PLoS Comput. Biol. **2**(9), e87 (2006)
3. Briand, L., El Emam, K., Melo, W.L.: ANSI-an inductive method for software process improvement: concrete steps and guidelines (1995)
4. Chrissis, M.B., Konrad, M., Shrum, S.: CMMI Guidelines for Process Integration and Product Improvement. Addison-Wesley Longman Publishing Co., Inc., Boston (2003)
5. Deming, W.E.: Elementary Principles of the Statistical Control of Quality: A Series of Lectures. Nippon Kegaku Gijutsu Remmei, Tokyo (1950)
6. Eisty, N.U., Thiruvathukal, G.K., Carver, J.C.: Use of software process in research software development: a survey. In: Proceedings of the Evaluation and Assessment on Software Engineering, pp. 276–282. ACM (2019)
7. Emam, K.E., Melo, W., Drouin, J.N.: SPICE: The Theory and Practice of Software Process Improvement and Capability Determination. IEEE Computer Society Press, Washington, D.C. (1997)
8. Heroux, M., et al.: Developer productivity and software sustainability report: advancing scientific productivity through better scientific software, September 2018
9. Holdren, J.P., Donovan, S.: National strategic computing initiative strategic plan. Technical report, National Strategic Computing Initiative Executive Council (2016)

10. Klünder, J., et al.: Catching up with method and process practice: an industry-informed baseline for researchers. In: Proceedings of the 41st International Conference on Software Engineering: Software Engineering in Practice, pp. 255–264. IEEE Press (2019)
11. Kuhrmann, M., Diebold, P., Münch, J.: Software process improvement: a systematic mapping study on the state of the art. PeerJ Comput. Sci. **2**, e62 (2016)
12. McIlroy, M.: Software engineering: report on a conference sponsored by the NATO science committee. In: NATO Software Engineering Conference, NATO Scientific Affairs Division, pp. 138–155 (1968)
13. Mesh, E.S.: Supporting scientific SE process improvement. In: Proceedings of the 37th International Conference on Software Engineering-Volume 2, pp. 923–926. IEEE Press (2015)
14. Osterweil, L.: Software processes are software too. In: ICSE 1987: Proceedings of the 9th International Conference on Software Engineering, Monterey (1987)
15. Paulk, M.C., Curtis, B., Chrissis, M.B., Weber, C.V.: Capability maturity model, version 1.1. IEEE Softw. **10**(4), 18–27 (1993)
16. Pettersson, F., Ivarsson, M., Gorschek, T., Öhman, P.: A practitioner's guide to light weight software process assessment and improvement planning. J. Syst. Softw. **81**(6), 972–995 (2008)
17. Pinto, G., Wiese, I., Dias, L.F.: How do scientists develop scientific software? An external replication. In: 25th International Conference on Software Analysis, Evolution and Reengineering, SANER 2018, Campobasso, Italy, 20–23 March 2018, pp. 582–591 (2018)
18. Stojanov, Z., Dobrilovic, D.: Learning in software process assessment based on feedback sessions outputs. In: Information Technology and Development of Education (ITRO) 2015, p. 259 (2015)
19. Stojanov, Z.: Inductive approaches in software process assessment. In: International Conference on Applied Internet and Information Technologies (2016)
20. Tell, P., et al.: What are hybrid development methods made of?: an evidence-based characterization. In: Proceedings of the International Conference on Software and System Processes, pp. 105–114. IEEE Press (2019)

Role-Oriented Code Generation in an Engine for Solving Hyperbolic PDE Systems

Jean-Matthieu Gallard[(✉)], Lukas Krenz, Leonhard Rannabauer,
Anne Reinarz, and Michael Bader

Department of Informatics, Technical University of Munich, Munich, Germany
{gallard,lukas.krenz,leonhard.rannabauer,reinarz,bader}@in.tum.de

Abstract. The development of a high performance PDE solver requires the combined expertise of interdisciplinary teams with respect to application domain, numerical scheme and low-level optimization. In this paper, we present how the ExaHyPE engine facilitates the collaboration of such teams by isolating three roles: application, algorithms, and optimization expert. We thus support team members in letting them focus on their own area of expertise while integrating their contributions into an HPC production code.

Inspired by web application development practices, ExaHyPE relies on two custom code generation modules, the Toolkit and the Kernel Generator, which follow a Model-View-Controller architectural pattern on top of the Jinja2 template engine library. Using Jinja2's templates to abstract the critical components of the engine and generated glue code, we isolate the application development from the engine. The template language also allows us to define and use custom template macros that isolate low-level optimizations from the numerical scheme described in the templates.

We present three use cases, each focusing on one of our user roles, showcasing how the design of the code generation modules allows to easily expand the solver schemes to support novel demands from applications, to add optimized algorithmic schemes (with reduced memory footprint, e.g.), or provide improved low-level SIMD vectorization support.

Keywords: ExaHyPE · Code generation · High-order discontinuous Galerkin · Hyperbolic PDE systems · Model-View-Controller · Jinja2

1 Introduction

ExaHyPE ("An Exascale Hyperbolic PDE Engine", www.exahype.eu) is an EU Horizon 2020 project to develop an exascale-ready general solver for hyperbolic systems of partial differential equations (PDEs). Intended as an *engine*

© Springer Nature Switzerland AG 2020
G. Juckeland and S. Chandrasekaran (Eds.): HUST 2019/SE-HER 2019/WIHPC 2019,
CCIS 1190, pp. 111–128, 2020.
https://doi.org/10.1007/978-3-030-44728-1_7

(as in "game engine"), it concentrates on a dedicated numerical scheme and on a fixed mesh infrastructure, but provides flexibility in the PDE system to be solved [14]. Its mission statement is "to enable medium-sized interdisciplinary research teams to realize extreme-scale simulations of grand challenges modelled by hyperbolic conservation laws". We anticipate (and have observed in our project) that such endeavours progress in phases: from first attempts to implement the desired PDE model in the engine (realizing simple analytic setups) via application-oriented benchmark setups (to validate numerical schemes) towards large-scale demonstrator scenarios that establish the viability of the engine to tackle grand challenges. We also need to envisage that successful demonstrators shall be further developed into production codes or even services.

Orthogonal to the requirements of designing more and more complex applications, we are facing the challenges of upcoming exascale architectures. The engine needs to take into account architecture-specific optimizations, which, however, again need to be tailored to the specific PDE system and variants of the numerical schemes. A common approach is to rely on C++ templating, in practice this approach is often limited and thus supplemented by the use of a domain-specific language such as UFL [1] and code generation for hardware-specific optimisations, see e.g. [10,16]. To solve the contradictory goals of being both an optimized custom-made solver and a broad general-purpose framework, ExaHyPE uses code generation and modularity. The ExaHyPE engine isolates its most compute intensive routines into modular kernels. These kernels are created using code generation to be able to choose the most appropriate numerical schemes for a given application and further tailor them to a given set of requirements. Code generation also allows the engine to rely on tailored glue code to bind user written functions that implement the desired PDE system, and the suitable kernels to its engine.

The generation of the glue code and kernels is performed by two custom Python 3 modules, the *Toolkit* and the *Kernel Generator*. They are designed to be expandable and accommodate for new user requirements.

This interplay of user-provided PDE-specific code, generated glue code and kernels, and hardware-aware optimization of both, typically requires the combined expertise of interdisciplinary teams. We have observed that in such teams the following roles exist and need to be addressed by the engine:

The **application expert** implements the PDE system for a given application, as well as problem-specific initial and boundary conditions or criteria for mesh refinement and admissibility of solutions. This role desires a straightforward user API that requires only knowledge about the application and hides the complexity of the solver and its optimizations. It expects a general-purpose framework with best-possible flexibility in terms of implementing various PDE systems, respective application scenarios and postprocessing of results.

The **algorithms expert** tunes the numerical solvers, for performance or numerical properties, breaking them down into sequences of kernel calls. New algorithmic schemes need to be made available, to expand ExaHyPE's capabilities to tailor itself toward applications matching specific numerical requirements.

The algorithms expert needs to be able to design these parts in an architecture-oblivious way, while still getting low-level optimizations automatically in the generated code.

The **optimization expert** contributes architecture specific knowledge and optimizes all performance-critical components of the solver. This role requires tools to impact in the background the work done by the other two, while being able to efficiently support multiple architectures.

The three roles might be taken by a single person, but will usually be distributed to teams, such that each role might even be adopted by several persons. While a separation of concerns is used in other PDE frameworks, such as Firedrake [11,13] (following a compiler-based approach), we put a special emphasis on the ability of the three experts to extend the code generation itself. ExaHyPE thus uses its code generation utilities to isolate the roles, allowing users to focus on their area of expertise, while integrating their cumulative work. To achieve this, we took inspiration from web application development practices and designed both code generation modules using a Model-View-Controller (MVC) architectural pattern on top of a template engine library, Jinja2 (http://jinja.pocoo.org/). Such template engines are not often used in HPC software – an exception being the MESA-PD particle dynamics code developed within the waLBerla framework [6]. There, template logic is used to decouple physical interaction models from the remaining framework. For a general PDE framework, such as ExaHyPE, a similar decoupling is not sufficient, however, due to the large number of supported use cases, the use of external libraries and the strong interdependence of the numerical methods. In this paper, we show how ExaHyPE's code generation utilities and their design choices support the separation of roles and foster optimization of ExaHyPE towards an exascale PDE engine.

We start with a brief overview of the engine, its ADER-DG scheme, kernels and pre-compile-time code generation utilities in the Toolkit and Kernel Generator. In Sect. 3 we discuss the architecture of our code generation utilities and how the MVC pattern and Jinja2 are used to make code generation and optimization more straightforward. We then discuss on three use cases how these choices translate into a simplified workflow for each of the three identified roles.

2   The ExaHyPE Engine

In this section, we provide the numerics of the ADER-DG scheme used by ExaHyPE and how it allows to design a framework for solving a wide range of applications. We then motivate the use of code generation to provide a smooth user experience for the application expert while providing opportunities for algorithms and optimization experts.

2.1   A High-Order ADER-DG Solver with A-Posteriori Limiting

The ExaHyPE engine [14] can solve a large class of systems of first-order hyperbolic PDEs, which are expressed in the following canonical form:

$$\frac{\partial \mathbf{Q}}{\partial t}(x, t) + \nabla \cdot \mathbf{F}(\mathbf{Q}) + \mathbf{B}(\mathbf{Q}) \cdot \nabla \mathbf{Q}(x, t) = \mathbf{S}(\mathbf{Q}). \tag{1}$$

$\mathbf{Q}(x, t) \subset \mathbb{R}^q$ is a space- and time-dependent state vector for any $x \in \Omega \subset \mathbb{R}^d$ ($d = 2, 3$) and $t \in \mathbb{R}_0^+$. $\mathbf{F}$ denotes the conserved flux vector, $\mathbf{B}$ the (system) matrix composing the non-conservative fluxes and $\mathbf{S}(\mathbf{Q})$ the source terms.

To solve equations of this form, ExaHyPE uses the arbitrary high-order accurate ADER Discontinuous Galerkin (DG) method in the formulation by Dumbser et al. [18]. The computational domain Ω is discretized with a tree-structured Cartesian grid using the Peano framework [17] as mesh infrastructure, allowing for dynamic adaptive mesh refinement. As understanding the kernels described in the following sections relies on an understanding of the numerical scheme we will briefly sketch the ADER-DG method. More details on the implementation in the engine are given in [2].

The ADER-DG method consists of two phases, a predictor step in which the weak formulation of (1) is solved locally in each cell, and a corrector step in which the contributions of neighboring cells are taken into account. To derive the weak solution of the problem we insert the DG ansatz function from the space of piecewise polynomials into Eq. (1) and multiply with a test function from the same space of piecewise polynomials. We then integrate over a space-time control volume. The solution of the resulting element-local problem makes up one of our most compute-intensive kernels, the *space-time predictor*. In non-linear problems the solution of this element-local weak form is calculated using Picard iterations, in the linear setting it can be computed directly using the Cauchy-Kowalewski procedure.

In the second phase the element-local predictor solution is corrected, using contributions from neighboring cells. To solve the surface integrals we introduce a classical Riemann solver as it is used in Godunov-type FV schemes. After this correction the next time-step can be calculated. The next time step size depends on the CFL number.

However, this high-order approach suffers from oscillations at shocks and discontinuities. We therefore apply an a-posteriori Finite Volume limiter [4]. We identify cells as troubled using the following detection criteria: a relaxed discrete maximum principle in the sense of polynomials, absence of floating point errors (NaN, e.g.) and positivity (or similar physical constraints) of the solution. If one of these criteria is violated after a time step, the scheme recomputes the solution in the troubled cells, using a more robust high resolution shock capturing FV scheme on a subgrid composed of $(2N + 1)^d$ cells. This procedure is composed of several kernels, the computation of the discrete maximum principle, and a projection from DG to FV solution and vice versa.

ExaHyPE thus provides building blocks to solve specific PDE systems with a tailored scheme: DG vs. FV-only, DG with or without limiting, Cauchy-Kowalewski procedure or Picard loops for linear or non-linear schemes, various choices of Riemann solvers, etc. – presenting this complexity to users (depending on their roles) and thus keeping the engine and derived simulation software manageable are consequently intrinsic challenges for the engine development.

2.2 Application-Specific Programming Interface

The canonical PDE system (1) can model a wide array of applications, including relativistic astrophysics [3,7], seismic wave propagation [5,15] or several variants of fluid equations (see [14] for an overview). All these problems can be formulated via Eq. (1) via specific $\mathbf{F}(\mathbf{Q})$, $\mathbf{B}(\mathbf{Q}) \cdot \nabla \mathbf{Q}$ and $\mathbf{S}(\mathbf{Q})$. However, not all these terms occur in every PDE; the engine should therefore not force the user to provide a useless zero function.

Hence, as the first step, the application expert is expected to provide a *specification file* to describe the application and its runtime parameters. This includes but is not limited to:

- Application parameters such as the number of quantities in the vector $\mathbf{Q}$ or the polynomial order for the ADER-DG scheme;
- Which terms of the canonical PDE (1) will be required;
- Whether the application will require an a-posteriori limiter (as described in Sect. 2.1);
- Optimization specific options that can be enabled to further improve the application performance.

The specification file relies on a Domain Specific Language (DSL) defined via JSON Schema (https://json-schema.org/). Using JSON Schema and its open source tools simplifies both the validation of a given specification file and the modification the DSL (e.g., to introduce new options) as will be described in the use cases.

The specification file is passed to the code generation utilities that set up the engine, and generate glue code and kernels. This includes a class `UserSolver` where the application expert shall implement the required *user functions*:

- PDE-related functions that provide an implementation of the required terms in (1), such as a flux function to compute $\mathbf{F}(q_h)$;
- Initial and boundaries conditions;
- Eigenvalues and physical admissibility;
- Mesh refinement criteria (if mesh refinement is enabled).

The application can then be compiled using a generated Makefile and executed with the specification file as argument for its runtime parameters.

Thus, from an application expert's perspective, ExaHyPE allows to solve complicated PDE systems with minimal code writing and without considering the complex issues of designing a performance-oriented high-order solver on a parallel compute cluster. Hence, ExaHyPE is well suited to quickly build an application for a given PDE system and obtain first insights whether the engine will fit the problem to be tackled.

2.3 Architecture-Aware Optimization of Kernels

Toolkit and Kernel Generator aim to tailor the engine toward its applications and a target architecture, such that an HPC-worthy production code is produced. To enable this tailoring, the ExaHyPE engine itself is modular.

This is motivated by the fact that the element-local computation of ADER-DG updates (cf. Sect. 2.1) naturally breaks down into substeps (space-time predictor, Riemann solver, etc.), which can often again be formulated as smaller substeps (such as tensor or matrix operations). In the engine, each of these substeps is isolated into a specific kernel. These kernels are the critical parts of ExaHyPE, both performance-wise and regarding the implementation of the numerical scheme [2].

Having more knowledge about the target application allows more specific but also more efficient numerical schemes, such as using a linear scheme instead of a general nonlinear one. Likewise, a specific numerical scheme may be required to satisfy certain stability constraints, such as using a special Riemann solver. Finally, knowing the target architecture enables different low-level optimization techniques, such as the supported SIMD features and the required array alignment and padding settings.

The Kernel Generator uses all information provided in the specification file to choose the correct scheme for each kernel and uses code generation to add application- and architecture-aware optimizations to them. Using code generation also facilitates the inclusion of external performance related libraries and code generators. The generated kernels are bound to the engine core using the Toolkit's generated glue code.

We cannot expect that the set of alternative schemes and supported optimizations provided by the Kernel Generator will ever be complete. New user and hardware requirements will arise constantly. Therefore, to facilitate the work of algorithm and optimization experts, the Kernel Generator is designed with ease of modification in mind, so that they can enrich the available customization options of the engine. As adding new options for the Kernel Generator translates into expanding the specification file DSL and adapting the glue code, the Toolkit's design follows the same philosophy.

3 Code Generation in ExaHyPE

3.1 Model-View-Controller Design

The Toolkit and the Kernel Generator are implemented as Python 3 modules. Python was chosen for its ease of use and development, as well as for its mature open source ecosystem. Both modules follow the Model-View-Controller (MVC) architectural pattern, which is widely used, especially in web applications. Our motivation toward using an MVC pattern is twofold. First, the goal of generating user-tailored HTML pages and building an application by combining multiple separate developer roles is quite similar to our own situation. MVC has managed to become an industry standard, being recognized for the ease of development, code reusability and useful abstraction layers it provides. Second, we can re-purpose mature open source tools, such as the Jinja2 template engine, to generate C++ code instead of its intended HTML output. Using a template engine allows us to streamline the development of new features and to separate the implementation of a new numerical scheme to its low-level optimization.

Reformulated in the MVC paradigm, each of our desired C++ files to be generated (kernel and glue code alike) is a *View* to be rendered by a *Model* responsible for it and the specification file is the input of the *Controller*. The Toolkit implements the MVC pattern in the following way:

Controller. The Toolkit's Controller class validates the specification file, parses it, and builds multiple contexts, implemented by Python dictionaries. Each context contains only the relevant information for a given Model, thus providing an abstraction layer between the specification file grammar and the internal Toolkit API. The Controller calls the application relevant models only and passes them their respective context. For example a Python dictionary containing the application name, path and target architecture (if provided) is generated and passed as context to the Model responsible for generating the `Makefile`, while the Model responsible for building the `UserSolver` contains the solver relevant information, such as the polynomial order of the ADER-DG scheme or the used terms of the canonical PDE form (1).

Model. Each Model is responsible for generating a specific View, or group of Views. After receiving its context from the Controller, a Model may expand it using its own internal logic to add relevant internal parameters. In situations where different versions of a View exist, it decides which one is required. For example, it might choose a View to generate the glue code for either a finite volume solver or an ADER-DG solver, which require different kernels. It selects the appropriate template that represents the desired View version, or in a simpler case uses the sole template for this View.

View. Views are implemented by templates which are a generalized representation of a given C++ code that may be tailored to a specific context. The Jinja2 template engine is invoked to render a template with a Model-provided context. Jinja2 parses its input template and uses the context to interpret it. Its output is then written as a valid C++ file that matches the context, and thus specification file, requirements. For example, it may hard-code the selected polynomial order and use the generated kernels.

The Kernel Generator follows the same MVC architecture and is called by a special Model of the Toolkit. This Model translates its context into the required format for the Kernel Generator API and passes it to its Controller. The same MVC schema is then replicated. The separation of Toolkit and Kernel Generator into two utilities is dictated by their different purpose: The Toolkit generates glue code and code the application expert is expected to interact with, while the Kernel Generator handles numerical schemes and low-level optimizations for the other two roles.

3.2 Templates

As mentioned in Sect. 3.1, a template is a generalized representation of a given C++ file that we want the code generation utilities to generate – e.g., a kernel or some glue code. By using templates, we are able to put some logic in the code representation while keeping it close to the generated code and thus easily readable and expendable.

To express this logic, we use the templating language implemented by Jinja2. Its language syntax is designed to be both easy to learn and to work with, and is therefore well suited to allow ExaHyPE's users to modify the behavior of its code generation utilities. It also provides some advanced functionalities that can be used directly in the code abstraction.

```
// template
{% if initA %}
{{allocateArray('A', nDof)}}
for(int i=0; i<{{nDof}}; ++i) {
  A[i] = B[i+{{nDof*nVar}}] * {{C}}[i];
}
{% endif %}

// generated code
double A[5] __attribute__((aligned(32)));
for(int i=0; i<5; ++i) {
  A[i] = B[i+20] * foo[i];
}
```

Fig. 1. Example of a template and the resulting generated code

The code fragment in Fig. 1 illustrates how we use templates to generate C++ code: At its simplest any given string or number can be abstracted behind a variable in a template's context. This is used, for example, to abstract the application's namespace, which depends on the user specification, in the template. Mathematical computations can also be done and the result directly written in the generated code, In the code of Fig. 1 this is used to hard-code the loop boundary nDof, the index shift of the array B and the name of the third array.

Furthermore, boolean operations and branchings are used to selectively enable or disable certain parts of the generated code. For example in the glue code responsible for binding the kernels to the engine, choosing linear or non-linear kernels is done using Jinja2's branching. This allows us to efficiently deal with the multitude of options ExaHyPE offers its users, without having to duplicate code or use slower runtime branching. In the code of Fig. 1, branching is used to include the whole fragment only if the context's boolean initA is true.

Jinja2's logic also includes subtemplating, i.e. including and rendering a template inside another one, and custom macros. With this we can factorize repeating portions of the templates, thus making them easier to maintain and expand.

We also use macros to provide architecture-aware optimizations. In Fig. 1, we use the macro `allocateArray` to allocate a new array `A`. This macro abstracts the optimized allocation of an array of a given size. In our example, it produces the C++ code to allocate the array `A` on the stack and on a 32-bytes boundary for more efficient AVX2 operations.

3.3 Architecture-Oblivious Templates and Architecture-Aware Optimization Macros

```
{% macro allocateArray(name, size, setToZero=False) %}
{% if tempVarsOnStack %}
double {{name}}[{{size}}] __attribute__((aligned(        \
    {{alignment}}))) {{"={0.}" if setToZero}} ;
{% else %}
double* {{name}} = ((double*) _mm_malloc(sizeof(double) \
    *{{size}}, {{alignment}}));
{% if setToZero %}
std::memset({{name}}, 0, sizeof(double)*{{size}});
{% endif %}
{% endif %}
{% endmacro %}
```

Fig. 2. Example of an optimization macro to allocate arrays

The Kernel Generator provides kernels that are optimized toward both given application requirements and a target architecture. The former is done via algorithmic adaptations: choosing the appropriate scheme, enabling or disabling features, hard-coding specific values, etc. The latter requires low-level code optimizations (e.g., array padding and alignment), compiler specific pragmas and instructions, or external libraries. Performing both at the same time on a given kernel template would make it hard to read, maintain and expand. Hence the separation of the role of algorithms and optimization experts.

Using Jinja2's macros and variables, we can design an architecture-oblivious template that will be rendered with architecture-aware optimizations. Thus, most templates in the Kernel Generator are *algorithmic templates*: templates that focus on describing a given scheme with some algorithmic optimizations but without any complex logic for architecture related ones. A second smaller set of templates define *optimization macros* and the subtemplates used by these macros to perform a specific task or output a specific architecture-aware optimization. The macros defined this way can then be used by the algorithmic templates.

The code excerpt in Fig. 2 shows a simplified version of the `allocateArray` macro that was used in Fig. 1. It takes the array's **name** and **size** as positional inputs and optionally a boolean **setToZero** to indicate if the array should be initialized to zero. Then, depending on a global optimization flag `tempVarsOnStack`, it allocates the array either on the stack or on the heap. Enabling this feature depends on the target hardware setting, as a limited stack size could cause crashes. The `allocateArray` macro takes care of array alignment to optimize for SIMD using a global `alignment` context parameter that is set by the Kernel Generator's Controller depending on the specified target architecture, and thus the target AVX settings. For heap allocation, a compiler-specific instruction is used (e.g., `_mm_malloc` for the Intel compiler).

Thus every time a temporary array is needed, it can be allocated using this macro, hiding the low-level optimization from the algorithms expert. If the optimization expert needs to add support for a different compiler, e.g., expanding this macro provides it to all kernels. A complementing `freeArray` macro exists to free the memory correctly, as for example using `_mm_malloc` requires using the Intel-specific `_mm_free` instruction, whereas the pointer should not be freed at all, if a stack allocation was used.

Macros can also be used to include external libraries. For example ExaHyPE's kernels spend a lot of computational effort in performing small dense matrix products that result from expanding respective element-local tensor operations. For these we employ LIBXSMM [9], which generates architecture specific function kernels to perform small matrix products at best-possible performance on a given Intel architecture. Using a custom `matmul` macro and with some modification to the controller and models to properly define the parameters of each matrix products in the template, LIBXSMM can be selected and integrated into the kernels. By expanding the `matmul` macro, an optimization expert can also easily switch to another library to support another kind of architecture.

Thus the development of new numerical schemes and the low-level architecture-aware optimization can be kept separated. This ensures that the role of algorithm and optimization expert are independent from one another.

4   Expanding the PDE: Navier-Stokes Equations

In this section, we discuss the solution of the compressible Navier-Stokes equations using the ExaHyPE engine [14]. Following our PDE system (1), we can write the compressible Navier-Stokes equations as

$$
\frac{\partial}{\partial t} \underbrace{\begin{pmatrix} \rho \\ \rho v \\ \rho E \end{pmatrix}}_{=\mathbf{Q}} + \nabla \cdot \underbrace{\begin{pmatrix} \rho v \\ v \otimes \rho v + Ip + \sigma(\mathbf{Q}, \nabla \mathbf{Q}) \\ v \cdot (I\rho E + Ip + \sigma(\mathbf{Q}, \nabla \mathbf{Q})) - \kappa \nabla(T) \end{pmatrix}}_{=\mathbf{F}(\mathbf{Q}, \nabla \mathbf{Q})} = S(Q). \tag{2}
$$

where ρ denotes the density, ρv the momentum, ρE the energy density, T the temperature and p the pressure (including hydrostatic pressure, e.g., gravitational effects). The temperature diffusion is given by $\kappa \nabla T$ with constant κ. Note that the stress tensor $\sigma(\mathbf{Q}, \nabla \mathbf{Q})$ involves a parabolic component, expressed via the dependence on $\nabla \mathbf{Q}$. While we can largely stay with the existing numerical approach to solve the equations in ExaHyPE, we had to extend the API to allow for flux terms $\mathbf{F}(\mathbf{Q}, \nabla\mathbf{Q})$ that depend on $\nabla\mathbf{Q}$ in the canonical PDE (1). For example, the gradient of the state vector $\mathbf{Q}$ had to be added as argument of the flux function, which was also renamed to `viscousFlux`. Further changes are modifications to the space-time predictor, the boundary conditions and the introduction of a new Riemann solver [8].

As only minor modifications to the existing numerical schemes and none to the optimizations are required, we followed a straightforward linear workflow:

4.1 Expanding the DSL

We modified the DSL of our specification file to include a new optional flag enabling the viscous flux terms in the PDE system as an opt-in feature. In the JSON schema, this meant adding a `viscous_flux` option to the already existing list of optional PDE components for an ADER-DG Solver:

```
"items":{
  "type":"string",
  "enum":["flux","source","ncp","viscous_flux"]
}
```

The Schema processing library only performs basic input validation. Here `flux` and `viscous_flux` should not appear together, thus a new test was added to the validation method of the Toolkit's Controller class, such that an error message is issued if a user selects both options simultaneously.

4.2 Processing the New Specification File Option

The new `viscous_flux` option is processed by the Controller and passed on as a boolean flag `useViscousFlux` in the context of the Models needing to act on it. In the MVC architecture, the addition of a few lines of code is sufficient to provide the Views with such a boolean flag.

4.3 Expanding the Views

The code to be generated is abstracted in the Views of the Toolkit and Kernel Generator by Jinja2's templates. Using Jinja2's template branching logic, the application expert is asked to provide a `viscousFlux` user function in the generated UserSolver, if the `useViscousFlux` flag is set. Then in all kernels using `flux`, the gradient $\nabla\mathbf{Q}$ is computed using already existing macros, which deal with the optimization of this computation, and the `viscousFlux` function is called instead with it as additional argument.

The branching also ensured that the expanded Views generate the same code as before if the flag is not set (opt-in option). Since every part of the code generation is compartmentalized into separate Models, modifying a Model or expanding the Controller has no side effects on the other generated code.

4.4   Result Evaluation

An application using this new feature was written and tested. It is able to simulate cloud formation processes in scenarios incorporating a background atmosphere that is in hydrostatic balance [12]. At the end of this use case, the ExaHyPE engine's canonical PDE system (1) is expanded and can now, as an opt-in option, work with further applications requiring a viscous flux term instead of a classical flux.

The modifications needed to implement the features required roughly 100 lines for the kernels and additionally less than 100 lines for the Toolkit. This includes all code, comments and all needed API changes. We want to emphasize that theses changes required only a basic algorithmic understanding and minimal optimization knowledge, thanks to the reuse of existing optimization macros.

5   Improved Space-Time Predictor for Linear Applications

Benchmarks of the linear PDE solver at high polynomial orders revealed significant loss of performances due to cache misses inside the SpaceTimePredictor kernel. This was caused by the temporary arrays required by the algorithm to implement the Cauchy Kowalewski scheme inside this kernel. The size of these arrays depends on the polynomial order used, and increased beyond the L2 cache size of our test hardware during benchmarks. Thus, to reduce the memory footprint, we reformulated the algorithm toward cache efficiency.

Instead of storing all time derivatives for later integration, the time integration is performed on the fly. Thus the full time dimension is removed from temporary arrays. As a result, the spatial directions of the PDE system are processed one at a time. The algorithm therefore requires three directional `flux` functions instead of one for all dimensions. Depending on the application specific formulation this might lead to redundant computations. Therefore, despite being more memory efficient, the new algorithm is offered as an optional kernel variant (opt-in option). To introduce this new SpaceTimePredictor kernel variant, we used an iterative and incremental approach:

5.1   Prototyping the New Algorithm

The new algorithm was first prototyped on a test application with fixed settings. We generated the default SpaceTimePredictor kernel for the test case and edited it locally to get to the new algorithm. This way we could test the new algorithm, verify it against the default one and validate our assumption on improving the memory footprint. We then iterated upon the prototype to incrementally add new optimizations, as tests revealed bottlenecks and possible areas of improvements.

5.2 Inclusion in the Kernel Generator

Once the prototype was finished and validated, it was incorporated directly into the Kernel Generator. The prototype source code was directly used as the first iteration of a new template, since a template can also exist of explicit code without any template logic. Then using the existing MVC structure of the Kernel Generator, its generation behavior was modified by introducing a new optional input parameter to trigger the generation of this new template (as in the use case of Sect. 4). At this stage the Kernel Generator was able to generate the prototype kernel variant only for the application and setting it was designed for during the prototyping step.

5.3 Template Generalization and Optimization

Finally the template was generalized, such that it can be used with other settings or by other applications. The hard-coded settings from the prototyping steps (e.g., the name of the solver, the polynomial order) were replaced by their respective abstractions, as defined in the provided template context, thus enabling the new kernel variant to be properly generated for all settings. This transformed the prototype template to an algorithmic template as described in Sect. 3.3.

To provide architecture-aware optimizations, we used the existing optimization macros, for example to perform optimized matrix products. Thus, this new kernel variant was immediately optimized toward all the supported architecture without needing any optimization knowledge.

5.4 Performance Evaluation

Once the new kernel variant was fully supported by the code generation utilities, we used ExaHyPE's internal benchmarking tools to compare it with the default one on a set of test applications, settings and architectures. These tests confirmed our early intuition that the new algorithm provides no runtime benefits for applications with low memory footprint, but leads to speedups of >2 for bigger settings that are severely affected by cache misses with the default algorithm. The threshold depends on the application, its settings (esp. the polynomial order) and the hardware specification (esp. the L2 cache size).

Using the Kernel Generator MVC architecture and the optimization macro, the development of this new kernel variant, from building a prototype to the benchmarking of the feature, required almost exclusively the numeric and algorithmic optimization expertise, expected from an algorithm expert role.

6 Vectorization of User Functions

The last use case addresses the exploitation of SIMD capabilities of modern CPUs. Here, ExaHyPE faces a conflict of API and optimization requirements. For the implementation of user functions, such as the flux function $\mathbf{F}(\mathbf{Q})$, the most intuitive API is like the function flux(Q,F) in Fig. 3: flux acts on a contiguous vector of quantities. This Array of Structure (AoS) data layout also supports the optimized execution of 4D tensor operations (3D space plus the quantity dimension) via sequences of matrix operations – the matrices always have the quantities as a dimension that is contiguous in memory. However, AoS becomes inefficient, when calling the user functions for multiple spatial positions, such as evaluating the flux function at all integration points to evaluate the Riemann problem on element faces. The kernels then loop over all spatial coordinates, but call the user functions on the vector **Q** for each single spatial point. These calls cannot be vectorized, as the accessed components Q[0], Q[1], etc. (similar for F[0][0], ...) are not stored in unit-stride.

To solve this data layout conflict, we introduced SIMD user functions as opt-in features. Instead of processing a single quantity vector, they take as parameter a vector of quantities in a Structure of Array (SoA) layout, so that the resulting loop in the implementation can be vectorized. Figure 3 illustrates how to implement such a SIMD flux function (fluxVect): The input arrays of fluxVect now have a new fastest-running dimension that matches the loop iteration, such that compiler auto-vectorization may be enabled.

```
void Euler::flux(double* Q, double** F) {
  //[...] constants
  // x direction
  F[0][0] = Q[1];
  F[0][1] = irho*Q[1]*Q[1] + p;
  F[0][2] = irho*Q[2]*Q[1];
  F[0][3] = irho*(Q[3]+p)*Q[1];
  //[...] y direction
}

void Euler::fluxVect(double** Q, double*** F){
  #pragma vector aligned
  #pragma ivdep
  for(int i=0; i<VECTSIZE; i++){
    //[...] constants
    // x direction
    F[0][0][i] = Q[1][i];
    F[0][1][i] = irho*Q[1][i]*Q[1][i] + p;
    F[0][2][i] = irho*Q[2][i]*Q[1][i];
    F[0][3][i] = irho*(Q[3][i]+p)*Q[1][i];
    //[...] y direction
  }
}
```

Fig. 3. Example implementation (for the 2D Euler equations) of a flux function **F(Q)** for a single flux vector **Q** (flux(...), top) or for an array of flux vectors (fluxVect(...), bottom). Note that in F[0][0][i], etc., i is the fastest-running index.

In this use case, we describe the integration of these new user functions to all existing kernels using new optimization macros. By using macros, only optimization specific knowledge is required during development and they can be reused by algorithms experts when implementing new schemes. We will describe only the work for the flux user function, the same being done for the others.

6.1 Optimized Transpose – from AoS to SoA (and Back)

To be able to use a SIMD user function, the data layout has to be transformed on the fly from AoS to SoA and back. This is achieved by transposing a slice of the input array to a new temporary array. Processing with slices instead of the whole array optimizes caching behaviors.

We therefore introduced a new optimization macro called transpose. By default it falls back to a naive loop-based transpose. However, more optimized transpose implementations are offered, such as ones using architecture-specific intrinsic operations like _mm256_permute2f128_pd and _mm256_shuffle_pd for AVX. At rendering, the best available implementation for the given context is chosen. It can easily be expanded to better support other architectures and could be expanded to use an external library like the matrix product matmul macro with LIBXSMM.

6.2 Abstracting the Call to the User Function Behind a Macro

The choice between the flux and fluxVect user functions and the required supporting logic is complex and repeated at each instance where the flux function $\mathbf{F(Q)}$ is evaluated in the kernels. As described in Sect. 3.3, we can factorize this template code and abstract it behind a new optimization macro named callFlux. We started by abstracting the current behavior behind the callFlux macro:

```
{% macro callFlux(Q, F, size) %}
{% set F_shift = nDof**nDim*size %}
double* F[{{nDim}}];
for (int i = 0; i < {{nDof**nDim}}; i++) {
  F[0] = {{F}}+i*{{size}};
  F[1] = {{F}}+i*{{size}}+{{F_shift}};
{% if nDim == 3 %}
  F[2] = {{F}}+i*{{size}}+2*{{F_shift}};
{% endif %}
  {{solverName}}.flux({{Q}}+i*{{size}},F);
}
{% endmacro %}
```

At that point it performed only the existing default case to call the flux function: loop over all spatial points of the cell, initialize the array F and call the function with the correct shift in the data arrays as they use an AoS layout. The evaluations of the flux function in all kernels are replaced by callFlux.

6.3   Expanding the `callFlux` Macro

As in the two previous use cases, we introduced a new context boolean flag `useFluxVect`. We then expanded the `callFlux` macro with a branch on this flag. If the flag is set, the `callFlux` macro uses the `transpose` macro defined earlier to switch on the fly between AoS and SoA data layout and call a new `fluxVect` user function with its altered signature compared to `flux` as shown in Fig. 3. As we modified a macro, this work is automatically propagated to all existing templates using it.

6.4   Performance Evaluation

We evaluated the SIMD user functions on two example PDEs: the 3D Euler equations (EulerFlow), where the flux function is quite simple, and the Einstein equations from relativistic astrophysics (CCZ4), where the user functions are highly complex and comprise most of the runtime. The benchmark was done on Super-MUC phase 2 (Intel Haswell architecture, supporting AVX2). For EulerFlow we compared the default version with the auto-vectorized one and with an intrinsics-version for AVX2. The auto-vectorized and the intrinsics implementations both achieved similar performances, illustrating that for simple user functions a quick adaptation of the scalar implementation to enable auto-vectorization is enough. Compared to the default version, both SIMD implementations provided an end-to-end speedup by a factor 1.04. Here the low cost of the simple user function is barely enough to compensate for the cost of the required transpositions.

With the help of an application expert, we implemented a partially auto-vectorized version of the complex CCZ4 user functions. We measured a speedup factor of 1.27. While the user functions were not fully vectorized due to their complexity, their high computational cost is enough to offset the transpose one. A better vectorized implementation of the user functions would provide even more performance gain.

Here by working with macros, we not only provide these new features to all existing schemes, but also ensure that future ones can easily use them. The implementation of the macros required mostly low-level optimization knowledge. All architecture-specific optimizations are fully handled by the macros, enabling an optimization expert to easily improve them or expand them for other architectures.

7   Conclusions

This paper details how code generation is used in a PDE engine to offer a tailored application-specific programming interface for users, while at the same time selecting the most appropriate (regarding the target application) numerical scheme and implementation for each of its critical components, and tuning it with low-level architecture-aware optimizations. The choice of a MVC architecture for code generation facilitates the collaboration of three identified user roles

– application, algorithm and optimization experts – as they use and expand the engine. In the Views, Jinja2's template logic and macros support the implementation of new algorithms and low-level code optimization independently of each other.

The three presented use cases show how a user assuming only one single role can work with the engine and contribute to it by expanding the code generation utilities, cumulatively improving its capabilities. Thus, the presented design solves a common issue encountered when building complex HPC simulation software: to support users with different areas of expertise in their effective collaboration.

Acknowledgements and Funding. This project has received funding from the European Union's Horizon 2020 research and innovation programme under grant agreement No 671698. We thank the Gauss Centre for Supercomputing e.V. (www.gauss-centre.eu) for providing computing resources on the GCS Supercomputer SuperMUC at Leibniz Supercomputing Centre (www.lrz.de).

References

1. Alnaes, M.S., Logg, A., Ølgaard, K.B., Rognes, M.E., Wells, G.N.: Unified form language: a domain-specific language for weak formulations of partial differential equations. ACM Trans. Math. Softw. **40**(2) (2014)
2. Charrier, D., Hazelwood, B., Weinzierl, T.: Enclave tasking for discontinuous Galerkin methods on dynamically adaptive meshes. SIAM J. Scient. Comput. (in press). arXiv:1806.07984
3. Dumbser, M., Fambri, F., Tavelli, M., Bader, M., Weinzierl, T.: Efficient implementation of ADER discontinuous Galerkin schemes for a scalable hyperbolic PDE engine. Axioms **278** (2018).https://doi.org/10.3390/axioms7030063
4. Dumbser, M., Zanotti, O., Loubère, R., Diot, S.: A posteriori subcell limiting of the discontinuous Galerkin finite element method for hyperbolic conservation laws. J. Comput. Phys. **278**(C), 47–75 (2013)
5. Duru, K., Rannabauer, L., Ling, O.K.A., Gabriel, A.A., Igel, H., Bader, M.: A stable discontinuous Galerkin method for linear elastodynamics in geometrically complex media using physics based numerical fluxes (2019). arXiv:1907.02658
6. Eibl, S., Rüde, U.: A modular and extensible software architecture for particle dynamics. In: 8th International Conference on Discrete Element Methods (2019). arXiv:1906.1096
7. Fambri, F., Dumbser, M., Köppel, S., Rezzolla, L., Zanotti, O.: ADER discontinuous Galerkin schemes for general-relativistic ideal magnetohydrodynamics. Mon. Not. R. Astron. Soc. **477**, 4543–4564 (2018)
8. Gassner, G., Lörcher, F., Munz, C.D.: A discontinuous Galerkin scheme based on a space-time expansion II. Viscous flow equations in multi dimensions. J. Sci. Comput. **34**(3), 260–286 (2008)
9. Heinecke, A., Henry, G., Hutchinson, M., Pabst, H.: LIBXSMM: accelerating small matrix multiplications by runtime code generation. In: SC 2016: International Conference for HPC, Networking, Storage and Analysis, pp. 981–991 (2016)
10. Kempf, D., Heß, R., Müthing, S., Bastian, P.: Automatic Code Generation for High-Performance Discontinuous Galerkin Methods on Modern Architectures. arXiv e-prints (2018). arXiv:1812.08075

11. Kirby, R.C., Mitchell, L.: Code generation for generally mapped finite elements. ACM Trans. Math. Softw. **45**(4) (2019)
12. Krenz, L., Rannabauer, L., Bader, M.: A high-order discontinuous Galerkin solver with dynamic adaptive mesh refinement to simulate cloud formation processes. In: 13th International Conference on Parallel Processing and Applied Mathematics (PPAM 2019). LNCS, vol. 12043 (2020). arXiv:1905.05524
13. Rathgeber, F., Ham, D.A., Mitchell, L., Lange, M., Luporini, F., McRae, A.T.T., Bercea, G.T., Markall, G.R., Kelly, P.H.J.: Firedrake: automating the finite element method by composing abstractions. ACM Trans. Math. Softw. **43**(3), 24 (2017)
14. Reinarz, A., Charrier, D.E., Bader, M., Bovard, L., Dumbser, M., Duru, K., Fambri, F., Gabriel, A.A., Gallard, J.M., Köppel, S., Krenz, L., Rannabauer, L., Rezzolla, L., Samfass, P., Tavelli, M., Weinzierl, T.: ExaHyPE: an engine for parallel dynamically adaptive simulations of wave problems. Comp. Phys. Comm. 107251 (2020)
15. Tavelli, M., Dumbser, M., Charrier, D.E., Rannabauer, L., Weinzierl, T., Bader, M.: A simple diffuse interface approach on adaptive Cartesian grids for the linear elastic wave equations with complex topography. J. Comp. Phys. **386**, 158–189 (2019)
16. Uphoff, C., Bader, M.: Yet another tensor toolbox for discontinuous Galerkin methods and other applications. ACM Trans. Math. Softw. (under review). arXiv:1903.11521
17. Weinzierl, T.: The Peano software-parallel, automaton-based, dynamically adaptive grid traversals. ACM Trans. Math. Softw. **45**(2), 14:1–14:41 (2019)
18. Zanotti, O., Fambri, F., Dumbser, M., Hidalgo, A.: Space-time adaptive ADER discontinuous Galerkin finite element schemes with a posteriori sub-cell finite volume limiting. Comput. Fluids **118**, 204–224 (2015)

FQL: An Extensible Feature Query Language and Toolkit on Searching Software Characteristics for HPC Applications

Weijian Zheng[1] , Dali Wang[2(✉)] , and Fengguang Song[1]

[1] Indiana University-Purdue University, Indianapolis, IN 46202, USA
zheng273@purdue.edu, fgsong@iupui.edu
[2] Oak Ridge National Laboratory, P.O. Box 2008, MS 6301,
Oak Ridge, TN 37831, USA
wangd@ornl.gov

Abstract. The amount of large-scale scientific computing software is dramatically increasing. In this work, we designed a new query language, named Feature Query Language (FQL), to collect and extract HPC-related software features or metadata from a quick static code analysis. We also designed and implemented an FQL-based toolkit to automatically detect and present software features using an extensible query repository. A number of large-scale, high performance computing (HPC) scientific applications have been studied in the paper with the FQL toolkit to demonstrate the HPC-related feature extraction and information/metadata collection. Different from the existing static software analysis and refactoring tools which focus on software debug, development and code transformation, the FQL toolkit is simpler, significantly lightweight and strives to collect various and diverse software metadata with ease and rapidly.

Keywords: Feature Query Language · Static code analysis · High-performance computing

1 Introduction

Open source scientific software projects are growing explosively in number and size. Many companies, universities, and national laboratories build their software ecosystems around the open-source software projects. There are also a lot of ongoing efforts to combine different software modules to create a larger scale software system (e.g., climate modeling and simulation [1], fluid/solid dynamics computations [20], material science [17], etc.). The complexity of large-scale scientific

This research was funded by the U.S. Department of Energy, Office of Science, Advanced Scientific Computing Research (Interoperable Design of Extreme-scale Application Software).

G. Juckeland and S. Chandrasekaran (Eds.): HUST 2019/SE-HER 2019/WIHPC 2019,
CCIS 1190, pp. 129–142, 2020.
https://doi.org/10.1007/978-3-030-44728-1_8

models developed for specific machine architectures and application requirements has become a barrier that impedes continuous software development. Furthermore, more and more scientific codes have incorporated high-performance computing (HPC) features that, in turn, create machine configuration, computer architecture, user and system library dependency issues.

Hence, given a large number of open source software projects, it is critical to provide an efficient way for decision makers (such as users, administrators, customers, developers, investors, and software managers) to quickly evaluate the software and understand its structure and characteristics [18, 32]. Also, as numerous codes have been released and published every day in the open repositories (such as GitHub and bitbucket) as well as institution-owned repositories (such as DOECode at the Office of Scientific and Technical Information (www. osti.gov/doecode)), we need to develop a portable tool that can automatically extract and collect essential features from these scientific codes.

In this paper, we target at creating a software toolkit to discover open source software projects' features. Here, "features" refer to any characteristic and metadata related to the software, including programming languages, third-party library dependency, special hardware requirement, particular tools, adopted programming models, and so on.

We use open source science and engineering application software on high performance computing (HPC) systems as examples to drive the design and development of our toolkit due to the science and engineering software's large scale, high complexity, and utilization of a wide variety of computer hardware. For instance, we experiment with a number of science codes from several large-scale DOE programs to harvest HPC features for code archive purpose and beyond.

In order to handle nearly "arbitrary" queries of interest from users, we need a flexible and extensible solution that can process any number/type of features in any open source software and can also efficiently answer these feature-related questions. Our proposed solution is based upon a new language called *Feature Query Language* (FQL) that lets users describe their queries (or questions) in the FQL language. Given an FQL query, we then design a new software toolkit, which can parse the user input, execute the query, scan open source software, and present the final results. Our design shares the same philosophy with the popular Structured Query Language (SQL) to support users' arbitrary queries about databases [11]. The distinction between FQL and SQL is that FQL is designed to query open source code repository, which is being viewed as another type of database, meanwhile achieving SQL's portable, regular, structured, and simple characteristics. We expect that this new toolkit will significantly benefit broader scientific computing communities who are facing similar challenges.

The rest of the paper is organized as follows. Next section presents the related work. Section 3 describes our toolkit from three perspectives: (1) FQL language, (2) overall software workflow, and (3) FQL toolkit implementation. Section 4 presents the results obtained by executing predefined queries. Section 5 concludes the impact and the possible future directions for our work.

2   Related Work

This paper introduces a SQL-like query language and supporting toolkit, called Feature Query Language (FQL), to collect HPC-related software metadata from a quick static code analysis. We present the related work in two categories: (1) software analysis tools without using domain-specific languages; and (2) software analysis tools using domain-specific languages.

2.1   Software Analysis Tools Without Using Domain-Specific Languages

There is a lot of software engineering work on code analysis that does not use any domain specific language. A few software analysis tools are designed to obtain low level code information. For instance, security flaws may be detected effectively [35]. In the work of Bush et al., an analyzer for program errors is created [5]. Buffer overflow and function dependencies can be found in the work [14] and [33] respectively. On the other hand, a number of tools focus on providing a higher level overview of the code. For example, the open source toolkits Scan-Code [26] and Fossology [16] are used to extract the license, copyright, package dependency and other information. Oss-review-toolkit is designed to provide the dependencies of different open source libraries for software [25].

Although these software tools can detect specific software information, they are not generic enough to query any type of features that may be interesting to different users. Our FQL is designed to provide an abstract query interface to users so that one can define any new queries in FQL and get answers quickly.

2.2   Software Analysis Tools Using Domain-Specific Languages

On the other hand, many software engineering tools define new programming languages that are of domain purpose only (i.e., DSL) [21]. As described by Deursen et al. [29], DSL has the following advantages: (1) more expressiveness in the specific domain, (2) more friendly to domain experts, and (3) more verification and optimization can be performed at the domain level. Hence, DSL has been widely used in various static code analysis and refactoring tools. In this subsection, we present software tools that use DSL in two classes: (1) static code analysis and (2) code transformation.

Static Code Analysis: Static analysis tools such as crocopat [3], JRelCal [23], JTL [6], SOUL [13], .QL and SemmleCode [12,30] use their own languages and patterns to represent the desired features in the target code. For instance, cro-coPat uses patterns that are described by binary decision diagrams for detecting inter-class structures, which consist of good object-oriented (OO) design patterns, weak anti-patterns, etc. [3]. JRelCal is a library to obtain different kinds of relations in the source code based on the binary relational calculus [23]. JTL (Java Tools Language) is a Java programming language extension to represent

Java code patterns by providing native and predefined first-order logical predicates [6]. By using the new JTL representation, a JTL processor can analyze queries for object-oriented Java programs. SOUL is a Prolog-like language to query a program's structure and is mainly used for detecting source code structures of Java and Smalltalk programs [13]. .QL is an object-oriented query language for measuring code quality, observing bugs and other analysis tasks [12], meanwhile SemmleCode [30] is a free Eclipse plugin, which adopts the .QL language.

However, the above programming languages or tools have different goals from ours, and they are intended to query software development related questions (e.g., design defect, implementation bug, suboptimal code structure, inter-class relationship, design violation, etc.), while our work targets at collecting software's meta-data, parallel library requirements, architecture or device dependency, and other HPC-related questions.

Code Transformation: Another influential line of work aims to support automatic code transformation or refactoring instead of static code analysis only [2,4,7,9,18,22,31]. SrcML is a platform for both code analysis and code manipulation via representing the code in a language called XPath that is similar to XML [7]. Rascal is a programming language designed to integrate program analysis with code manipulation [18]. By defining new basic data types and statically checking the types, Rascal allows programmers to represent a program then transform the program automatically under a number of constraints. DMS is a commercial code transformation tool, which has different performance optimizations [2]. The TXL (Tree Transformation Language) and ELAN [4] languages are used for rule-based code refactoring [9]. Unlike TXL/ELAN, Stratego is able to describe both refactoring strategies and refactoring rules [31]. Moreover, Coccinelle is a special tool to automatically transform Linux kernel drivers by using a language based on the *patch* syntax [22].

Nevertheless, the above code transformation tools require users to write new programs or representations by using the new languages provided by the tools. While they are efficient in code refactoring, they are overly complicated and time-consuming for one's simple goal of software metadata collection.

3   The FQL Language and Toolkit

In this section, we introduce the Feature Query Language (FQL) definition in Subsect. 3.1, then describe the overall workflow of using the FQL toolkit in Subsect. 3.2 followed by the design and implementation of our software toolkit in Subsect. 3.3.

3.1   Feature Query Language (FQL)

The Feature Query Language (FQL) is designed for users to ask any software feature or metadata related questions such as "Does the software require MPI-2?", "Does the software need GPUs", "Does the software depend on a special

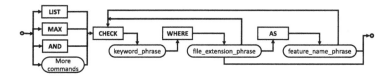

Fig. 1. FQL syntax diagram.

compiler or parallel system library?", "Does the software take advantage parallel I/O", etc. Since a user's questions could be greatly diverse, our FQL must have an extensible architecture and can incorporate any questions of interest. As long as the user knows the keywords of targeted software features, he or she can write a corresponding query in FQL (i.e., an FQL *sentence*) quickly.

3.1.1 FQL Syntax

FQL is defined by the FQL syntax, which is comprised of one or more *clauses* (defined in the next paragraph).

If there is one clause, we return the query result of the specific clause. If there are multiple clauses, results from the various clauses will be summarized by an *FQL command*. An FQL *sentence* with multiple clauses can be expressed in the following form:

$$FQL\_command\ (Clause1, Clause2, ...) \tag{1}$$

An FQL *Clause* is defined as a combination of *phrases* and FQL *reserved keywords*. An example of *clause* is provided below:

$$CHECK\ (keyword\_phrase)\ WHERE\ (file\_extension\_phrase)$$
$$AS\ (feature\_name\_phrase) \tag{2}$$

In the above syntax, *CHECK*, *WHERE* and *AS* are reserved keywords in FQL. They are not case sensitive. Here, a *phrase* is just a set of strings. The current version of FQL has three types of phrases: (i) *keyword_phrase*, (ii) *file_extension_phrase*, and (iii) *feature_name_phrase*.

(i) *keyword_phrase*: A keyword phrase has a few keywords that describe a specific software feature. Each keyword is simply a string. Different keywords are concatenated by "||" or "&&". Symbol "||" means that if one of the keywords is found, we claim that the feature is found. Symbol "&&" means that only if all keywords are found, we then claim that the feature is found.

(ii) *file_extension_phrase*: This phrase is used to tell the FQL software toolkit where to search for the keywords. It consists of a list of file extensions connected by ",". If it is specified as "*", the FQL toolkit will check all types of files.

(iii) *feature_name_phrase*: This *feature_name* phrase is optional and used to specify how to interpret (or name) the query result. For instance, if the *keyword_phrase* is found to exist in the target software, the toolkit will return the specified meaningful *feature name*. Otherwise (i.e., if there is no *feature_name_phrase* provided), the toolkit will only return True or False based upon the query result.

3.1.2 FQL Command

It is common that users may need more than one phrase to define a query. When there are several clauses in a query sentence, results from different clauses will be summarized by executing an FQL command. Currently, FQL provides three commands:

- **LIST:** The LIST command enumerates all the features whose query results are true.
- **MAX:** The MAX command returns the largest query value found in the available features. It can be used to check the software version required by a project.
- **AND:** The AND command returns True only if all clauses' features have been found.

The provided FQL commands can answer many frequently asked questions. In addition, both our FQL syntax and toolkit implementation are designed to be flexible and extensible. Such an extensible design allows new FQL commands to be added to the FQL language quickly whenever needed. We expect to add more commands as the types of queries increase.

To summarize the FQL grammar, we use Fig. 1 to illustrate the syntax of a valid FQL sentence containing more than one clause. FQL-provided commands and FQL-reserved keywords are written in bold uppercase inside rectangles. Phrases and FQL-provided commands are written in lowercase inside ovals. By following the arrows from left to right in Fig. 1, we can construct a valid FQL query.

3.1.3 FQL Query Examples

Here, we list five examples of HPC related questions that may be asked by users and the corresponding FQL queries as well as our remarks. For more examples, please refer to Table 1.

Question 1: Whether OpenMP is used in the code?
FQL: CHECK (!$OMP || #pragma omp) WHERE (*)
       AS (OpenMP)

Note: OpenMP is a widely used API for shared-memory programming [10] in HPC.

Question 2: Is one-sided MPI communication used?
FQL: CHECK (MPI_Put || MPI_RPut || MPI_Get
       || MPI_RGet) WHERE (*)
Note: This query is used to check the MPI one-side communication feature. Since no feature name is provided, our FQL toolkit will return True if one of those keywords is found.

Table 1. Examples of HPC-related asked questions and corresponding queries

Number	User's Interesting Question	Corresponding FQL Query
1	Is OpenACC used?	CHECK (!$acc || #pragma acc) WHERE (*) AS (OpenACC)
2	Is OpenACC atomic operation used?	CHECK (acc atomic) WHERE (*) AS (atomicACC)
3	Is CUDA programming used?	CHECK (__device__ || __global__ || __host__ || __noinline__ || __forceinline__) WHERE (.cu,.cuh) AS (CUDA)
4	What OpenMP scheduling method is used?	LIST (CHECK (schedule(static) WHERE(*) AS (Static), CHECK (schedule(dynamic) WHERE(*) AS (Dynamic), CHECK (schedule(guided) WHERE(*) AS (Guided), CHECK (schedule(auto) WHERE(*) AS (Auto), CHECK (schedule(runtime) WHERE(*) AS (Runtime))
5	Does it use OpenMP Task programming constructs?	CHECK (omp task || end task || omp taskloop || omp taskloop simd || omp taskyield) WHERE (*)

Question 3: What is the minimum version requirement of MPI?
FQL: MAX (
      CHECK (MPI_AINT_ADD \|\| MPI_AINT_DIFF)
        WHERE (*) AS (3.1),
      CHECK (MPI_COMM_DUP_WITH_INFO \|\|
        MPI_COMM_SET_INFO) WHERE (*) AS (3.0),
      CHECK (MPI_DIST_GRAPH_CREATE_ADJACENT
        \|\| MPI_DIST_GRAPH_CREATE) WHERE (*)
        AS (2.2),
      CHECK (mpi.h \|\| use mpi \|\| mpif.h) WHERE (*)
        AS (2.0))
Note: This query is used to search for the minimum version requirement of the MPI in the code. Please note that if our FQL toolkit finds that MPI is not used by the project, it will return "Not found".

Question 4: What kind of MPI process topology (topologies) is (are) used?
FQL: LIST (
      CHECK (MPI_CART_Create) WHERE(*)
        AS (Cartesian),

CHECK (MPI_GRAPH_Create) WHERE(*)
    AS (Graph),
CHECK (MPI_DIST_GRAPH_CREATE_Adjacent
    || MPI_DIST_GRAPH_Create) WHERE(*)
    AS (Distributed Graph))

Note: This query uses the command LIST, whose function is to list all the features found in the code. For this query, all the MPI process topologies used in the code will be listed by our toolkit.

Question 5: Does the project use a hybrid MPI/OpenMP programming model? FQL: AND (
    CHECK (mpi.h || use mpi || mpif.h) WHERE (*)
    AS (MPI),
    CHECK (!$OMP || #pragma omp) WHERE (*)
    AS (OpenMP))

Note: This query uses the command AND, which is used to summarize whether all the features are found. As to this sentence, if both MPI and OpenMP are found, our toolkit will return True.

3.1.4   Predefined FQL Queries and User-Defined FQL Queries

Our software toolkit can support two types of FQL queries: predefined queries and user-defined queries. Predefined queries correspond to frequently asked questions, which are offered as a list of question choices by our software toolkit. User-defined FQL queries are written by a user based on his or her special questions. Both types of queries can be parsed and executed by our toolkit automatically. In our implementation, all the predefined FQL queries and their corresponding questions (in plain English) are stored in a text file. The user-defined queries can also be added to the text file for future use.

3.2   Overall Workflow of the FQL Software Toolkit

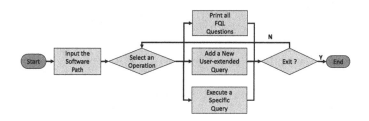

Fig. 2. Overall workflow of the software

Figure 2 shows the workflow of using the FQL toolkit. There are three major steps to use the software: (i) Users input the targeted software's file path

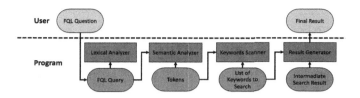

Fig. 3. Software components implemented for parsing and executing FQL queries in the FQL toolkit.

(shown as the first rectangle from the left); (ii) Next, the toolkit pre-scans the targeted software (shown as the second rectangle); and (iii) Based on the user's choice, the FQL toolkit executes particular operations till the user exits the program.

More details of the three major steps are shown as follows:

 (i) *Input the software path by users*: Our toolkit will firstly ask the user to input a file path to search for. This path should be the top-level directory of the targeted software. All files in the specific file path will be scanned by the FQL toolkit recursively.
 (ii) *Select an operation*: In the second step, our software will ask the user to select an operation to operate. There are three available operations.
(iii) *Execute a selected operation*: Our software will execute an operation based on the user's selection in the previous step. Three operations are as follows:
   – To list all the predefined questions. This operation is to remind a user of all predefined FQL queries and corresponding questions (in plain English). The user can then execute a specific query by entering the index number of the question.
   – To add a new user-defined query. The FQL toolkit will also make sure the query entered by a user is valid. It will repeatedly ask the user to input the query until a valid query is received.
   – To execute a specific query. Section 3.3 provides details about how to execute an FQL query by the FQL toolkit.
   After executing one of the above three additional operations, the toolkit will check whether the user wants to repeat Step iii or not.

3.3   Implementation of the FQL Toolkit

To support FQL, we develop a new software toolkit to parse and execute FQL queries. An overview of the process that parses and executes FQL queries is illustrated in Fig. 3.

As shown in Fig. 3, the two yellow round-corner boxes (above the dotted line) represent a user's input and output. The four green round-corner boxes (at the bottom) represent the data exchanged between several major program components.

Table 2. HPC features of the different software

	QMC-Pack	ParFlow	E3SM	SICM	Truchas	Tusas	ExaMPM	MEUM-APPS
MPI	✓	✓	✓	✓	✓	✗	✗	✓
MPI min. version required	2.0	2.0	2.0	2.0	2.0	–	–	2.0
MPI process topology	Carte-sian, Graph	None	Cartesian	Cartesian	None	–	–	None
MPI one-sided communication	✓	✗	✓	✗	✓	–	–	✗
MPI I/O	✗	✗	✓	✗	✗	–	–	✗
OpenMP	✓	✗	✓	✓	✗	✓	✗	✗
Task pro- gramming constructs	✓	–	✓	✗	–	✗	–	–
Hybrid MPI/ OpenMP	✓	–	✓	✓	–	✗	–	–
Scheduling method	Static	–	Static	Static, Dynamic	–	Static	–	–
CUDA	✓	✗	✗	✗	✗	✗	✗	✗
Single/double precision	Both	–	–	–	–	–	–	–
Support multiple GPUs	✓	–	–	–	–	–	–	–
OpenACC	✗	✗	✓	✗	✗	✗	✗	✗
Asynch-ronous operation	–	–	✗	–	–	–	–	–
Atomic operation	–	–	✗	–	–	–	–	–
Min required C compiler	C99	C99	C99	C99	C89	–	C99	–
Fortran standard	Fortran 77	Fortran 77	Fortran 2003	Fortran 2003	Fortran 90	–	Fortran 90	Fortran 77

In total, there are four major program components in the toolkit, which are displayed as four blue rectangles in Fig. 3. They are *lexical analyzer, semantic analyzer, keyword scanner*, and *result generator*. We will introduce the four major components in details as follows.

(i) *Lexical Analyzer*: The input of this component is an FQL query which is an array of characters. The *lexical analyzer* will parse the query into a list of tokens. Here, each token is a string with an assigned or predefined meaning.

(ii) *Semantic Analyzer*: The objective of the *semantic analyzer* component is to find a feature's corresponding keywords from a sequence of tokens. The component translates a list of tokens into keywords. Keywords refer to a set of significant strings that can be used as an indicator of the software feature. For instance, if we find the string *#pragma omp* in the source code, we can say OpenMP is used.

(iii) *Keywords Scanner*: The objective of the *keywords scanner* component is to find whether the desired keywords exist in the source code or not. This component searches for the keywords derived from the semantic analyzer, then prints out a list of boolean variables (illustrated as the Intermediate Search Result in Fig. 3) to indicate whether each keyword is found or not in the source code.

(iv) *Result Generator*: The *result generator* component imports the intermediate results from the *keywords scanner*, and presents the results in an easy-to-understand way to users.

In summary, the *lexical analyzer* and *semantic analyzer* components generate a list of keywords from an FQL query. Then, this list is passed to the *keywords scanner* component, which searches the open source code of interest by using the keywords. Finally, the *result generator* component presents the *keywords scanner* results to users.

4   Exemplar Applications

For the demonstration purpose, we present the searching results of scientific computing software packages supported by several large-scale DOE programs, such as the Innovative and Novel Computational Impact on Theory and Experiment (INCITE) program (www.doeleadership-computing.org), Exascale Computing Projects (www.exascaleproject.org), Earth System Modeling (climatemodeling.science.energy.gov), and Subsurface Biogeochemical Research (doesbr.org). For the demonstration purpose, we use five applications in this paper:

1. QMCPACK: A quantum Monte Carlo package designed for the *ab initio* electronic structure calculations [17]. It includes the implementation of a number of numerous Quantum Monte Carlo (QMC) algorithms.
2. ParFlow A parallel watershed flow model used to simulate different kinds of hydrological processes [20].

3. E3SM: A model used to simulate the interaction between human and Earth systems [1].
4. SICM: A tool provides a simple unified interface to simplify the process of managing the complex memory hierarchies [24].
5. ExaAM (includes Truchas, Tusas, ExaMPM and MEUMAPPS) : ExaAM is a software environment to simulate the complex additive manufacturing process (AM) [19]. Since it is an integration of many software, we use the Truchas [27], Tusas [28], ExaMPM [15] and MEUMAPPS [8] as our test cases. As shown in Table 2, there are four columns for each of them.

Exemplar FQL results of these applications are listed in the Table 2. It is obviously that MPI and OpenMP are two of the most widely used HPC features.

5   Conclusions

In this paper, we design and develop a software toolkit that automatically collects the software features from scientific codes using a new language, called Feature Query Language (FQL). For specific user-defined questions, we translate and formulate them into FQL queries using the FQL syntax. Then, the toolkit parses and executes the FQL queries over source code to collect information about the software features, such as special hardware, software and architecture requirements. Although we emphasize collecting the HPC features in this study, the capability of the toolkit can be easily extended to other software engineering tasks, such as coding pattern, hardware dependency and portability, as long as these questions can be formulated as valid FQL sentences following the defined FQL syntax that combines command, keyword, and phrase. FQL can also be integrated into other code analysis tools. For instance, FQL is included in an integrated tool called XScan. As described in [34], XScan can be used to analyze the Open Source Community-based Scientific Code.

References

1. Bader, D., et al.: Accelerated climate modeling for energy (ACME) project strategy and initial implementation plan (2014)
2. Baxter, I.D., Pidgeon, C., Mehlich, M.: DMS®: program transformations for practical scalable software evolution. In: Proceedings of the 26th International Conference on Software Engineering, pp. 625–634. IEEE Computer Society (2004)
3. Beyer, D., Lewerentz, C.: CrocoPat: efficient pattern analysis in object-oriented programs. In: 2003 11th IEEE International Workshop on Program Comprehension, pp. 294–295. IEEE (2003)
4. Borovanskỳ, P., Kirchner, C., Kirchner, H., Moreau, P.E., Vittek, M.: ELAN: a logical framework based on computational systems. Electron. Notes Theor. Comput. Sci. 4, 35–50 (1996)
5. Bush, W.R., Pincus, J.D., Sielaff, D.J.: A static analyzer for finding dynamic programming errors. Softw. Pract. Exp. 30(7), 775–802 (2000)

6. Cohen, T., Gil, J.Y., Maman, I.: JTL: the Java tools language. In: ACM SIGPLAN Notices, vol. 41, pp. 89–108. ACM (2006)
7. Collard, M.L., Decker, M.J., Maletic, J.I.: srcML: an infrastructure for the exploration, analysis, and manipulation of source code: a tool demonstration. In: 2013 IEEE International Conference on Software Maintenance, pp. 516–519. IEEE (2013)
8. Cook, J., Finkel, H., Junghans, C., McCorquodale, P., Pavel, R., Richards, D.: Proxy app prospectus for ECP application development projects. Technical report, Lawrence Livermore National Lab (LLNL), Livermore, CA, United States (2017)
9. Cordy, J.R., Dean, T.R., Malton, A.J., Schneider, K.A.: Software engineering by source transformation-experience with TXL. In: Proceedings First IEEE International Workshop on Source Code Analysis and Manipulation, pp. 168–178. IEEE (2001)
10. Dagum, L., Menon, R.: OpenMP: an industry standard API for shared-memory programming. IEEE Comput. Sci. Eng. **5**(1), 46–55 (1998)
11. Date, C.J., Darwen, H.: A Guide to the SQL Standard: A User's Guide to the Standard Relational Language SQL. Addison-Wesley, Reading (1989)
12. de Moor, O., et al.: QL: object-oriented queries made easy. In: Lämmel, R., Visser, J., Saraiva, J. (eds.) GTTSE 2007. LNCS, vol. 5235, pp. 78–133. Springer, Heidelberg (2008). https://doi.org/10.1007/978-3-540-88643-3_3
13. De Roover, C., Noguera, C., Kellens, A., Jonckers, V.: The soul tool suite for querying programs in symbiosis with eclipse. In: Proceedings of the 9th International Conference on Principles and Practice of Programming in Java, pp. 71–80. ACM (2011)
14. Dor, N., Rodeh, M., Sagiv, M.: CSSV: towards a realistic tool for statically detecting all buffer overows in C. In: ACM Sigplan Notices, vol. 38, pp. 155–167. ACM (2003)
15. ExaMPM (2017). https://github.com/ECP-copa/ExaMPM
16. Gobeille, R.: The FOSSology project. In: Proceedings of the 2008 International Working Conference on Mining Software Repositories, pp. 47–50. ACM (2008)
17. Kim, J., et al.: QMCPACK simulation suite (2014)
18. Klint, P., Van Der Storm, T., Vinju, J.: RASCAL: a domain specific language for source code analysis and manipulation. In: 2009 Ninth IEEE International Working Conference on Source Code Analysis and Manipulation, SCAM 2009, pp. 168–177. IEEE (2009)
19. Exascale Simulation for Additive Manufacturing (2017). https://github.com/ExascaleAM
20. Maxwell, R.M., et al.: ParFlow user's manual. International Ground Water Modeling Center Report GWMI 1(2009), p. 129 (2009)
21. Mernik, M., Heering, J., Sloane, A.M.: When and how to develop domain-specific languages. ACM Comput. Surv. (CSUR) **37**(4), 316–344 (2005)
22. Padioleau, Y., Lawall, J., Hansen, R.R., Muller, G.: Documenting and automating collateral evolutions in Linux device drivers. In: ACM SIGOPS Operating Systems Review, vol. 42, pp. 247–260. ACM (2008)
23. Rademaker, P.: Binary relational querying for structural source code analysis. University Utrecht, Netherlands (2008)
24. SICM (2018). https://github.com/lanl/SICM
25. oss-review-toolkit (2017). https://github.com/heremaps/oss-review-toolkit
26. scancode-toolkit (2016). https://github.com/nexB/scancode-toolkit
27. Truchas (2017). https://github.com/truchas/truchas-release

28. Tusas (2018). https://github.com/chrisknewman/tusas
29. Van Deursen, A., Klint, P., Visser, J.: Domain-specific languages: an annotated bibliography. ACM SIGPLAN Not. **35**(6), 26–36 (2000)
30. Verbaere, M., Hajiyev, E., De Moor, O.: Improve software quality with Semmle-Code: an eclipse plugin for semantic code search. In: Companion to the 22nd ACM SIGPLAN Conference on Object-Oriented Programming Systems and Applications Companion, pp. 880–881. ACM (2007)
31. Visser, E.: Stratego: a language for program transformation based on rewriting strategies system description of stratego 0.5. In: Middeldorp, A. (ed.) RTA 2001. LNCS, vol. 2051, pp. 357–361. Springer, Heidelberg (2001). https://doi.org/10.1007/3-540-45127-7_27
32. Wang, D., Zheng, W., Song, F.: Application software analytics toolkit for facilitating the understanding, componentization, and refactoring of large-scale scientific models. Technical report, Oak Ridge National Lab (ORNL), Oak Ridge, TN, United States (2018)
33. Wilde, N., Huitt, R., Huitt, S.: Dependency analysis tools: reusable components for software maintenance. In: Proceedings. Conference on Software Maintenance, pp. 126–131. IEEE (1989)
34. Zheng, W., Wang, D., Song, F.: XScan: an integrated tool for understanding open source community-based scientific code. In: Rodrigues, J.M.F., et al. (eds.) ICCS 2019. LNCS, vol. 11536, pp. 226–237. Springer, Cham (2019). https://doi.org/10.1007/978-3-030-22734-0_17
35. Zitser, M.: Securing software: an evaluation of static source code analyzers. Ph.D. thesis, Massachusetts Institute of Technology (2003)

WIHPC – Workshop on Interactive High-Performance Computing

Accelerating Experimental Science Using Jupyter and NERSC HPC

Matthew L. Henderson[1,3(✉)], William Krinsman[1,3], Shreyas Cholia[1,2,3], Rollin Thomas[2,3], and Trevor Slaton[2,3]

[1] Computational Research Division, Berkeley, USA
{mhenderson,williamkrinsman,scholia}@lbl.gov
[2] NERSC, Berkeley, USA
{rcthomas,tslaton}@lbl.gov
[3] Lawrence Berkeley National Laboratory, Berkeley, CA 94720, USA

Abstract. Large scale experimental science workflows require support for a unified, interactive, real-time platform that can manage a distributed set of resources connected to High Performance Computing (HPC) systems. What is needed is a tool that provides the ease-of-use and interactivity of a web science gateway, while providing the scientist the ability to build custom, ad-hoc workflows in a composable way. The Jupyter platform can play a key role here to enable the ingestion and analysis of real-time streaming data, integrate with HPC resources in a closed-loop, and enable interactive ad-hoc analyses with running workflows.

We want to enable high-quality reproducible human-in-the-loop science using HPC and Jupyter at the National Energy Research Scientific Computing Center (NERSC). Achieving that goal is challenging in the general case because scientific workflows and data can vary significantly in size and type between disciplines. There are many areas of work to achieve highly reproducible science, let alone human-in-the-loop interactive scientific workflows, but we focus here on some basic elements for enabling an improved interactive HPC experience including creating reusable recipes and workflows with Notebooks, sharing and cloning Notebooks, and parallelization and scaling of scientific code requiring HPC and using Jupyter.

Keywords: HPC · Interactive · Jupyter · Scientific workflows · Reuse · Parameters

1 Introduction

Experimental science typically involves designing an experiment to perform, setting up the experiment, running the experiment, collecting resulting data, and finally, analyzing the results. User facilities such as the Advanced Light Source (ALS) and the National Center for Electron Microscopy (NCEM) are examples

G. Juckeland and S. Chandrasekaran (Eds.): HUST 2019/SE-HER 2019/WIHPC 2019,
CCIS 1190, pp. 145–163, 2020.
https://doi.org/10.1007/978-3-030-44728-1_9

at Lawrence Berkeley National Laboratory of high volume experimental science, with many researchers collecting and storing data. Teams of researchers travel to these centers, reserving time slots in advance to collect data, and then analyze the data afterward. The data analysis used to be achievable on a laptop or workstation, but with larger data sizes and faster data collection, researchers are turning to HPC for experimental data analysis. If we think of this as the outer loop of the experimental workflow, there is a strong impetus to reduce the end-to-end time required to iterate over an experimental run, through real-time interactive analyses that allow scientists to quickly validate and analyze their results. This, in turn, feeds back into subsequent data acquisition cycles and can help create a more intelligent and efficient process at the instrument level, and can greatly reduce costs associated with expensive instrument time.

The Jupyter [27] platform can play an important facilitating role in this type of interactive human-in-the-loop analysis of experimental workflows. Jupyter Notebooks combine live executable code cells, with inline documentation and embedded interactive visualizations. This allows us to capture an experiment in a fully contained runnable Notebook that is self-documenting and incorporates live rendering of outputs and results as they are generated. The Notebook format lends itself to a highly modular and composable workflow, where individual steps and parameters can be adjusted on the fly. Additionally, with the advent of JupyterLab [9], the updated and plugin-based Notebook user interface, the Jupyter platform can support custom applications and extensions that live alongside the core Notebook interface.

The National Energy Research Scientific Computing Center (NERSC) connects data from several experimental facilities, such as the ALS and NCEM to HPC resources to enable these data analyses. The supercomputing resource currently available at NERSC is Cori, a Cray XC40 supercomputer consisting of 2,388 Intel Haswell nodes, 9,688 Intel Knights Landing nodes, 1.8 PB of integrated flash storage for bursty I/O, and 30 PB of high-performance Lustre "scratch" storage. The NERSC Global Filesystem provides longer-term medium-performance storage.

Given that Jupyter is already well-established in the scientific toolbox for small scale, single node exploratory analysis, it would be extremely useful to be able to scale these analyses up on larger datasets and compute resources. There is a growing ecosystem of tools that make Jupyter useful for larger collaborative workflows on HPC platforms. By creating and integrating tools and extensions that allow Jupyter to scale up workflows in a reproducible manner, we expect to enhance overall productivity across large scientific projects. We are working to provide interactive analysis of experimental data using Jupyter Notebooks and the Jupyter ecosystem while taking advantage of NERSC's HPC resources to handle large computations on big datasets.

In this paper, we discuss the underlying Jupyter and JupyterHub infrastructure at NERSC that makes it possible to serve and deploy Jupyter Notebooks for thousands of users and provides us the flexibility to set up these extensions and customizations in the Jupyter environment. In our previous work, we began exploring Deep Learning on HPC using Jupyter [20]. We seek to build upon this early work, particularly in the context of large scale experimental science, while also considering the broader scope of collaboration and data exploration using Jupyter in these domains. We focus on three key areas of modern scientific workflows:

Scaling Up Analyses on HPC: In a scientific workflow utilizing Jupyter, the Notebook serves as an executable data processing and analysis run, with the potential for scaling up certain steps (or cells in the Notebook) by running these steps in parallel across multiple HPC nodes. Specifically, we look at vectorizing certain loops or running steps concurrently across multiple backend nodes. To do this, we attach a parallel execution framework to our Notebook (e.g., Dask [13] or IPyParallel [6]) and farm out specific code elements as function calls to this backend execution engine to scale up. The NCEM py4DSTEM [16] analysis fits this model. We expect this methodology to apply for other scientific domains as well.

Streamlining Exploration of Parameter Spaces: While Jupyter Notebooks are very useful at capturing a specific analysis, in certain cases we may want to repeat this analysis across a broad parameter space and analyze the results. In the case of 3D tomographic reconstruction from ALS beamlines [26], we would like to adjust parameters and capture the resulting analyses as separate Notebooks so that we have a family of Notebooks representing the parameter space. Tools like Papermill [28] allow us to run the same Notebook using different parameters. This may be useful in other contexts such as simulations, where parameter exploration is also important.

Reproducible and Replicable Workflows: Given the collaborative nature of large experimental science projects, it becomes critical to be able to curate and capture certain analysis workflows as Jupyter Notebooks, such that users of the project can then launch these Notebooks in their environments, and re-run the workflows on different datasets or with their mutations. We are extending the nbviewer [24] Jupyter tool to allow projects to curate a set of Notebooks for users to clone (along with the accompanying computing environment and related dependencies), so that they may run their version of the workflow. Parameterized Notebooks also play an important role here, allowing them to be incorporated easily as immutable objects.

2   NERSC Jupyter Infrastructure

Cori has been in service at NERSC since late 2015. It is designed with the goal of enabling both simulation and data processing workloads to run side-by-side in the same system. Among a number of features that are deemed especially friendly to "data users", Cori includes a larger number of front-end nodes than previous NERSC systems. These nodes support long-running workflow and service engines, data transfer, large-memory jobs, and interactive platforms—specifically, Jupyter. Originally one node was set aside for running Jupyter Notebooks on Cori, but over the past four years, demand for Jupyter at NERSC has surged to the point where two more of these nodes have been repurposed for running Jupyter. On any given day approximately 200 Notebook servers are running on Cori's Jupyter nodes, and the number of users who have run a Notebook server at NERSC exceeds 1,000. Since August of 2018, the JupyterLab interface has been used as the default Jupyter client at NERSC.

NERSC runs a JupyterHub service to manage its multi-user Jupyter deployment. This web service runs in a Docker container outside Cori in NERSC's container-as-a-service platform, Spin [14]. Once a user has authenticated to JupyterHub at NERSC using their NERSC credentials, they select a target system setup (Cori or another Docker container in Spin) where they want a Jupyter Notebook to launch. Round-robin DNS assigns the user to one of the Cori Jupyter nodes where their Notebooks spawn. The authenticator and spawner logic is custom-developed by NERSC and easily plugs into JupyterHub. This allows for a tiered model, where the external-facing JupyterHub runs outside Cori but can route web traffic to each user's JupyterLab instance running inside Cori. This provides access to file systems, batch queues, and Cori's high-speed network. The NERSC JupyterHub deployment model is captured in Fig. 1.

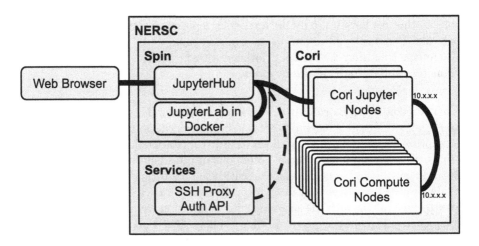

Fig. 1. Jupyter at NERSC. A user authenticates through a web browser connected to the JupyterHub process running in Spin. The Hub uses the secure NERSC SSH Proxy authentication API to enable the spawning of Notebooks on other systems at NERSC. The user may spawn JupyterLab in another container in Spin or on dedicated Jupyter nodes akin to login nodes. These nodes have an internal-facing interface that enables connections between Jupyter processes running on the Jupyter nodes and compute nodes. This enables interactive distributed IPyParallel or Dask computing through job allocations.

When deploying Jupyter on HPC systems, HPC center staff must make a number of decisions within a set of constraints. For instance, inbound connections to compute nodes may not be easy to orchestrate or even possible. In that case, running Jupyter Notebooks on compute nodes may be "clunky" or impossible. At NERSC we have been able to add interfaces to the Cori Jupyter nodes that enable Notebooks to communicate with processes running in batch jobs on the compute nodes. This relatively simple change to the networking rules on a few nodes means that we can scale up deployment of scientific analyses by launching jobs on Cori and interacting with them through JupyterLab via distributed execution engines like IPyParallel and Dask. This may be the best fit for Jupyter on Cori at this point. Users expect JupyterLab to behave like a long-lived secure shell (SSH) or remote desktop connection and retain state almost indefinitely (within appropriate use guidelines), something that is incompatible with time-limited batch jobs. This means that part of our focus is on making JupyterLab "HPC-aware" and exposing HPC resources and capabilities through Jupyter's user-friendly interface.

Traditional HPC supercomputers like Cori at NERSC are homogeneous bare metal servers, providing a low latency interconnect, high network bandwidth, a large number of CPU cores, shared parallel file systems and access to large scientific data sets and software libraries that are optimized for HPC hardware. Users submit job requests to a queue system, which allocates available time and resources for the job, normally with those resources exclusive to the user. Many HPC parallel codes use the message passing interface (MPI) to communicate between units of code. Data storage volumes on HPC systems can be large but do not increase in capacity rapidly.

This can be contrasted with typical cloud computing environments, such as Amazon Web Services and Microsoft Azure. These are generally heterogeneous, with different virtualized hardware environments to choose from. Resources can be requested more dynamically in a cloud environment, but performance metrics can vary more and applications need to be more resilient to failures on individual nodes. In a virtualized hardware environment, the local node resources and network are shared by other cloud tenants, which could mean drastically different latencies and compute times per node. Software that runs well in a cloud environment at scale tends to be more asynchronous by nature and may also exhibit more data parallelism with individual units not needing to communicate with each other. Data storage volumes can be large, and they can rapidly increase in capacity, with multiple centers providing geographically distributed data and compute resources.

Much of the prior Jupyter development for computing at scale has emerged from cloud deployments and carries with it assumptions that don't fit the HPC model (e.g., isolated resources without a common user namespace, no large shared parallel filesystems, high latency between nodes). HPC environments present unique challenges when it comes to running Jupyter for interactive computing. Our efforts at NERSC have been focused on tighter integration with many of the HPC features described above.

3   Scaling up Analyses on HPC

3.1   NCEM Bragg Disk Detection with Py4DSTEM

Scanning transmission electron microscopy (STEM) is used for spectroscopy, diffraction, and imaging of materials. The microscope scans an atomic scale beam of electrons across a thin sample of material in a raster pattern, using interactions between electrons from the beam and atoms from the sample to investigate material structure. In a 4D-STEM experiment, a two-dimensional diffraction pattern is recorded at every beam position, encoding which electrons scattered into which directions for every raster position. For crystalline and semicrystalline materials, it is possible to determine many structural properties using 4D-STEM by identifying the directions of Bragg scattering, where the periodicities of the crystal create reflections of the electron beam in different locations in the diffraction patterns. To find these directions, a vacuum probe is used as a template, a correlation is taken between each diffraction pattern and the template, and the positions and intensities of all local correlation maxima are used to identify the Bragg disks. Measurement of the positions of these diffraction disks are commonly used for strain mapping, orientation mapping, and phase mapping [30]. Currently, Bragg disk detection [18,31,32] is the most computationally expensive step for py4DSTEM-based analyses.

The original version of the Bragg disk detection algorithm was in serial form, run from inside of a Jupyter Notebook where images of the data were rendered for inspection and analysis. The Bragg disk detection step took several minutes to process a 2 GB dataset using either a workstation or a shared Cori login node. A 65 GB dataset took 11 h to process on a workstation, and a 300 GB dataset was expected to take days to complete on a workstation.

3.2   Transforming the Code for Parallel Execution

Because the function that performs disk detection could operate on an individual diffraction pattern, a slice of the data, a data-parallel algorithm was formed by simply running the same function simultaneously on multiple diffraction patterns. The original function was written in Python and makes heavy use of NumPy [29,34] for array manipulation and calculations, so a natural fit to parallelize this would be a tool like IPyParallel or Dask. Both IPyParallel and Dask provide a mechanism for instantiating a cluster of workers and can provide remote execution of Python functions from a Python interpreter or a Jupyter Notebook running a Python Jupyter Kernel. We started with IPyParallel first to see how well a parallel version would scale and how much code refactoring may be needed. By keeping all of the new code in a Notebook initially, it was easy to iteratively test what was working and check results. A basic initial version was already promising, reducing runtimes but not scaling quite as well as expected. Performance using Dask was slower than IPyParallel for this implementation, and it became evident that there were bottlenecks in our initial implementation when attempting to scale beyond a few nodes. Even with a less than ideal improvement initially, it was relatively easy and fast to use IPyParallel to create and test a parallel implementation, with minimal changes needed from the original code.

One of the issues with the initial implementation was that there was an assumption that there was a low overhead to calling the function an arbitrary number of times using IPyParallel or Dask. Because each function call completed quickly for processing a single slice, there was a high relative overhead for pushing input data over the network, calling the function, and returning the results each time. To address this, a wrapper function was created that calls the original function in bulk based on the number of data slices provided. The full dataset is split as evenly as possible based on the number of workers available, and then each of these chunks is passed to the wrapper function on a worker. That change made a noticeable improvement in throughput from the original implementation.

Additionally, moving input data to and from the workers was also a bottleneck. This had to be addressed in three parts, (i) the parameter inputs to the function, (ii) the data slice to process, and (iii) the function output data. The inputs were serialized to disk, and then the file path was passed to the wrapper function for deserialization. The data slices could be read from the original data file, so slice offsets were passed to the wrapper function with the path to the input data to extract the relevant data slices for processing. Finally, the output data from each function call was assembled into a data structure and serialized to disk, with the wrapper function returning the path to that file for retrieving the result data. By eliminating bottlenecks, overall throughput improved, but there was also an improvement in scalability, expanding the size of the cluster that could be effectively used to process the data, reducing processing time substantially by increasing available compute resources.

3.3 Upgrading Disk Detection

While this parallel work was being performed, the py4DSTEM authors were busy upgrading their software to improve their analyses. Some initial results of the parallel work had already improved processing time for larger data, but it did not improve yet beyond about 640 cores or 20 Haswell nodes. The py4DSTEM developers added a different computational method to Bragg disk detection (subpixel method 'multicorr' instead of 'poly') for computing image subpixels during disk detection to gain more accuracy, but this also changed the running time from fixed to variable. The 'poly' version is simpler and fits a parabola to pixels around each peak and finds the maximum without upsampling. The 'multicorr' version upsamples the image selectively using Discrete Fourier Transforms (DFT) instead of upsampling all pixels using Fast Fourier Transforms (FFT) [22,33]. FFTs have well-optimized libraries, but for this data, many of the upsampled pixels are not useful and end up being discarded, increasing memory consumption and computation increasingly inefficiently as the upsampling factor is increased.

This algorithmic change altered how evenly the work gets distributed to workers since some data slices require more work to upsample. The uneven distribution of work becomes more clear at larger cluster scales, as shown in Fig. 3.

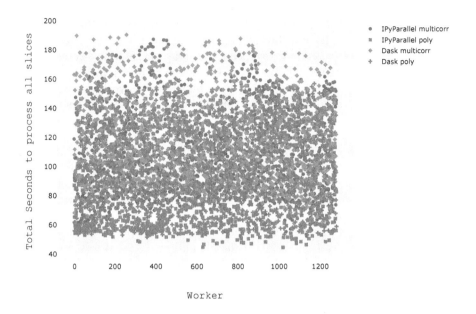

300GB py4DSTEM Bragg Disk Detection on Cori Haswell using 40 nodes

Fig. 2. Total seconds to process Bragg disk detection per worker on Cori Haswell with 300 GB data using 40 nodes.

For a 40 node cluster, using 1,280 cores on a 300 GB dataset, a noticeable split was present in the processing time for each slice, as shown in Fig. 2. About half of the slices took longer to complete, meaning some of the workers would spend more time idle if they received more slices requiring less work.

3.4   Integrating the Parallel Version Back into Py4DSTEM

The original py4DSTEM code was refactored to incorporate this work, including adding a module with parallel implementations for IPyParallel and Dask and wrapping the original serial code and parallel code in a common function interface, maintaining backward compatibility with existing software using py4DSTEM but adding new parameters for specifying an IPyParallel or Dask cluster to submit work to.

3.5   NCEM Impact

Building a parallel implementation for the Bragg disk detection code significantly improved processing time for large data. Now a 300 GB dataset takes only minutes to process instead of days, as captured in Fig. 4. Figure 5 shows wall clock time to process a 65 GB dataset using up to 40 Cori Haswell nodes, or 1,280 workers. This performance improvement directly impacts NCEM users

300GB py4DSTEM Bragg Disk Detection on Cori Haswell using 40 nodes

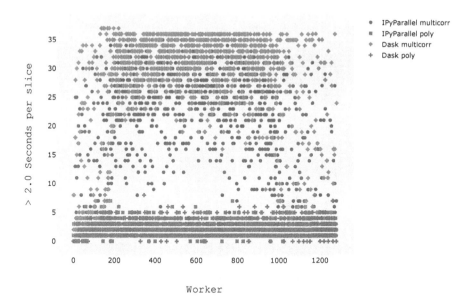

Fig. 3. Number of slices taking longer than 2 s for Bragg disk detection per worker on Cori Haswell with 300 GB data using 40 nodes. This figure shows the significant difference in performance characteristics between the 'poly' and 'multicorr' algorithms.

that no longer need to take home hard drives packed with raw data to process on their own later. Additionally, it is difficult to evaluate data utility during a 4D-STEM experiment without analyzing the data. Processing data much faster allows time to evaluate collected data, update the experiment, and collect better results with available instrument time. Data transfer to Cori from the microscope is now more time consuming than the analysis. These improvements are bringing real-time analyses during data collection closer to a reality for NCEM.

This speedup is also opening up computational analyses that were not previously practical. One of the main advantages of 4D-STEM is the ability to get both atomic-scale structural information with fine spatial sampling and very large fields of view. Without HPC and the parallel implementation, this multiscale advantage would not be possible. It would be necessary to sacrifice either spatial sampling or field-of-view to achieve the analysis for current data.

Approximately 50% of 4D-STEM experiments at NCEM involve Bragg disk detection, and this enhancement to py4DSTEM will be applied to that data going forward. Currently, the data collection rate is about 2–4 TB per day, but this will be increasing with the introduction of new high-speed cameras that have a data rate of 50 GB per second. In 1–2 years it is realistic for data volumes to increase when more microscopes contain high-speed cameras. Having this parallel processing available from a Jupyter Notebook cell also means that NCEM users

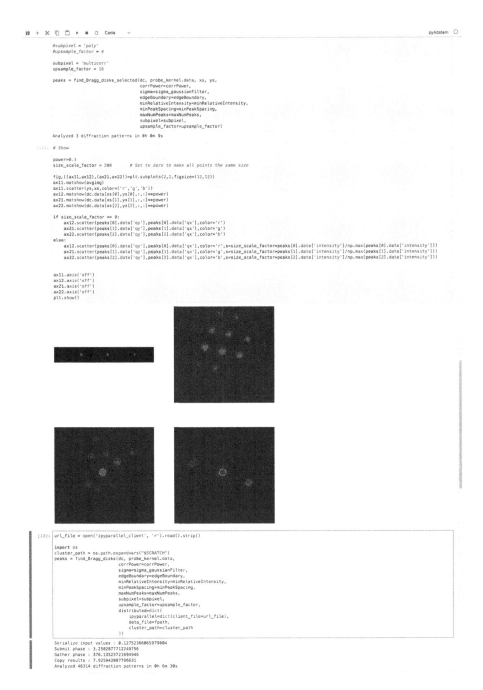

Fig. 4. py4DSTEM Notebook with 300 GB dataset using 320 engines IPyParallel cluster

65GB py4DSTEM Bragg Disk Detection on Cori Haswell

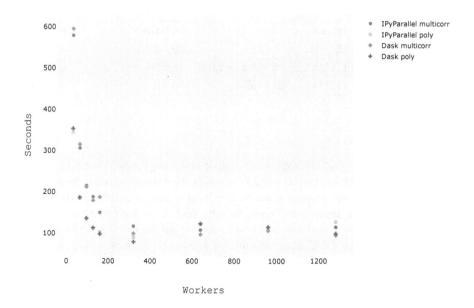

Fig. 5. Bragg disk detection on Cori Haswell with 65 GB data.

can utilize existing recipe Notebooks from NCEM to help them in processing their data, while able to take advantage of HPC resources from NERSC in an interactive session. Approximate peak data rates for the K2 microscope and high-speed 4D microscope are shown in Table 1.

3.6   Insights for Parallel Performance of Scientific Software

Efficient data access is very important for parallel work in general and in this case efficient use of memory was also important. Data readers need to be memory efficient to support many instances running on a single node, which can occur in a data-parallel implementation. In an earlier parallel implementation, memory was not an issue because the data was read in once during submission and slices were transferred over the network to workers. In a later implementation, to reduce overhead we opened the file at each worker, but this resulted in running out of memory with many workers per node when the data reader expected to load everything into memory at once. Some of the data readers used by py4DSTEM utilize memory-mapped files, which worked well for this paradigm.

Data movement can also be expensive, with costs increasing by data volume. The scheduler does not understand the data or workflow as well as the end-user, and will not be able to completely optimize processing or moving data - the user can do this more effectively on their end in some cases.

Table 1. NCEM microscope approximate peak data rates

Microscope	Peak rate
TitanX	50 MB/s
Themis	300 MB/s
TEAM 0.5/TEAM I (K2/K3)	16 GB/s
TEAM 0.5/4D Camera	50 GB/s

3.7   Future Work

As data collection at NCEM increases, scaling the Bragg disk detection further will be important. One way to achieve greater performance with more CPU cores would be to more evenly balance the load among workers. Performance improvements to the underlying code for the multicorr algorithm would also help, potentially using Numba or Cython to accelerate the existing Python code. Adapting the code for GPU usage is another avenue to explore.

The NCEM Gatan K2 IS microscopes record data in a raw format that users can convert at the microscope to the more commonly used Gatan Digital Micrograph [5] file format. For larger 300 GB files, this conversion takes about an hour. The py4DSTEM developers are working on a data reader for the Gatan K2 raw format partly based on prior open source work by the LiberTEM [17] developers that is also compatible with the py4DSTEM datacube interface, but read performance is about five times slower for Bragg disk detection in py4DSTEM compared to the Digital Micrographand HDF5 [21] readers in py4DSTEM. This is an active work area to either be able to process the original format data comparatively fast or be able to rapidly reformat the data without needing the microscope.

IPyParallel and Dask clusters here were manually instantiated on Cori from the shell outside of a Notebook, but Dask does have tools such as dask-jobqueue [4] and a Dask JupyterLab extension [19] for controlling and monitoring Dask clusters from the JupyterLab interface. There is ongoing work to better integrate these tools into the NERSC Jupyter environment for users. IPyParallel does not yet have a JupyterLab equivalent control center for cluster management as in the classic Notebook interface, but that is another area we are working to enable.

4   Streamlining Exploration of Parameter Spaces

The ALS Beamline 8.3.2 is a Synchrotron-based Hard X-ray Micro-Tomography instrument. Tomography analysis requires processing of datasets (many GBs) that contain 32-bit image stacks. Standard raw datasets contain X-ray images of a sample taken at many angles as the sample is rotated with respect to the imaging system. These raw images are 2D horizontal slices of the sample which are inspected by researchers and a process of filtering and adjustment takes place to determine the best parameters to choose for proper tuning and alignment of all the slice images. Finally, a combined image is produced that merges the 2D slices into a 3D view of the object. When analyzing the slices, it is incredibly useful to explore the parameter space to help determine the best fit for each dataset and capture the parameters and results. Applications already exist for Beamline 8.3.2 users that offer visualization of the image stack and some exploration of the parameter space, however, these are meant to run on a laptop or workstation. Researchers do not have a unified way to process these images and rely on scripts and collections of code snippets to experiment with the image stacks during alignment. Jupyter offers a broader feature set as discussed above, including the ability to perform custom ad-hoc analyses as needed within the same Notebook context.

A common use case we have encountered in talking to different groups of scientific users of Jupyter, including at the ALS, is that there is a desire to use Notebooks as reusable curated recipes or apps. This means having the ability to run a Notebook on different data or with different inputs without having to copy and edit the Notebook each time, to simply execute it like a packaged piece of software. The ALS and NCEM analyses would both benefit from being able to parameterize their Notebooks so that facility users can start with curated reusable analyses and simply plug data in and adjust parameters. Consolidating analyses into reusable forms using Notebooks also aids in the repeatability of results, and makes it simpler to compare results.

Using Jupyter Notebooks as a means to explore parameter spaces is another use case that frequently comes up in discussions with scientific users. It is possible to explore parameter spaces by making many copies of Notebooks and editing each for a different parameter set or data set, but this is a cumbersome process and makes it more difficult to track and compare results, in addition to being error-prone.

The Papermill tool, originating from Netflix, allows one to execute a Notebook with input parameters, maintaining the original Notebook as an immutable document. The underlying mechanism for parameterizing Notebooks with Papermill relies on applying and parsing Notebook metadata, specifically "parameters" tags that can be applied to cells in a Notebook document. Papermill then uses the nbconvert [3] Jupyter tool to execute the modified Notebook, injecting inputs based on tagged parameters while leaving the original Notebook untouched. This mechanism allows us to build in automation around Notebook execution and bridges the gap between the Notebook as an interactive document and as an executable program.

For example, when doing 3D tomographic reconstruction from the ALS beamline, it is useful to look at a single slice of an image taken from the beamline and optimize the parameters for generating the reconstruction interactively. In other words, the user would attempt to run the Notebook across a different set of parameters and pick the optimal set, by browsing through a series of generated Notebooks and images. These parameters would then be saved and applied across subsequent datasets and experimental runs.

Parameterized Notebooks also play an important role in preserving provenance in a workflow. Since any given run across a set of parameters can be preserved as a complete Notebook, this serves as a self-documenting representation of that particular run. We can review the results from this parameter set as a stand-alone Notebook, and even reproduce the results by re-running it.

4.1 Future Work

We are investigating comparing the use of Papermill with more inline single-Notebook approaches for the exploration of parameter spaces with tomographic data and workflows used at the ALS Beamline. We are looking at inline widgets and interfaces within a single Notebook that can expose this type of parameter exploration as an alternative to generating multiple Notebooks across the parameter space. In practice, we expect to see a combination of these approaches, since the inline approach may be more suited for exploratory analysis, while a set of Notebooks would be more useful for maintaining provenance and batch processing. We are also working on making these tools and services broadly available to NERSC Jupyter users so that they can be seamlessly incorporated into their workflows.

5   Reproducible and Replicable Workflows

5.1   Sharing and Cloning Jupyter Notebooks

Jupyter Notebooks are becoming increasingly common in scientific communities as a mechanism for publishing analyses and sharing them with colleagues. Because Notebooks are just files, it is not difficult to email or otherwise share these files through the usual mechanisms, and there are publishing mechanisms for viewing and running Notebooks in a cloud environment (e.g., Binder, Pangeo). However, currently, there is no built-in mechanism in the JupyterLab or classic Jupyter interfaces, or in JupyterHub (the shared Jupyter gateway deployed at NERSC and many other locations), to copy or share a Notebook. Additionally, when copying a Notebook, it can also be important to replicate the execution environment the Notebook expects, namely software dependencies required by the contents of the Notebook (Fig. 6).

For the ALS and NCEM use cases, there is a need to provide curated recipe Notebooks for users that do not have software development or coding experience to expertly process and analyze their data. This also merges with the need for parameterized Notebooks since it makes more sense in this context to treat the Notebooks as "apps" that can be run on many different inputs without needing to edit their contents. In the workflow context, each parameterized Notebook can be assumed to be immutable, greatly enhancing the repeatability and reproducibility of the results.

Specifically, we are developing modifications to our JupyterHub deployment and the addition of a modified version of nbviewer to bring Notebook sharing

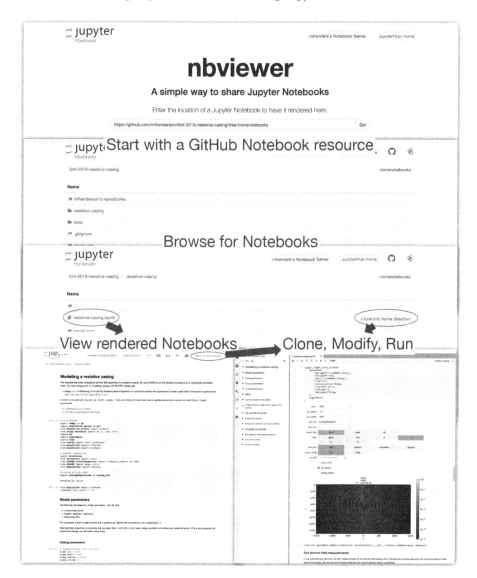

Fig. 6. The nbviewer tool, running as a JupyterHub service, allows a project within an HPC system to provide a set of curated Notebooks that users can browse and preview a static rendering of. Users can then clone a Notebook and its associated Jupyter kernelspec into their environment to modify and execute a live Notebook. This figure shows an example geoscience Notebook [10, 11, 23].

functionality to NERSC users. The nbviewer tool acts as a web service for rendering Jupyter Notebooks as static web pages using nbconvert. There is a public instance of this service [12] that accepts a URL or GitHub identifier for a given Notebook and then renders the Notebook as a static web page.

By creating an area for users to deposit Notebooks for sharing, we can expose that to nbviewer, and add a hook to nbviewer that copies the Notebook into a user's home area. Our service clonenotebooks [1] consists of two parts: a version of nbviewer modified to facilitate extensibility and custom configuration, and an extension to the Jupyter Notebook server. It uses nbviewer to enable browsing and viewing of Notebooks and enables a special "clone" button within the nbviewer interface which makes an HTTP request to an endpoint served by the extended Jupyter Notebook server. The extension to the Notebook server invokes the JupyterLab Contents API [7] (an API for filesystem-level operations in the Jupyter backend) to copy the Notebook file into the user's workspace as well as updating the Notebook's format when necessary to be compatible with the current version of Jupyter. Additionally, the Jupyter Notebook server extension uses the existing Jupyter client to install the Jupyter kernelspec file that specifies which kernel goes along with the Notebook, to capture the underlying software environment and library dependencies. This means that the user now has a live working copy of the Notebook-based workflow in their workspace, and they are free to modify and tweak this reference Notebook to suit their own needs. At the same time, since nbviewer only allows users to view Notebooks, not modify them, the original curated Notebook remains unaffected by the user's actions and therefore remains suitable to share with other users.

We note that this is different from direct sharing, as in Google Docs, where users instantly receive access to a shared document, but it does provide a mechanism for users to publish Notebooks locally and share them in the general sense with others. A challenge here is making sure that the environment needed to execute the Notebook is available to anyone running a copy of these Notebooks. Since there is not currently a general solution to this problem, we have users that want to share Notebooks also provide a Conda [2] environment that can be used as the basis for a Jupyter Kernel that would run the Notebook. The kernelspec file that the user shares with the Notebook, and which is installed automatically by clonenotebooks, makes it simple for other users to run the Notebook using the correct Kernel.

5.2 Future Work

There are existing efforts in the Jupyter ecosystem that enable reproducible science in the cloud. The Binder [25] project enables a set of Notebooks along with a specification for software dependencies in a GitHub repo to be cloned, provisioned and run as Docker containers on cloud resources. While Binder is focused on small ephemeral cloud resources, our goal is to create this kind of reproducible Notebook in an HPC setting for large workflows, such that we can run these workflows against large datasets that are being generated from experimental workflows. We are looking at taking Binder's container-based approach and applying it to reproducible environments at NERSC.

We also note the Pangeo [15] effort in the geosciences space. Pangeo uses public cloud infrastructure to pair Jupyter with a predefined stack that includes relevant scientific Python libraries and enables a scalable backend through Dask to run large analyses. There are many high-level similarities to this work, but our focus is on the interactive HPC component of the workflow. Our infrastructure is geared towards shared HPC resources rather than containerized cloud resources that Pangeo currently focuses on.

Moving forward we would like to explore the possibility of integrating our work with projects like Binder and Pangeo. Since the persistence of resources and data play a key role in most of our work, it would be useful to discuss how this could apply to some of these other efforts that take a more ephemeral cloud-based view of things.

The Jupyter developers are also working on a collaborative mechanism [8] for multiple users to interact with a single Notebook, which will provide a more built-in interface for sharing. As these features take shape, we hope to integrate them with our Notebook sharing services to provide another dimension to real-time, interactive collaboration.

6   Conclusions

By relying on specific use cases from NCEM and ALS to improve an interactive HPC experience with Jupyter at NERSC, we are moving closer to human-in-the-loop scientific workflows. We believe focusing on Notebooks as a reusable element of workflows will improve reproducibility for scientists, as well as quality when community effort is directed at curating high-quality Notebook recipes.

The Jupyter platform has been a remarkably robust and extensible solution for interactive computing, and we have been able to enhance collaborative, experimental workflows by integrating and building a suite of tools and enhancements into our setup at NERSC. Enabling parallel backend execution engines such as IPyParallel and Dask has given us a powerful and simple mechanism to scale up Python-based analyses in Jupyter. This is critical when it comes to enabling interactive analyses on very large datasets. Tools to explore parameter spaces like Papermill have added a level of provenance and automation to the experimental workflow. Finally, Notebook sharing is a key element in enabling flexible, reproducible, interactive computing across a large project, since this allows for reference Notebooks to capture a common base workflow that can then be modified and extended by individuals.

Taking a broader view, Jupyter can lower the barrier for entry to experimental science. Jupyter Notebooks function as de facto canned "apps" that can be re-run by users without a deep computational background - these users can simply modify parameters, data inputs or specific cells without disturbing the rest of the workflow logic. At the same time, the entire workflow process is transparent and can be modified and re-composed as needed, so that more advanced users can implement deeper changes to the code.

Our success in engaging with early users at NCEM and ALS have reinforced our belief that interactive computing is a key element in large experimental workflows, and user-friendly Notebook interfaces like Jupyter, that can be accessed from anywhere on the web, will be critical in driving the scientific discovery loop.

Acknowledgements. This research used resources of the National Energy Research Scientific Computing Center (NERSC), a U.S. Department of Energy Office of Science User Facility operated under Contract No. DE-AC02-05CH11231.

We wish to thank the Jupyter team; Colin Ophus, Benjamin Savitzky, and Steven Zeltmann at NCEM; and Dilworth Parkinson at ALS Beamline 8.3.2. We would also like to thank Lindsey Heagy for the geoscience Notebook example.

References

1. Clonenotebooks. https://github.com/krinsman/clonenotebooks/
2. Conda. https://docs.conda.io/projects/conda/en/latest/
3. Convert notebooks to other formats. https://nbconvert.readthedocs.io/en/latest/
4. dask-jobqueue. https://jobqueue.dask.org/en/latest/
5. Gif quantum k2 system. https://www.gatan.com/products/tem-imaging-spectroscopy/gif-quantum-k2-system
6. Ipyparallel: Using ipython for parallel computing. https://ipyparallel.readthedocs.io/en/latest/
7. Jupyter contents api. https://jupyter-notebook.readthedocs.io/en/stable/extending/contents.html
8. Jupyterlab: Real time collaboration. https://github.com/jupyterlab/jupyterlab/issues/5382
9. Jupyterlab: The next generation web-based user interface for project jupyter. https://github.com/jupyterlab/jupyterlab
10. lbnl-2019-resistive-casing notebook. https://github.com/simpeg-research/lbnl-2019-resistive-casing
11. mlhenderson fork of lbnl-2019-resistive-casing notebook. https://github.com/mlhenderson/lbnl-2019-resistive-casing
12. nbviewer. https://nbviewer.jupyter.org/
13. Scalable analytics in python. https://dask.org/
14. Spin. https://www.nersc.gov/users/data-analytics/spin/
15. Pangeo (2018). https://pangeo.io/
16. Bsavitzky, et al.: py4dstem/py4dstem: Doi release, July 2019. https://doi.org/10.5281/zenodo.3333960
17. Clausen, A., et al.: Libertem/libertem: 0.1.0, November 2018. https://doi.org/10.5281/zenodo.1478763
18. Das, S., et al.: Observation of room-temperature polar skyrmions. Nature **568**(7752), 368 (2019)
19. Dask: dask-labextension, September 2019. https://github.com/dask/dask-labextension
20. Farrell, S., et al.: Interactive distributed deep learning with Jupyter notebooks. In: Yokota, R., Weiland, M., Shalf, J., Alam, S. (eds.) ISC High Performance 2018. LNCS, vol. 11203, pp. 678–687. Springer, Cham (2018). https://doi.org/10.1007/978-3-030-02465-9_49
21. Folk, M., Cheng, A., Yates, K.: HDF5: a file format and I/O library for high performance computing applications. In: Proceedings of Supercomputing, vol. 99, pp. 5–33 (1999)
22. Guizar-Sicairos, M., Thurman, S.T., Fienup, J.R.: Efficient subpixel image registration algorithms. Opt. Lett. **33**(2), 156–158 (2008)

23. Heagy, L.J., Oldenburg, D.W.: Modeling electromagnetics on cylindrical meshes with applications to steel-cased wells. Comput. Geosci. **125**, 115–130 (2019). https://doi.org/10.1016/j.cageo.2018.11.010
24. Jupyter: jupyter/nbviewer, September 2019. https://github.com/jupyter/nbviewer
25. Project Jupyter, et al.: Binder 2.0 - reproducible, interactive, sharable environments for science at scale. In: Akici, F., Lippa, D., Niederhut, D., Pacer, M. (eds.) Proceedings of the 17th Python in Science Conference, pp. 113–120 (2018). https://doi.org/10.25080/Majora-4af1f417-011
26. Kanitpanyacharoen, W., et al.: A comparative study of x-ray tomographic microscopy on shales at different synchrotron facilities: ALS, APS and SLS. J. Synchrotron Radiat. **20**(1), 172–180 (2013)
27. Kluyver, T., et al.: Jupyter notebooks-a publishing format for reproducible computational workflows. In: ELPUB, pp. 87–90 (2016)
28. Nteract: nteract/papermill, September 2019. https://github.com/nteract/papermill
29. Oliphant, T.E.: A Guide to NumPy, vol. 1. Trelgol Publishing USA (2006)
30. Ophus, C.: Four-dimensional scanning transmission electron microscopy (4D-STEM): from scanning nanodiffraction to ptychography and beyond. Microsc. Microanal. **25**(3), 563–582 (2019)
31. Panova, O., et al.: Diffraction imaging of nanocrystalline structures in organic semiconductor molecular thin films. Nat. Mater. **18**, 860–865 (2019). https://doi.org/10.1038/s41563-019-0387-3
32. Pekin, T.C., et al.: Direct measurement of nanostructural change during in situ deformation of a bulk metallic glass. Nat. Commun. **10**(1), 2445 (2019)
33. Soummer, R., Pueyo, L., Sivaramakrishnan, A., Vanderbei, R.J.: Fast computation of Lyot-style coronagraph propagation. Opt. Express **15**(24), 15935–15951 (2007)
34. Van Der Walt, S., Colbert, S.C., Varoquaux, G.: The NumPy array: a structure for efficient numerical computation. Comput. Sci. Eng. **13**(2), 22 (2011)

Interactive Supercomputing
for Experimental Data-Driven Workflows

Mark Klein, Maxime Martinasso, Siew Hoon Leong$^{(\boxtimes)}$, and Sadaf R. Alam

Swiss National Supercomputing Centre, ETH Zurich, Lugano, Switzerland
`cerlane.leong@cscs.ch`

Abstract. Large scale experimental facilities such as the Swiss Light Source and the free-electron X-ray laser SwissFEL at the Paul Scherrer Institute, and the particle accelerators and detectors at CERN are experiencing unprecedented data generation growth rates. Consequently, management, processing and storage requirements of data are increasing rapidly. Historically, online and on-demand processing of data generated by the instruments used to be tightly-coupled with a dedicated, domains-specific, site-local IT infrastructure. Cost and performance scaling of these facilities not only pose technical but also planning and scheduling challenges. Supercomputing ecosystems optimize cost and scaling for computing and storage resources but typically exploit a shared batch access model, which is optimized for high utilization of compute resources. In comparison, in public clouds, on-demand service delivery models address the concept of elasticity while maintaining isolation with performance trade-offs. Furthermore, these on-demand access models allow for different degrees of privileges to users for managing IT infrastructure services, in contrast with shared, bare-metal supercomputing ecosystems. This paper outlines an approach for enabling interactive, on-demand supercomputing for experimental data-driven workflows, which are characterised by a managed but bursty data and computing requirements. We present a delegated batch reservation model, controlled by the customer and provisioned by the supercomputing site, that allows scientists at the experimental facility to couple generation of data to the allocation of compute, data and network resources at the supercomputing centre. Scientists are then able to manage resources both at the experimental and supercomputing facilities interactively for managing their scientific workflows. Prototype implementation demonstrates that this rather simple co-designed extension to a supercomputing classic batch scheduling system with a controlled degree of privilege can be easily incorporated to the experimental facilities existing IT resource management and scheduling pipelines.

1 Introduction

The Swiss National Supercomputing Centre (CSCS) develops and operates cutting-edge high-performance computing systems as an essential service facility

© Springer Nature Switzerland AG 2020
G. Juckeland and S. Chandrasekaran (Eds.): HUST 2019/SE-HER 2019/WIHPC 2019,
CCIS 1190, pp. 164–178, 2020.
https://doi.org/10.1007/978-3-030-44728-1_10

for Swiss researchers. CSCS flagship supercomputing system is called Piz Daint, which is a hybrid and heterogeneous Cray XC40/XC50 platform [AGMS19]. HPC and data services at CSCS are used by scientists for a diverse range of purposes from high-resolution simulations to the analysis of complex data. Swiss scientists, research institutions and projects with their own funding can access the computational resources at CSCS as contractual partners. The environment provided is either shared with the User Lab[1], or a dedicated solution can be deployed, depending on specific needs. Examples of services provided by CSCS to contractual partners are the analysis of data from the Large Hadron Collider (LHC) at CERN, the archiving of data from the Swiss Light Source (SLS) and the Swiss Free Electron Laser (SwissFEL) for the Paul Scherrer Institute and the provision of computational resources for the numerical weather forecasts of MeteoSwiss.

Historically, CSCS had a dedicated system per customer i.e. one for MeteoSwiss due to their unique operational needs, one for CHIPP for complex WLCG grid middleware, etc. With the recent upgrade of Piz Daint that enabled a few cloud technologies such as containers [BCMM17], availability of public IPs to compute nodes and access to multiple storage targets, almost all customers except MeteoSwiss have been moved to a shared supercomputing platform. However, these customers and their workflows largely abide by the rules and policies of a shared supercomputing ecosystem i.e. batch processing constraints, length of jobs, storage policies, etc. An exception is the Grid middleware, which CSCS is responsible for the deployment, management and operation on behalf of the Swiss high energy physics community [CKOS+08]. In general, workflows that require dedicated access to resources with some levels of quality of service for availability and response times cannot be readily mapped onto Piz Daint and likely other shared supercomputing ecosystems [AMS18]. In this paper, we consider a data-driven workflow requirements for on-demand, interactive supercomputing, within existing constraints of a shared, bare-metal, production HPC ecosystem.

The Paul Scherrer Institute (PSI) is the largest research institute for natural and engineering sciences in Switzerland by conducting cutting-edge research. It develops, builds and operates complex large research facilities [MSA+17]. PSI data driven workflows can be largely classified in two categories: online analysis and offline analysis. Online analysis refers to processing of data while the scientist is using an instrument (and has a dedicated allocation to an instrument and is typically onsite at PSI for a fixed period of time). Hence, scientists need interactive and dedicated access to large-scale data and computing infrastructure while they have a limited time window. In other words, they need a tight feedback loop to guide their experiments and cannot wait for the availability of IT resources (waiting times in a batch queue). Offline data processing refers to processing of archived data (mostly on tape at the data centre) once the scientist is no longer at the experimental site. In this paper, we consider the online data processing workflows.

---

[1] https://www.cscs.ch/user-lab/overview/.

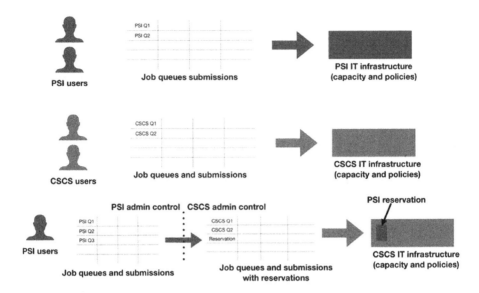

Fig. 1. Overview of the reservation service concept from a facility and user point of view. Traditionally, users and system administrators work on allocating resources according to local compute capacities and policies. This is highlighted in the first two workflows at PSI and CSCS. In this example, the third workflow, a PSI system administrator can create a reservation such that the workflow for interactive access from a user point of view remain unchanged as a dedicated reservation for PSI will not be governed by CSCS batch job queuing policies.

Our incremental, co-design approach for enabling a data-driven interactivity within an existing supercomputing ecosystem takes into consideration existing technical and policy constraints of the site as well existing workflows requirements of the experimental facility. The objective is to enable the service in a transparent manner to the end users and to have a minimal impact to the operators of the IT infrastructure, at both the experimental site and the supercomputing data centre. Slurm, the resource manager and scheduling system at CSCS, is one of the common point of interaction for the middleware to specify resource needs. We do not modify the system configuration of slurm but rather enable the execution of a privileged operation by an external customer in a secured and controlled manner. The IT administrator at the experimental facility can integrate process of reserving predefined resources in an external cluster (i.e. limited number of nodes on a supercomputing system plus other constraints) into their existing workflows (the experimental facility in this case uses slurm for their internal IT resource management and scheduling system). Such a concept is shown in Fig. 1. Both computing and data orchestration resources at CSCS can be coupled in slurm jobs through data staging services. To an end user, the supercomputing ecosystem resources can then be no different from the facility's on-site IT infrastructure resources for coupled, interactive access during the experiment.

The outline of the paper is as follows: Sect. 2 presents the background of other classic interactive usage in supercomputing environments in addition to the experimental data-driven interactivity. In Sect. 3, we present the scope and design of the reservation service in the context of interactive, data-driven workflows. Implementation details of the prototype tool is presented in Sect. 4 followed by a summary and future work in Sect. 5.

2 Background and Motivation

It is important to compare and contrast data-driven, interactive workflows with other use cases for interactivity in HPC. Classic use cases for interactive computing include visualization, workflow engines like Jupyter Notebooks and computational steering. For the data-driven workflows of PSI online analysis, there needs to be a co-location of the data and compute services. Unlike other PSI workflows, the source of data generation is typically under the control of users such as a simulation engine, data repositories, etc. while data collection at PSI [Pau] is tightly coupled with a complex instrument and its operation, which, like a supercomputing system is reserved for weeks or months in advance. Another distinction is the user expectation of request and response time. Typically, visualization applications and Jupyter Notebooks, require a near realtime feedback loop for resource request and availability of resources. Since an experimental equipment is reserved ahead of time and the time during which the instrument is running is rather limited, there could be a lag between the time a request for services is made for experimental data-driven workflows. However, unlike classical batch, the instrument time and supercomputing time must be tightly coupled as the cost of idle or underutilized resources for both data generation instruments at the experimental facility and the supercomputing ecosystem can be significantly high. Furthermore, for a scientist, it is a lost opportunity cost because there may not be an option to get back their allocation on the experimental facility in a timely manner. Table 1 summarises the comparison of different interactive workflows in supercomputing ecosystems.

2.1 Scientific IT Infrastructure Design Principles

Supercomputing ecosystems are designed, from ground up, for performance and scale. As a result, the hardware, software and system management characteristics as well as allocation and scheduling policies for using such resources reflect these priorities to support execution of large-scale applications. Consequently, dedicated IT services at a domain-specific experimental facility are typically optimized (compute, storage, network and software stack) for the custom applications and workflows and cannot scale out, without a redesign, to a supercomputing ecosystem that serves multiple scientific domains. Development of cloud technologies that introduced multiple levels of abstractions could, in theory, enable a subset of Infrastructure-as-s-Service (IaaS), Platform-as-a-Service (PaaS) and Software-as-a-Service (SaaS) features on a supercomputing ecosystem. This, however, in practice, would require a different system design to enable

Table 1. Comparison of different (canonical) use cases of interactivity in HPC in terms of flexibility for expected behavior for service availability and access latency. These parameters are considered in proposing the reservation service for the data-driven reservation services for coupling experiments and interactive access to HPC resources.

Use case	Data acquisition	Resource acquisition	Response latency	Service availability
Visualisation	Flexible	Flexible	Real time	Flexible
Jupyter Notebook	Flexible	Flexible	Real time	Flexible
Experimental facility	Static/coupled	Static/coupled	Deterministic	Time-constrained

virtualization of hardware technologies like computing, storage and network as well as automation for provisioning of resources. Virtualisation often comes at an expense of performance and scaling, specifically for compute, storage and network intensive MPI applications. Existing systems, like Piz Daint, employ an incremental approach for introducing cloud technologies and service delivery models for workflows, which need design of a supercomputing system for performance and scale while accessibility and control of a cloud infrastructure. This does not imply that Piz Daint can be considered as an OpenStack, full multi-tenant ecosystem for generic IaaS and PaaS service delivery models.

2.2 Dedicated vs. Shared Cluster Computing Resources

Dedicated IT resources, in the context of an experimental facility, are customized for computing, data and network needs of an equipment as well as its usage. We can consider WLCG Tiered environment as an example. The Worldwide LHC Computing Grid (WLCG) is composed of four levels, or Tiers, called 0, 1, 2 and 3. Each Tier is made up of several computer centres and provides a specific set of services. Between them the tiers process, store and analyse all the data from LHC. Tier 0 is the CERN Data Centre. All of the data from the LHC passes through this central hub, but it provides less than 20% of the Grid's total computing capacity. This infrastructure is therefore highly customized and optimized for storage capacity and distribution, not for generic high-end simulation needs of multiple scientific domains. CSCS operates Tier-2 services by incorporating a middleware on a supercomputing platform [CKOS+08]. However, Tier-2 services are by design not tightly coupled with a data generation instrument. The Tier 2s are defined by WLCG as universities and other scientific institutes, which can store sufficient data and provide adequate computing power for specific analysis tasks. They handle analysis requirements and proportional share of simulated event production and reconstruction. There are currently around 160 Tier 2 sites covering most of the globe.

In comparison, supercomputing systems are defined by their special high bandwidth global network, lightweight operating system to avoid OS jitters, no outward connectivity to internet from compute nodes, a high bandwidth files system (typically POSIX) and a batch file system that prioritises scalable jobs and high system utilization. Majority of system hardware and software characteristics for performance and scaling make it rather challenging for workflows that have external dependencies and coupling to map onto a scalable, shared, batch-oriented supercomputing system. Access control and tenancy models are rather weak on supercomputing systems that are primarily designed to execute multi-Petascale level simulation workloads. In fact, introducing rather lightweight virtualization technologies such as containers, pose several compatibility and security challenges in an HPC ecosystem [BCMM17].

2.3   Slurm Queues, Partitions and Fairshare

Piz Daint is a hybrid and heterogeneous system with 5704 GPU nodes and 1813 multi-core only nodes. Overall, all resources are connected with a high bandwidth Aries dragonfly interconnect. There is a shared Lustre parallel file system that serve all users and customer workloads with an exception of WLCG, which has a dedicated file system due to its unique high throughput storage needs.

While system utilization is a key criteria, there are service level agreements (SLA) with customers that must be managed within a shared environment on Piz Daint. Slurm controls and manages access to resources for jobs and it is configured with partitions and queues to fulfill SLAs. Jobs submitted inside a queue are scheduled following a fair-share principle among projects. Slurm scheduling policy allows to back-fill small jobs on preempted nodes required to schedule large jobs, which typically require draining of nodes. Table 2 lists the current set of system queues with description. Majority of resources are shared between logical queues and are differentiated by policies and priorities such as minimum and maximum number of nodes, length of jobs, etc. Note that the dedicated queues are relatively small to keep a higher system utilisation. WLCG queue is dedicated and has additional policies such as node sharing between jobs. This high throughput queue utilization is very high due to the nature of the workflows.

As indicated earlier and evident by the configuration of the queues and partitions of Piz Daint, it serves multiple classes of services already, albeit in a static, predefined manner. Table 3 lists key distinctions and similarities. Note that, by far, the majority of users and usage is managed through the scientific program called the User Lab. Interactive computing for JupyterHub is served by dedicated nodes but only for small scale jobs (small number of nodes are dedicated for interactive access) For details see https://jupyter.cscs.ch/. Large scale jobs wait in the batch queue. Policy exceptions are based on the default policy and quality of service model for the User Lab.

Another important aspect of resource allocation, sharing and fair usage is validity period of access to resources. A standard research project typically has a yearly quota, which is divided into four equal chunks. For instance, a project

Table 2. System queues and partitions

Name	Type	Description
normal	Shared	Standard queue for production work
long	Shared	Maximum 5 long jobs in total (one per user)
large	Shared	Large scale work, by arrangement only
low	Shared	Back-fill only when quota is exhausted
2go	Shared	Different policy for quota expiration
debug	Dedicated	Quick turnaround for test jobs (one per user)
prepost	Shared	High priority pre/post processing
wlcg	Dedicated	WLCG nodes for LHC workload
cscsci	Shared	Restricted for continuous integration
xfer	–	Data transfer queue

Table 3. Existing service classes on Piz Daint

	Shared resource	Privileged access	Scheduling model	Policy exceptions
User Lab	Yes	No	Batch	By default none
Customers	Yes	No	Batch	Yes, with restrictions
Interactive computing	No	No	(Interactive) Batch	Yes, with restrictions
LHC Grid	No	No	Batch	Yes, with restrictions
cscs2go	Yes	No	Batch	Yes, with restrictions

with 10000 node hours per year means 2500 node hours per quarter for a use or loose basis. This encourages a uniform usage of the system throughout the period but is more aligned with a batch oriented system usage where jobs can be queued based on the fairshare principles of usage, quota, wait times and size of jobs among other parameters. This, in turn, does not suit interactive usage of the resources without dedicating them for on-demand usage patterns.

3   Design and Scope of Data Driven Interactive Supercomputing

The co-design approach proposed in this paper leverages operational metrics and constraints for the facilities as well as productivity of the user though interactivity during the allocation of the equipment. One of the guiding principles for the workflow is high and effective utilization of expensive tools for scientific discoveries. On one side, there is allocation of the beamline time at the experimental facility that is generating scientific data, at a much faster rate than before after the upgrade. On the other side, there is a general-purpose, shared supercomputing ecosystem, where there are typically long batch queues of running and outstanding jobs to maximise system utilization.

3.1 Reservation Concepts and Use Cases

The concept of a reservation is not new to HPC resource management and job scheduling systems like slurm. It is a privileged operation, which has been routinely exercised but primarily used to override policies for user access and control. Some examples and use cases include:

- Maintenance: this special partition is used for scheduled maintenance, with system downtime. This is to avoid abrupt termination of jobs. System is essentially drained so it can go into the maintenance mode. This is an internal CSCS request, which is typically planned months in advance. The frequency is 3–5 times a year.
- Large scale runs: Often after scheduled maintenance, the full-scale system is reserved for debugging, troubleshooting as well as for large-scale runs for scientific publications such as Gordon Bell prize runs. Reservation for the Gordon Bell runs is a user driven activity but they are expected to contact weeks ahead of time. Frequency is a few times a year.
- Courses: Dedicated resources are needed for CSCS user and non-users who attend a course that is organized by CSCS or in collaboration with partners. A reservation is required to ensure that the required resources are available for hands-on exercises. These requests are of modest size i.e a couple of dozens of nodes maximum. Courses are planned in advance and these reservation requests can be made and approved in advance. Frequency is a couple of times per quarter.
- Debug: Often, in case of an issue related to system and software debugging and troubleshooting, certain nodes can be placed into a reservation to prevent user jobs from accidental running on these nodes. This is typically infrequent and incident driven to maintain overall health and service level of the system.
- JupyterHub: an elastic reservation system is used for maintaining availability of a small number of single, interactive node for Jupyter Notebook access where users ask for a single node interactive access. This is sort of a very small, persistent reservation.
- Other: there are user driven requests that are based on a valid reason and justification on why they need a specific set of resources for a given period of time. Such requests are approved on a case-by-case basis. These are rare and infrequent to maintain fairness among the users of a shared resource.

The common theme in the above use cases is that CSCS internal staff is involved in both the approval and execution pipeline of these exceptions to ensure the overall service commitments for users and high utilization of the IT resource. Therefore, the challenge is to re-purpose this tool without compromising the service level metrics for different customers in a shared supercomputing ecosystem.

3.2   Analysis of a Data-Driven Workflow

We describe a PSI online analysis workflow to understand the requirement for interactivity for a data-driven workload. For such online analysis, the following steps are performed in a chronological order:

- Users of PSI facility apply for a time allocation of PSI beam time
- Application is evaluated and the request is granted of rejected
- If the request is granted, a fixed schedule is created to access beam time
- On the scheduled days, users come physically to PSI and operate the beamline by following a precise workflow
- This workflow starts by a series of experiments to calibrate the beamline and to find area of interest on the object to visualize
- Once the beamline is calibrated, the real experiment starts and the object is exposed to the beam (the bean is always on). Depending on the experiment, several overlapping images are captured at regular interval. This steps takes several hours as the object is progressively rotated. For example and for one specific experiment, a complete rotation of the object is achieved after 1000 small rotations.
- After each exposure the set of generated data obtained by sensors is processed to reconstruct the internals of the object. In the general case, the object is discretized into pixel and for each pixel light intensity and phase are reconstructed.
- Data size generated for each exposure depends on the experiments but it varies in the range of GB. A full experiment can have thousands of exposures generating TB of data to process by the workflow.
- Once the users are satisfied about the obtained image or their allocation is completed, the experiment ends and users retrieved (transfer, physical disks) their data.

For PSI it is important to maximize the utilization of the beam time as it is the most expensive resource, and, therefore, after each exposure the computation time should be fast enough not to limit and reduce beam time usage.

With the new facility coming online, due to the sheer volume of data (experiments will generate PB of data instead of TB), the local IT facility cannot cope with storage and fast processing. While the calibration step can still be done on PSI premises, the data of the experiment must be shipped while the experiment is ongoing to a supercomputing facility for scalable computing. A tight feedback loop is needed to guide experiment such as re-doing a set of exposure for more accurate outputs.

3.3   Co-Designed Reservation Service for Data-Driven Workflow

In order to propose a reservation service design that fulfills potentially competing needs, we explain workflow of an existing, user-driven reservation service. Figure 2 shows steps of communication process between CSCS and a customer where manual intervention and approvals take place. This workflow however does not show any details on access and accounting. For instance, in this workflow, the resource consumption of jobs will be treated the same way as any other job. Essentially, a reservation can be created without running any jobs hence impacting utilization of the system.

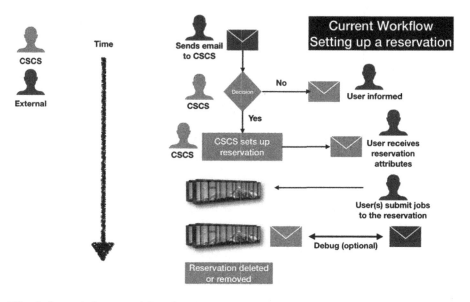

Fig. 2. Steps defining workflow for the reservation service for a user without automation and delegation. Once the reservation is in place, user can access it interactively. Often, approved users submit batch jobs to the reservation.

As shown in Fig. 2, the process starts with a user or a customer contacting CSCS through service desk or directly for a reservation, specifying and giving a justification for size and timings of a resource access request. The request is assessed and a decision is made in a couple of days to weeks. Once an approval is granted, a CSCS system IT staff member creates a reservation and share its handle with the requester. Approved users can then submit jobs to the reservation. Once reservation time expires, it is automatically removed.

Figure 3 shows a modified version of the workflow which can be delegated to selected representatives of a customer who are expected to setup an interactive workflow to Piz Daint. CSCS provides an interface or API to a customer to submit a request for reservation. It is the responsibility of the customer to evaluate technical and policy considerations before forwarding the request to CSCS. For instance, a customer may only selected users or a limited number of resources to be used in this manner. CSCS maintains its own access control lists and policies. In the absence of an issue, the process works in a similar manner as before except that a privileged operation is performed in an automated manner. Users can use

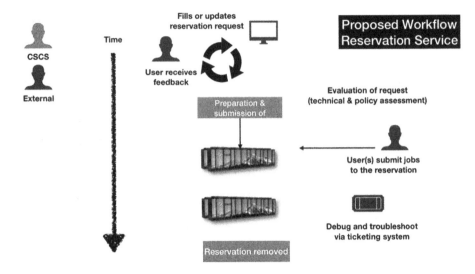

Fig. 3. Steps defining workflow for the reservation service by a customer on behalf of a user for coupling data and compute resources between an IT infrastructure and an experimental data facility. Steps are automated and delegated for control and access. Once the reservation is in place, user can access it interactively. This automated process is expected to reduce the time to request and to get approval to minutes from days to weeks. Note that the reservation may not be granted immediately because it may depend on attributes such as size of resources. Typically, for data driven workflows, reservation start times will be known weeks in advance so these reservations are in place for interactive analysis for users.

this reservation both as interactive and batch manner. CSCS and customer are expected to agree ahead of time access, usage and accounting guidelines for using this service.

3.4 Controlled Privileges and Limitations

As mentioned earlier, using a reservation is nothing new to an HPC resource management and scheduling system like slurm. In fact, any user is able to show reservations on the system they belong to using the scontrol command:

```
scontrol show reservation
```

However, the ability to create or modify a reservation in Slurm requires at least an operator level of privilege [Scha]. The restricted operations related to reservations are:

```
scontrol create reservation
scontrol update reservation
scontrol delete reservation
```

Operator level access gives much more ability to the users than simply related to reservations [Schb]. It is a good practice to avoid granting this level of control to normal users as they could then create reservations which bill to other projects, remove active reservations belonging to other users, or modify/suspend jobs not belonging to them. Ideally for this service, an unprivileged user is only able to create and modify reservations for projects that they belong to.

3.5   Reservation Management Tool

A tool that was previously created for CSCS user support representatives to assist in modifying partition permissions was adapted as a proof of concept utility for this service. The tool sanitizes user input, checks group membership to validate request, and elevates to an operator user to submit the underlying scontrol command if everything is valid. While in early user testing, access to the tool is further limited and controlled by a list of approved users (by CSCS). The following functionality exists in the initial release of the tool:

```
list owned reservation
add reservation
delete owned reservations
```

4   Implementation and Analysis

Although the tools have been used for internal CSCS use cases in operation, the redesigned version for the proof of concept is evaluated for the PSI online workflow as an example. A subset of features are selected to evaluate whether the design and implementation of the tool is feasible in operation. On the customer side, features include the look and feel of slurm reservation commands, ability to restrict and control a reservation per beamline, ability to define a start time and ability to modify and cancel a reservation. The scientist or end user perspective of this service is shown in Fig. 5. The interactive or on-demand access is guaranteed provided the user is not competing with his/her own resource access within the allocated reservation. For instance, is a reservation is made with 50 compute nodes and a user submit 10 jobs with 5 nodes each, the 11th job will have to wait until resources are released by one of the running jobs by the user.

For CSCS, key features are an ability to manage and control access to the service, restrict attributes of a reservation and workflows for graceful failure of service in case of an issue so customers do not loose key time allocation windows. There are several technical and policy consideration that are omitted in the proof of concept. Among these are design of the API, accounting workflows, and understanding overall impact of using a reservation service on the utilization and fairshare usage of Piz Daint.

The reservation service enables users to transparently manage their reservations with only minor modifications to the underlying system. As a proof of concept, only basic functionalities, create, delete and list reservation(s), are provided but they are sufficient to demonstrate the potential of offering such a service to support interactive computing for the PSI use case. The example in Fig. 4 shows some features of the tool and how it can be used in practice. For instance, an approved user cannot create a reservation for a project that he/she does not belong or submit a job to the reservation it does not own. A user can specify size and length of a reservation. The prototype version has been evaluated and tested on a Cray XC system with 100+ Intel Xeon Phi processors. Currently, a manually defined access control list manages access to the tool.

```
rsvmgmt: the reservation management tool
subcommands:

-l                       lists current project reservations
-a project #nodes #hours adds reservation
example: -a group-d 10 10 creates group-d reservation for 10 nodes 10 hours
-d [reservation id]      delete reservation
-V                       displays version number
ser_user@tave102:~> rsvmgmt -l
rsvmgmt: Current Reservations
--------------------------
ReservationName=group-d_7 StartTime=Tomorr 16:30 EndTime=Fri 02:30
Duration=10:00:00 Nodes=nid000[00-11,24-31]
NodeCnt=20 CoreCnt=1280 Features=(null)
PartitionName=normal Flags= TRES=cpu=5120 Users=(null)
Accounts=group-d Licenses=(null) State=INACTIVE BurstBuffer=(null) Watts=n/a
--------------------------
ser_user@tave102:~> rsvmgmt -a g34 10 10
rsvmgmt: Error: You are not a member of the g34 project
ser_user@tave102:~> rsvmgmt -d maintenance
rsvmgmt: Error: You are not an owner of the maintenance reservation
ser_user@tave102:~> rsvmgmt -d group-d_7
rsvmgmt: Reservation group-d_7 removed
ser_user@tave102:~> rsvmgmt -a group-d 10 10
Reservation created: group-d_8
```

Fig. 4. Outputs from the prototype version of the reservation management tool showing features and capabilities on a Cray XC system. The tool at the moment prevents simplified access controls and monitoring capabilities.

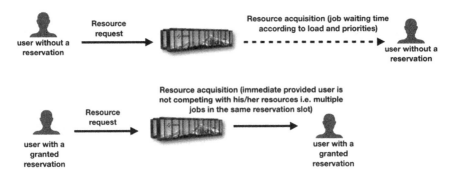

Fig. 5. Interactive access to Supercomputing resources for an experimental facility scientist. This assumes that the experimental facility admin workflows are in place to setup the reservation.

As a next step, as the tool continues to be co-designed and co-developed for the use cases, the PSI IT staff will integrate this tool to their existing slurm workflows. The reservation service in turn can then enable the PSI scientists to coordinate well in advance both the reservations of their instruments and the required compute resources at CSCS. The service is expected to bypass the traditional human-in-the-loop steps and facilitate improved time-to-solution by allowing scientists to focus on their actual scientific activities as opposed to administrative overheads for coordinating distributed IT resources.

The existing implementation serves as a good demonstrator but has a few shortcomings, which will be addressed in future updates and improvements:

- Role based access control
- Usage and administration policies
- Business model for on-demand usage in a shared batch environment
- Technical functionalities
  - Additional attributed to the reservation
  - Modification of an existing reservation
  - An API for development and integration into customer tools
  - Reservation of dependent resources/services/tools
  - Monitoring and logging

Furthermore, as a next step with continued improvements to the implementation and evaluation together with PSI, CSCS will use a tool called RM-replay to study the impact of creating these reservations on overall utilization targets of Piz Daint and job waiting times for users [MGB+18]. RM-replay is a fast replay engine for production workloads where we can use actual Piz Daint workload traces and inject workload for the reservation service. These studies would help us in tuning technical and policy constraints for the delegated reservation management service.

5 Summary and Future Work

We have demonstrated a co-design approach to data-driven interactive supercomputing that allows scientists to couple their data generation experiments at an experimental facility and IT resources at a shared, supercomputing data centre. The interactive, high performance and scalable access to computing and storage resources is key for the productivity of scientists to sustain exponential growth in data from experimental instruments. The incremental approach is not expected to disrupt key performance indicators of a supercomputing ecosystem namely utilization of the computing resources. Nevertheless, additional analysis is needed to understand necessary constraints for enabling such a service for customers. The usage and administration policies need to the be updated as the availability of such a service allows users to manage their own reservations, which is traditionally under the jurisdiction of system administrators, to prevent potential abuse. Additionally, monitoring and logging of operations will be extended to assist with troubleshooting and diagnostics.

Additional technical functionalities will be addressed as we continue co-designing the tool with the experimental facilities IT staff. The service would have to allow the scientists to specify a fixed start-time of the reservation, handles contentions, provides reminders, etc. Naturally it is also crucial to allow for minor modification of reservations without affecting their priorities. Typically, the scientists will require more than just compute CPU cores/GPUs to perform their computations. Additional resources/tools/services, e.g. extra storage in scratch folders, Kubernetes and on-demand storage, are also required. Ideally the reservation service should also provide an integrated interface to reserve diverse set of services.

Acknowledgements. We would like to thank our colleagues at PSI for their insightful remarks and their input for co-designing the early prototype. The work presented in this paper is partly funded by a swissuniversities P-5 grant called SELVEDAS (Services for Large Volume Experiment-Data Analysis utilising Supercomputing and Cloud technologies at CSCS).

References

[AGMS19] Alam, S.R., Gilly, L., McMurtrie, C., Schulthess, T.C.: CSCS and the Piz Daint System, pp. 149–174, May 2019

[AMS18] Alam, S.R., Martinasso, M., Schulthess, T.C.: Hybrid cloud and HPC services for extreme data workflows. In: Extreme Data: Demands, Technologies, and Services - A Community Workshop (2018)

[BCMM17] Benedicic, L., Cruz, F.A., Madonna, A., Mariotti, K.: Portable, high-performance containers for HPC. CoRR, abs/1704.03383 (2017)

[CKOS+08] Cameron, D., et al.: The advanced resource connector for distributed LHC computing. PoS (2008)

[MGB+18] Martinasso, M., Gila, M., Bianco, M., Alam, S.R., McMurtrie, C., Schulthess, T.C.: RM-replay: a high-fidelity tuning, optimization and exploration tool for resource management. In: Proceedings of the International Conference for High Performance Computing, Networking, Storage, and Analysis, SC 2018 (2018)

[MSA+17] Milne, C., et al.: SwissFEL: the Swiss X-ray free electron laser. Appl. Sci. **7**(7), 720 (2017)

[Pau] Paul Scherrer Institut: cSAXS X12SA: Coherent Small-Angle X-ray Scattering. https://www.psi.ch/en/sls/csaxs. Accessed 20 Sept 2019

[Scha] SchedMD: Slurm workload manager - scontrol. https://slurm.schedmd.com/scontrol.html. Accessed 20 Sept 2019

[Schb] SchedMD: Slurm workload manager - user permissions. https://slurm.schedmd.com/user_permissions.html. Accessed 20 Sept 2019

Portals for Interactive Steering
of HPC Workflows

Robert Settlage[1]([⊠]) [iD], Srijith Rajamohan[1] [iD], Kevin Lahmers[2] [iD],
Alan Chalker[3] [iD], Eric Franz[3] [iD], Steve Gallo[4] [iD], and David Hudak[3] [iD]

[1] Advanced Research Computing, Virginia Tech, Blacksburg, VA 24060, USA
rsettlag@vt.edu
[2] Virginia Maryland College of Veterinary Medicine, Blacksburg, VA 24060, USA
[3] Ohio Supercomputer Center, Columbus, OH, USA
[4] University of Buffalo, Buffalo, NY, USA

Abstract. High performance computing workloads often benefit from human in the loop interactions. Steps in complex pipelines ranging from quality control to parameter adjustments are critical to the successful and efficient completion of modern problems. We give several example workflows in bioinformatics and deep learning where computing decisions are made throughout the processing pipelines ultimately changing the course of the compute. We also show how users can interact with the pipeline using Open OnDemand plus XDMoD or Plot.ly.

Keywords: HPC · OnDemand · XDMoD · Steering · Workflow · Deep learning · Bioinformatics

1 Introduction

The need and scale of computing requirements continue to grow. Daily, we are collecting zettabytes of data which requires computing to transform it into knowledge [1] and actionable insights. As with the data, the associated data analysis pipelines and simulations have grown in size and computational complexity often needing large cluster based computing approaches such as those enabled by high performance computing (HPC) clusters. Traditionally, high performance computing (HPC) workloads have consisted of a series of static shell scripts that are run via the command line. Changes to the pipeline, i.e. scripts, are manual, error prone, and not usually intuitive. For interactive workflows, command line intervention is not desirable and has limited adoption within mainstream HPC computing pipelines.

As an endpoint, we are looking to create user friendly, intuitive and resilient tools for use of HPC resources to handle arbitrary and potentially complex computational pipelines. As the pipelines grow in size and complexity, the computational workflows may need branching or other decisions made mid-stream.

Supported by National Science Foundation grant 1835725.

G. Juckeland and S. Chandrasekaran (Eds.): HUST 2019/SE-HER 2019/WIHPC 2019,
CCIS 1190, pp. 179–189, 2020.
https://doi.org/10.1007/978-3-030-44728-1_11

These decisions could be as simple as determining where the next step should run to get to result faster or as complex as clustering for data classification. Bioinformatics and Deep Learning are two compute heavy domains where computing pipelines with potentially complex workflows could benefit from some human intervention at run time.

The Big Bang in analytical and discovery biology could be viewed as the rise of -Omics data acquisition technologies. Today it is possible, in a single hour, using modern DNA sequencing technology to sequence the genome of hundreds of bacteria simultaneously, or using mass spectrometry, collect full metabolite profiles from humans, or using protein array technology, collect the entire human phospoproteome profile. Analyzing and making sense of all this data is a massive computational challenge. By using a combination of web forms and GUI apps in Open OnDemand complete with job and cluster status statistics provided by XDMoD, we are endeavoring to make our clusters more accessible and efficiently utilized. Here we highlight two workflows we are designing to chaperone the data from raw to result with the aim of making the workflows computationally efficient and easy to use.

Open OnDemand [2] and XDMoD [3] are open source projects with overarching goals of improving the accessibility and usage of HPC clusters. Historically, HPC cluster access has been limited to command line access via ssh. Compute jobs require creation of shell scripts and interaction with schedulers that are often unfamiliar to most new users. Combined, these normal HPC modes of operation have created barriers to use of the computational power contained in the clusters. Open OnDemand provides a rich set of browser based tools and apps to facilitate use of HPC clusters through more familiar interfaces. For instance, OnDemand has a browser based files app that allows users to interact with the HPC file system through a graphical interface. In addition to the native apps included in the standard OnDemand installation, Open OnDemand allows creation of custom user apps. XDMoD focuses more on the performance and utilization of HPC resources. XDMoD gives administrators and users tools to gauge how well the system and their jobs are running. Open OnDemand and XDMoD, combined, give users a unique set of interfaces and tools to access and utilize HPC clusters.

In traditional supervised Deep Learning, subject matter experts are required to provide accurately labeled data for training and evaluation of the model. However, this is usually either intractable or extremely labor-intensive whereas it is far easier to procure labelled data with labels that are only partially accurate. This type of weak supervision is referred to as inaccurate supervision [4]. Airflow [5] was used to orchestrate this decision-making, i.e. learning and post-processing, workflow. Airflow is built on the notion of tasks as Directed Acyclic Graphs (DAGs) which can be scheduled. Tasks can have dependencies and be restarted as needed thereby providing a repeatable pipeline for the interactive Visual Analytic framework based on Deep Learning presented here.

2   HPC Workflows

2.1   DNA Monitoring

As we move to personalized medicine and genomics, we will see more edge devices for data collection with data streams being sent to HPC clusters for efficient and timely data analysis. As an example, minION sequencers are being used in field monitoring of live stock health. In this scenario, the sequencer is brought to the farm, sequencing is performed locally, data is streamed to an HPC cluster, a perhaps complex and computationally intensive compute job is performed and near real time updates are provided via web portals to the veterinarian on-site.

In a simplistic case, this is a monitoring problem. During an outbreak, there could be additional data processing steps necessary. Here, we are only concerned with monitoring where ease of use by lab personnel and time to results is the primary interest. Using a combination of Open OnDemand and XDMoD, we are creating an interactive portal for choosing where (cluster and queue) to submit processing jobs based on cluster utilization and job performance statistics, see Fig. 1. The workflow includes DNA basecalling through the minION sequencer software (Guppy), bacterial DNA assignment and counting (Centrifuge [6]) and results viewing through Pavian [7]. Currently the portal includes a job submission form, job progress app and link to Pavian results viewer. As the portal matures, additional optional possibilities for data processing will be exposed and enabled as options in data review. The optional possibilities could include submitting additional processing jobs, pushing the data to archive, pushing the results to a database, etc. (Fig. 2).

Fig. 1. DNAmonitor main page and job progress viewer with Pavian results link.

Open OnDemand and XDMoD App. Open OnDemand [2], through familiar web-based access to HPC clusters, reduces barrier to use of HPC resources and has also been shown to reduce the time to science. In fact, the median time from initial login to first job submission for all new OSC clients in 2017 using OnDemand was 10 times faster than those using traditional access methods.

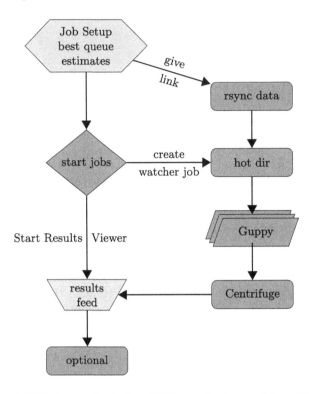

Fig. 2. Basic minION Guppy-Centrifuge DNA monitoring workflow. User interaction is indicated in orange. (Color figure online)

OnDemand greatly simplifies access to HPC resources, freeing disciplinary scientists from having to worry about the operating environment and instead focus on their research. Here, we will use OnDemand to assist users in pipeline setup and GUI access for data viewing.

Extensibility is a key component of the Open OnDemand App architecture by allowing for creation of *custom* applications. Apps can be developed to surface common GUI programs such as R, Shiny, Jupyter Notebooks etc. Additionally, apps could be developed as web forms as common job submission templates. Here we are looking to use both modes. First, we have created an app for job submission. The app takes in metadata related to the project (name, date, etc.), approximate sequencing run time, flowcell type, and gives users informed choices for where to run the analysis based on current HPC usage. Ideally, we will use both user based job statistics for jobs of similar size for the various queues the user has access to and system benchmarks for the codes used. This information will come from XDMoD [3]. Second, we are using OnDemand to surface a GUI (R Shiny) for viewing results as they are made available by the compute pipeline. This app updates as new results are available and allows users to influence future behavior of the full pipeline.

2.2   Basic NGS QC

We will start with a very basic workflow representing a common quality control (QC) step performed on Next Generation Sequencing (NGS) data as a starting point for more complete analysis including RNASeq discussed in the next section. In this case, the workflow consists of steps for data input, splitting the data for processing (more useful in later steps), raw data metric collection, and review of the collected metrics. The user interacts with the HPC clusters to define the inputs, desired cleaning steps and finally to look at the metrics related to the QC as show in Fig. 3. The form used to start the workflow includes the ability to specify which HPC queue will run the analysis as in the DNA monitoring workflow.

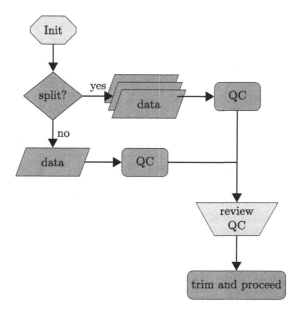

Fig. 3. Basic NGS QC workflow. User interaction is indicated in orange. (Color figure online)

2.3   RNASeq

Our RNASeq pipeline is really an extension of the NGS QC workflow. User intervention is enabled between major steps and includes options for failing samples and alternative RNASeq specific methods. Additional details and examples will be given in the session.

2.4   Weakly Supervised Deep Neural Network

The goal of this work [8] is to assess the feasibility of a weakly supervised Deep Neural Network (wsDNN) to produce projections for determining political affiliations. In a way, this can be seen as a type of target-based sentiment analysis also known as Aspect-Based Sentiment Analysis (ABSA) [9]. This is a form of 'inaccurate weak supervision' due to the presence of errors in the labels of the data used for training.

The data was downloaded periodically using the job scheduler RQ [10] for three months. The downloader was written using the Python library Tweepy [11] and around 2.6 million tweets were downloaded over this period. The tweet information was stored in a MongoDB [12] database with a Metabase [13] interface for database visualization and querying. This is the data acquisition stage. Once this step has been completed, the data is preprocessed and cleaned using a combination of PySpark and Spacy [14] to get a cleaner corpus for training purposes.

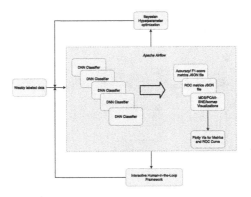

Fig. 4. Weakly supervised DNN workflow. User interaction is in green where reclassification of data points is enabled. (Color figure online)

The data, obtained after preprocessing, goes through a training and feedback loop as shown in the Fig. 4. A DNN based on static and contextual embeddings coupled with Attention mechanisms is trained on the corpus and is evaluated to produce metrics such as F1-Scores, Accuracy, ROC curves along with dimension-reduced projections as outputs. Visualizations are produced for the model metrics using the Plot.ly [15] framework from the several model runs. All of this is automated using the Airflow [5] tool.

The dimension-reduced projections are inspected by a human to assess model performance as described in [8]. Also, hyperparameter optimization is performed on the various configurations, as shown in Fig. 4, to identify the best-performing model using the Comet.ml [16] tool. The combination of the Human-in-the-loop process and the hyperparameter optimization process serves to iteratively refine the model.

Fig. 5. Framework for stance detection

Interactive and Exploratory Web-Based Application. The interactive web-based application (Fig. 5) that is created can be divided into two halves: the left half presents the projections and the right half presents the information associated with an entity selection. To interact with the visualization the user can single click on an entity in the visualization to select it, or the user can use any of the pan/zoom/select tools to explore the visualizations. The top projection is the result of the application of t-SNE to the output of the penultimate layer and the bottom projection is the MDS projection of the same output with euclidean distance functions.

Model Interpretability. With the prevalence and success of the predictive power of DNNs, it has also faced criticisms over how the results were generated. This has accelerated efforts to provide a solution to this concern, which is informally referred to as Interpretable AI. While the application shown in Fig. 5 allows us to assess stance with a measure of uncertainty, how this determination was made is not transparent to the user.

An attention layer takes as input a 'context' and 'query' and computes the similarity of the query vector to each vector in the context matrix. In self-attention, the context and query are the same and one computes the similarity of each word in the sequence to every other word in this sequence to form an attention weight matrix. The attention weights can be used to visualize the relevance of each individual word in a sentence with respect to its classification. An example of this is illustrated in Fig. 6. The emphasized words as indicated by the darker boxes have a larger contribution to the classification outcome, thereby informing the user what words are relevant from the network's perspective.

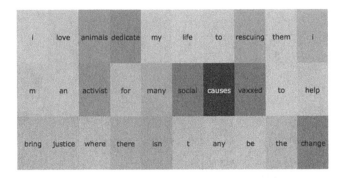

Fig. 6. Illustration of Attention weights for model interpretability

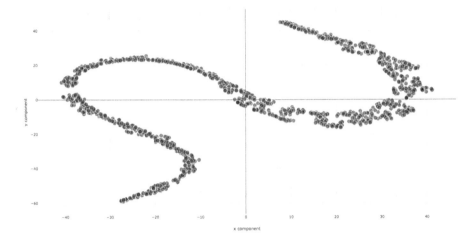

Fig. 7. Structure of t-SNE projections from the penultimate layer

Evaluation of Visualization Methods. Projections from the penultimate layer are dimension-reduced using PCA, MDS, Isomap and t-SNE to evaluate the suitability of these methods for representing the results of the networks and assessing political affiliation. MDS (Fig. 8), as a result of the nature of the projection allows quantification of stance as a function of 'distance' along the direction of the projection. t-SNE (Fig. 7) tended to reduce crowding. However, Isomap (Fig. 9) can be seen as a better technique for capturing non-linear relationships in the high-dimensional data.

Hyperparameter Optimization. Hyperparameter optimization was performed using the feature provided by the Comet.ml tool. This framework allows, through the use of APIs, the logging of model metrics and the optimization of the required hyperparameters over a desired metric such as accuracy or loss. Figure 10 shows the web interface for Comet.ml where one can inspect each pass

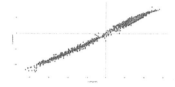

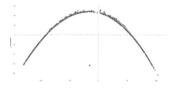

Fig. 8. Structure of MDS projections from the penultimate layer

Fig. 9. Structure of Isomap projections from the penultimate layer

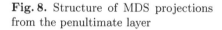

						Name	Tags	Server	File na	Duration	HIDDE	DROPO	LINEA	Loss
☐	⌄		✓	◉	■	75ba3c1	three	8/6/19 06:2	attention_p	00:01:09	75	0.21775777	55	0.02242653
☐	⌄		✓	◉	■	65d2790	three	8/6/19 06:2	attention_p	00:01:02	10	0.32994308	54	0.01715301
☐	⌄		✓	◉	■	17b9e7e	three	8/6/19 06:2	attention_p	00:01:08	102	0.50401669	12	0.01860596
☐	⌄		✓	◉	■	53fc961	three	8/6/19 06:2	attention_p	00:01:03	48	0.96513551	41	0.33428800
☐	⌄		✓	◉	■	dfd1928	three	8/6/19 06:2	attention_p	00:01:14	117	0.62109994	35	0.02168722
☐	⌄		✓	◉	■	df47395	three	8/6/19 06:2	attention_p	00:01:09	32	0.29615986	36	0.01531454
☐	⌄		✓	◉	■	b5658b0	three	8/6/19 06:3	attention_p	00:01:09	55	0.19085956	48	0.00567017
☐	⌄		✓	◉	■	8c68c45	three	8/6/19 06:3	attention_p	00:01:05	24	0.24194129	36	0.01355262
☐	⌄		✓	◉	■	cdde3c7	three	8/6/19 06:3	attention_p	00:01:07	82	0.16072706	53	0.00628004
☐	⌄		✓	◉	■	ad0941e	three	8/6/19 06:3	attention_p	00:01:03	17	0.14312883	40	0.00561240
☐	⌄		✓	◉	■	24c8abb5f	three	8/6/19 06:3	attention_p	00:01:06	71	0.44517077	42	0.01454407
☐	⌄		✓	◉	■	549298e	three	8/6/19 06:3	attention_p	00:01:11	73	0.32904065	18	0.01799950
☐	⌄		✓	◉	■	2d54721	three	8/6/19 06:3	attention_p	00:01:10	110	0.48485643	33	0.02082771
☐	⌄		✓	◉	■	e141ae5	three	8/6/19 06:3	attention_p	00:01:06	77	0.51328984	57	0.01738352
☐	⌄		✓	◉	■	346d1ee	three	8/6/19 06:4	attention_p	00:01:05	62	0.14503871	19	0.00693153
☐	⌄		✓	◉	■	6aca03e	three	8/6/19 06:4	attention_p	00:01:04	35	0.09961353	15	0.00363940

Fig. 10. Hyperparameter optimization with Comet.ml

of an optimization run. Figure 11 demonstrates visual filtering of the various passes with an interactive parallelogram chart that can be built using the tool. This allows the user to identify optimal hyperparameter configurations for the corpus.

Workflow. The purpose of this work was to determine how well the Bidirectional LSTM (BiLSTM) networks with various static embeddings perform compared to the same networks with pretrained contextual embeddings. In this work 'Elmo' [17] was used for the contextual embedding. For static embeddings, the 100-dimensional Glove embeddings were chosen as a tradeoff between expressiveness and availability of compute and memory resources. Along with the Glove

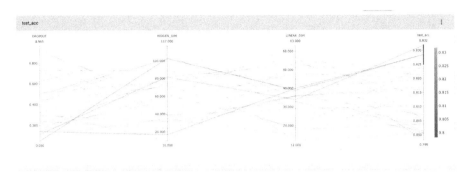

Fig. 11. Parallelogram with filters to identify optimal hyperparameter configurations

embeddings, the 'Glove.twitter.100d' embeddings and 'Charngram.100d' embeddings were also evaluated.

In order to evaluate these models, Airflow was used to automate the workflow associated with gathering metrics. Training and validation accuracy, precision, recall and F1-scores on a larger set of weakly-supervised data is noted along with the same metrics on the fully-supervised smaller test data. As a result of the class imbalance in our training data, it is critical to evaluate performance using all of the metrics above. ROC metrics are also recorded per configuration for each run so that an ROC curve can be generated. The raw metric files are processed by a script that generates the metric plots, i.e. box plots of accuracy, precision, recall and F1-scores, to compare model performance. The data files required to generate the visualizations are written out as pandas dataframes. These files are then read by the framework shown in Fig. 5 for interactive exploration. The users have the ability to interact with the documents in the corpus through the application. This allows them to correct the labels through inspection if it is deemed necessary, and export the corrected corpus back so that it can be fed back into the DNN for iterative refinement.

3   Conclusion and Future Work

In summary, case studies were presented that illustrated the use of HPC in knowledge mining. The availability of such resources expedited the iterative feedback loop necessary for the use-cases presented above. The work on the portals presented here lowered the barrier for access to HPC resources as well as increasing research productivity thereby effectively reducing the mean time to discovery and opening up HPC resource availability and use to more fields of science.

References

1. Reinsel, D., Grantz, J., Rydning, J.: The Digitization of the World - From Edge to Core. IDC White Paper - #US44413318 (2018)

2. Hudak, D., et al.: Open OnDemand: a web-based client portal for HPC centers. J. Open Source Softw. **3**(25), 622 (2018)
3. Palmer, J.T., et al.: Open XDMoD: a tool for the comprehensive management of high-performance computing resources. Comput. Sci. Eng. **17**(4), 52–62 (2015)
4. Zhou, Z.H.: A brief introduction to weakly supervised learning. Nat. Sci. Rev. **5**(1), 44–53 (2017)
5. Apache Airflow Documentation: Apache Airflow Documentation - Airflow Documentation. https://airflow.apache.org/. Accessed 13 Sept 2019
6. Kim, D., Song, L., Breitwieser, F.P., Salzberg, S.L.: Centrifuge: rapid and sensitive classification of metagenomic sequences. Genome Res. **26**(12), 1721–1729 (2016). Epub 2016 Oct 17. PubMed PMID: 27852649; PubMed Central PMCID: PMC5131823
7. Breitwieser, F.P., Salzberg, S.L.: Pavian: interactive analysis of metagenomics data for microbiome studies and pathogen identification. Bioinformatics (2019). https://doi.org/10.1093/bioinformatics/btz715. pii: btz715. [Epub ahead of print] PubMed PMID: 31553437
8. Rajamohan, S., Romanella, A., Ramesh, A.: A weakly-supervised attention-based visualization tool for assessing political affiliation. arXiv:1908.02282 [cs.CL] (2019)
9. Pontiki, M., et al.: SemEval-2016 task 5: aspect based sentiment analysis. In: Proceedings of the 10th International Workshop on Semantic Evaluation (SemEval 2016) (2016)
10. Python-rq.org: RQ: Simple job queues for Python (2019). http://python-rq.org/. Accessed 13 Sept 2019
11. Tweepy: tweepy/tweepy, GitHub, 04 September 2019. https://github.com/tweepy/tweepy. Accessed 13 Sept 2019
12. The most popular database for modern apps, MongoDB. https://www.mongodb.com/. Accessed 13 Sept 2019
13. Metabase is the easy, open source way for everyone in your company to ask questions and learn from data. Metabase. https://metabase.com/. Accessed 13 Sept 2019
14. Explosion: explosion/spaCy, GitHub. https://github.com/explosion/spaCy. Accessed 13 Sept 2019
15. Modern Analytic Apps for the Enterprise, Plotly. https://plot.ly/. Accessed 13 Sept 2019
16. Comet.ml: Comet.ml - Supercharging Machine Learning. https://www.comet.ml/. Accessed 13 Sept 2019
17. Peters, M.E., et al.: Deep contextualized word representations. arXiv preprint arXiv:1802.05365 (2018)

The Pangeo Ecosystem: Interactive Computing Tools for the Geosciences: Benchmarking on HPC

Tina Erica Odaka[1]([🖂]) , Anderson Banihirwe[2], Guillaume Eynard-Bontemps[3],
Aurelien Ponte[1] , Guillaume Maze[1] , Kevin Paul[2] , Jared Baker[2],
and Ryan Abernathey[4]

[1] Laboratory for Ocean Physics and Satellite Remote Sensing UMR LOPS, Ifremer,
Univ. Brest, CNRS, IRD, IUEM, Brest, France
{tina.odaka,aurelien.ponte,guillaume.maze}@ifremer.fr
[2] National Center for Atmospheric Research, Boulder, CO, USA
{abanihi,kpaul,jbaker}@ucar.edu
[3] CNES Computing Center Team, Centre National d'Etudes Spatiales,
Toulouse, France
guillaume.eynard-bontemps@cnes.fr
[4] Lamont Doherty Earth Observatory, Columbia University, New York, USA
rpa@ldeo.columbia.edu

Abstract. The Pangeo ecosystem is an interactive computing software stack for HPC and public cloud infrastructures. In this paper, we show benchmarking results of the Pangeo platform on two different HPC systems. Four different geoscience operations were considered in this benchmarking study with varying chunk sizes and chunking schemes. Both strong and weak scaling analyses were performed. Chunk sizes between 64 MB to 512 MB were considered, with the best scalability obtained for 512 MB. Compared to certain manual chunking schemes, the auto chunking scheme scaled well.

Keywords: Pangeo · Interactive computing · HPC · Cloud · Benchmarking · Dask · Xarray

1 Introduction

In the geosciences, simulation of physical systems has long been the focus of high-performance computing. Thanks to the excellent scaling properties of geoscientific simulations, scientists can now easily output petabytes of data, which together with the massive increase in the volume of observational data, is leading to a crisis for traditional data analytics workflows. In this community, traditional methods of analysis depend upon serial, non-scalable tools, such as the NetCDF Operators (NCO) [1], the NCAR Command Language (NCL) [2], or serial MATLAB and Python scripts. Alternatively, each scientist had to develop

© Springer Nature Switzerland AG 2020
G. Juckeland and S. Chandrasekaran (Eds.): HUST 2019/SE-HER 2019/WIHPC 2019,
CCIS 1190, pp. 190–204, 2020.
https://doi.org/10.1007/978-3-030-44728-1_12

parallel (*e.g.*, MPI) applications to perform specialized analysis on particular datasets, a task that is time-consuming, error prone, and leads to duplication of effort across the community. These methods of analysis are so time-consuming that scientists have accepted, for many years now, a *batch processing* style for conducting analysis, where the scientist spends considerable effort and time to write a data analysis script that is then submitted to a traditional HPC batch queuing system, such as PBS Pro [3] or SLURM [4]. These batch jobs can take hours to days to complete. This kind of batch-style data analysis (with non-scalable tools) interrupts the natural, iterative nature of the scientific process of data exploration. The geoscience community needs scalable tools that can free scientists to explore their data interactively, and it is to this end that the Pangeo [5–7] community exists.

2   Pangeo and the Pangeo Platform

Pangeo is a community devoted to the development of an ecosystem of interoperable, scalable, open source tools for interactive data analysis [8]. The community is diverse, comprising of members from traditional HPC as well as cloud computing backgrounds, scientists and technologists, and involving both industry and academia.

The Pangeo framework has allowed several scientific results already. Yu et al. [9], for example, processed global high resolution numerical simulation outputs of the ocean circulation (a 30 TB dataset) in order to quantify its frequency content and compare it with actual observations. The analysis required non-trivial rechunking of a large dataset which was achieved on an HPC platform with a remarkably light amount of code [10].

The Pangeo platform consists of five components: (a) a thin user interface, such as JupyterLab or Jupyter Notebook [11], (b) a data model, such as Xarray [12] or Iris [13], (c) a scalable computing system, such as Dask [14,15] or Spark [16], (d) a scalable storage system, such as a parallel file system or object storage, and (e) a resource management system, such as an HPC batch job scheduling system or Kubernetes. Exactly which choice you make for each component of the platform depends on how you can access the underlying computing system, the data you wish to analyze, and whether you are running the platform on a traditional HPC system or in the public cloud.

On HPC systems, Pangeo is used mainly with Dask. Dask's computing system is based on a central Dask scheduler and multiple Dask workers. The Dask scheduler orchestrates parallelisation tasks performed by Dask workers. Each parallel task assigned to the Dask workers is based on a 'chunk' of grided data in Xarray datasets. Users specify the size and shape of the 'chunk' and how many (and what kind of) Dask workers to provide to Dask. Then, Dask takes care of the parallelisation automatically. Dask-Jobqueue [15,17] works with traditional HPC job scheduling systems to launch Dask workers interactively, providing both fixed and adaptive scaling capabilities.

For the purposes of this paper, we consider two specific deployments of the Pangeo platform on HPC systems: (i) the HAL system at CNES [18], and

(ii) the Cheyenne system at NCAR's Wyoming Supercomputing Center (NWSC) [19]. The benchmarks performed for this paper consider only interactive compute (*i.e.*, no I/O), and so we only concern ourselves with the data model and scalable compute components of the Pangeo platform.

3   HPC Deployments of the Pangeo Platform

As mentioned in the previous section, and for the purposes of this paper, an HPC Pangeo deployment is distinguished from a cloud-based deployment by the use of a Pangeo Python environment (containing Xarray, Dask, and Dask-Jobqueue) and an HPC batch job scheduling system. Some HPC centers deploy the JupyterHub [20] service, which provides a platform for authenticating users and launching Pangeo Jupyter Notebooks on the remote HPC system.

3.1   Hal

CNES Cluster (Hal) Architecture. Hal is an intermediate size HPC cluster, with about 460 nodes, 12,000 cores and a 8.5 PB Spectrum Scale Storage. Nodes and storage are interconnected with Infiniband at 56 GB/s, and the storage system provides a bandwidth up to 100 GB/s.

Benchmarks for this paper were run on Lenovo compute nodes installed in Hal in 2017 with Intel Broadwell CPUs (2x E5-2650 per node, 24 cores per node) and 128 GB of RAM. Hal has several powerful frontal nodes equipped with more RAM and more powerful CPUs. Standard HPC users use the compute nodes by logging on to the frontal nodes with ssh, develop their applications, then submit their jobs on the command line through PBS Pro. Hal also provides Virtual Machines (VMs) configured as cluster clients. These VMs are integrated into the HPC's network, enrolled in its LDAP directory, mounting the GPFS file system through NFS, and have a PBS client installed and configured. Specific projects or groups of users can ask for one of these VMs in order to have their own environment upon cluster access.

Pangeo Deployment. On Hal, JupyterHub was deployed on a VM cluster client within a Conda environment. In order to launch the JupyterHub service, a systemctl service file was set up. ProfileSpawner [21] and BatchSpawner [22] are used to provide a selection of resource profiles for users through a web interface (*e.g.*, number of CPUs, amount of memory), and to start the user's Jupyter Notebook server in a batch job on HPC nodes. The Conda environment providing Pangeo's Python ecosystem Conda was copied from Pangeo's Docker images [5], installed and configured as a Jupyter kernel.

Lessons Learned. On the admin side, JupyterHub is the most complex component of the Pangeo deployment, but it was still relatively easy to set up. There is a lack of complete integration, like a provided service file for main linux distributions. BatchSpawner was not compatible with the latest versions of PBS

Pro, which resulted in some Pull Requests to the BatchSpawner codebase. The job script used by BatchSpawner was modified so that users could easily add custom shared kernel folders and configure the Python environment from which the Jupyter Notebook server is launched. Since the installation of JupyterHub in 2018 October, *i.e.* one year ago, more than 100 accounts out of 800 active accounts on Hal have used the service at least once, and nearly 50 accounts use on a weekly basis. About a quarter of JupyterHub users are using Dask for workload distribution. The principal feedback we've obtained on Dask is that it's really easy to start using it, but that it can be challenging to debug or optimize when problems scale up. Distributed computing may look simple, but understanding it and doing it well will always need some expertise, hence this benchmark to determine optimal parameters for common operations.

3.2   Cheyenne

NCAR Cluster (Cheyenne) Architecture. Cheyenne is a 5.34 petaflops peak, high-performance computer. It features 145, 152 Intel Xeon "Broadwell" processor cores in 4,032 dual-socket nodes (36 cores per node) and 313 TB total system memory (64 GB/node on 3,168 nodes and 128 GB/node on 864 nodes). Cheyenne uses Mellanox EDR InfiniBand in a partial 9D Enhanced Hypercube single-plane interconnect topology with a 25 GB/s bidirectional per link bandwidth. Standard users access the Cheyenne system via ssh with LDAP authentication to 6 dual-socket "Broadwell" login nodes with 256 GB memory/node. Resource management on Cheyenne is provided through PBS Pro.

A separate cluster, named Casper, exists for data analysis and visualization. The Casper system, procured from PCPC Direct, Ltd., is comprised of 28 Supermicro nodes featuring Intel Skylake processors (36 cores per node). Twenty (20) Casper nodes provide 384 GB of RAM for general purpose data analysis and visualization. Six (6) Casper nodes are high-memory nodes with 768 GB of RAM, and two (2) Casper nodes are login nodes. NCAR's JupyterHub provides access to both the Cheyenne and Casper systems, though the benchmarks for this paper where run only on Cheyenne.

Pangeo Deployment. Users can access Cheyenne's Pangeo deployment through an experimental JupyterHub deployment running on one of the Cheyenne login nodes, in a setup similar to CNES's Hal JupyterHub. Users are also allowed to launch their own personal installations of JupyterLab over ssh tunnels. NCAR is using this experimental JupyterHub deployment to assess how best to deploy an officially supported JupyterHub for the follow-on machine to Cheyenne in 2021.

Lessons Learned. Over the last year, we have made several observations that will help with agility, stability, and upgrades of the JupyterHub service in the future. We have learned that it is extremely beneficial to provide a single access point for the user community with a single web address. Leveraging a reverse proxy has really helped with this but not without difficulties. One issue was being too restrictive when proxying WebSocket connections as Jupyter applications can heavily rely on the protocol upgrade to function properly. Secondly, as data grows, the size of the Jupyter Notebooks increases as well, necessitating special attention to configuration and sizing of buffering capabilities on the reverse proxy. Additionally, Jupyter, and projects around Jupyter, move quite quickly, and therefore upgrades are expected to be delivered at a more rapid pace than other systems-based software. Currently all JupyterHub installations are kept around to revive them if needed. Separation of services is also critical. The reverse proxy, the different JupyterHub instances, and the site-provided kernels all run in different environments to allow each component to be updated individually. The site-provided kernels remain in a fixed state after they are validated to encourage as much repeatability as possible. Finally, the JupyterHub instances all run within a containerization environment called Inception that allow us to run with necessary changed system configuration files on already existing hardware as part of the machines. The site service has been well adopted and provided great value to workshops and hackathons that have taken place.

In the future, there are plans to increase database resilience by moving to PostgreSQL, or another potentially compatible database, and implementing better telemetry and utilization metric tracking. Finally, we are planning additional investigations into adaptively balancing the use of traditional batch schedulers (*e.g.*, PBS Pro, SLURM) for both batch jobs and interactive computing (via the JupyterHub and Dask-Jobqueue).

4   Benchmark of Pangeo on HPC

4.1   Benchmark Method

During this study, we varied our benchmarking computations in following ways:

– Dask chunk size, S_{chunk},
– cluster size (number of HPC nodes), N_{node}, and
– the chunking scheme used for Dask arrays.

To be able to compare the performance between different architectures we placed only one Dask worker with one thread on each HPC node. On Hal (Sect. 3.1), Dask-Jobqueue was used to submit jobs to PBS Pro job scheduler reserving 24 cores (the entire node) and 128 GB of memory for each Dask worker, ensuring that no other jobs would run on the node for benchmark. On Cheyenne (Sect. 3.2), Dask-Jobqueue was used to submit jobs to the `regular` queue, which reserves entire nodes for each job.

Dataset. For each chunk size, we created a random `float64` Xarray dataset called `ds` with the following 3 coordinates: `time`, `lon` (longitude) and `lat` (latitude). This synthetic dataset mirrors the structure of many real datasets in weather and climate research, such as satellite products or climate model outputs. The size of the total dataset S_{total} is a function of chunk size S_{chunk}, cluster size N_{node} and number of chunks per node F according to:

$$S_{total} = S_{chunk} \times N_{node} \times F. \qquad (1)$$

In this benchmark study, we used $F = 10$ chunks per node, fixing the number of points in `lon` and `lat` dimensions to 384 and 320, respectively.

The size of the temporal dimension is varied in order to meet the desired total dataset size as defined be (1). For example, a computation with a chunk size of $S_{chunk} = 128$ MB, $N_{node} = 16$ HPC nodes, leads to a total dataset size of 20.48 GB, and the `ds(time, lon, lat)` shape corresponds to (20834, 384, 320). For Hal, the time coordinate contained daily values ranging from 1 January 1980 to the year 2037. On Cheyenne, the time coordinate contained hourly data. The longitude varies from -180 to $+180°$, and latitude varies from -90 to $90°$.

Chunking Scheme. Three different chunking schemes were tested:

– The *auto* chunking scheme lets Dask automatically determine the shape of each chunk, given a particular chunk size. The auto chunking scheme subdivides every dimension in order to achieve the desired chink size.
– The *spatial* chunking scheme keeps the temporal dimension contiguous in one chunk, dividing data along spatial dimensions.
– The *temporal* chunking scheme keeps all spatial dimensions contiguous in one chunk, dividing data along temporal dimension.

With the above Dask dataset example, `ds(20834, 384, 320)`, the auto, spatial and temporal chunking schemes will lead respectively to the following chunk sizes: (251, 192, 160), (20834, 28, 28), and (131, 384, 320).

Geoscience Operations. The following four geoscience operations were used to measure performance:

– The **temporal mean** operation is a temporal average. It corresponds to the following code in Xarray:
  `ds.mean(dim='time')`
– The **spatial mean** operation is a spatial (*i.e.*, along `lon` and `lat`) average. On Hal, it corresponds to the following line of code in Xarray:
  `ds.mean(dim=['lat', 'lon'])`
  while on Cheyenne, the spatial mean includes weights.
– The **climatology** operation calculates a standard climatology analysis by calculating the seasonal mean value of `ds(time,lat,lon)`. This operation runs along the time axis. It corresponds to the following lines of code in Xarray:
  `ds_g = ds.groupby('time.season')`
  `climatology = ds_g.mean(dim='time')`

- The **anomaly** operation computes the anomaly of ds(time,lat,lon) with respect to the seasons (*i.e.*, the climatology result). It corresponds to the following line of code in Xarray:
  ds_g - climatology

The run time for each operation was measured after the dataset was created and loaded into memory. For each choice of chunk size, chunking scheme, the geoscience operation was performed multiple times, and the median run time for each operation in shown in this paper, reflect the real usage of an typical HPC user.

Strong Scaling Analysis. A strong scaling analysis keeps the total size of a problem constant (*i.e.*, the dataset) and evaluates computation times with an increasing number of processes. It allows the problem to possibly scale with the increase of parallel processors and to highlight critical values. Without parallel computing overhead, such as communication or synchronisation, the run time is expected to decrease as $1/N_{node}$. In this study, we fixed the total dataset size to 20.48 GB. The number of nodes N_{node} was varied over 1, 2, 4, 8 and 16, while the chunk size S_{chunk} was varied with the number of nodes from 2.048 GB to 128 MB, such that the total dataset size as defined in (1) stayed constant.

We produced and analyzed 60 sets of benchmark results (four geoscience operations × three chunking schemes × five values for N_{node}). We have performed this benchmark both on the Hal and Cheyenne supercomputers. Using Hal, a total of 1056 computations were performed, with each test set being performed 10 to 28 times. The run times on Hal varied from 1.25 to 77.61 s. Using Cheyenne, a total of 96 computations were performed, with each test set being performed one to three times. The run times on Cheyenne varied from 1.10 to 57.39 s.

Weak Scaling Analysis. A weak scaling analysis aims to determine how the time to solution varies with processor count for a fixed problem size *per processor*. In an ideal case, we expect to observe a constant time to solution, independent of the total number of processors in the system.

In this study, we fixed the chunk size S_{chunk} and varied the total dataset size S_{total} with the number of nodes N_{node}. We performed four different weak scaling analyses using a chunk size S_{chunk} of 64, 128, 256 and 512 MB. For each analysis, the number of nodes N_{node} varied over 1, 2, 4, 8, and 16. We produced and analyzed 240 sets of benchmark results (four geoscience operations × three chunking schemes × five values for N_{node} × four variations of chunk size).

At the time of this publication, the weak scaling study results for Cheyenne are incomplete and are not shown. However, a thorough weak scaling study was performed on Hal. In total, we performed 5268 computations using the Hal supercomputer. Each test set was computed from 20 to 28 times on Hal and from 1 to 2 times on Cheyenne. The run times on Hal varied from 0.49 to 125.22 s, and the run times on Cheyenne varied from 0.40 to 91.75 s. For each set of tests, the run time was normalized by the median of non-parallel ($N_{node} = 1$) test.

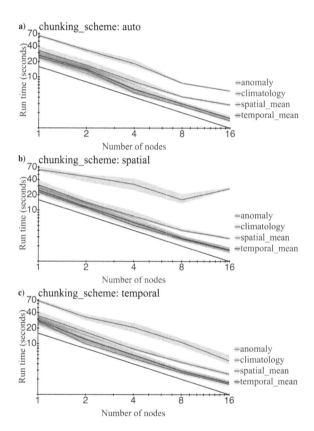

Fig. 1. Strong scaling analysis results for a total dataset size of 20.48 GB using the Hal supercomputer. The x axis shows number of nodes used for each test, shown on log scale. The y axis shows the run time in seconds on a log scale. The blue, orange, green and red lines correspond respectively to the run times for the anomaly, climatology, spatial mean and temporal mean operations. Curves corresponds to the median run time, and the shadowed area shows a single standard deviation from the mean run time. The black line corresponds to the expected strong scaling curve, a^{-1}. From the top, figures (a), (b) and (c) show the run times with auto, spatial and temporal chunking schemes, respectively. (Color figure online)

4.2   Results and Discussions

Strong Scaling Analysis. The benchmark results using Hal and Cheyenne are shown in Figs. 1 and 2, respectively. For the auto (Figs. 1-a and 2-a) and temporal (Figs. 1-c and 2-c) chunking schemes, the run time decreases for all four geoscience operations with a a^{-1} power law. This is consistent with the expectation.

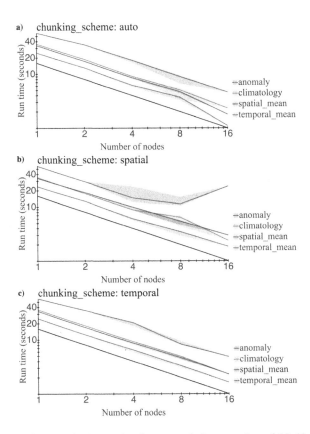

Fig. 2. Strong scaling analysis results for a total dataset size of 20.48 GB using the Cheyenne supercomputer. The x axis shows the number of nodes used for each test, shown on a log scale. The y axis shows the run time in seconds on a log scale. The blue, orange, green and red lines correspond respectively to the run times for the anomaly, climatology, spatial mean and temporal mean operations. Curves correspond to the median run time, and the shadowed area shows a single standard deviation from the mean run time. When only one run was performed, the standard deviation is displayed on plots as zero. The black line corresponds to the expected strong scaling curve, a^{-1}. From the top, figures (a), (b) and (c) show run times with auto, spatial and temporal chunking schemes, respectively. (Color figure online)

Dask's automatic parallelism scales well for this cluster size for most chunking schemes. With the spatial chunking scheme, each chunk holds all the data along the time dimension. It is appropriate for operations that run along time (*i.e.*, the temporal mean and climate operations). The anomaly operation also runs along the time coordinate, so we expect it to scale appropriately as well. Run time decreases for the temporal and climatology operations as expected (Figs. 1-b and 2-b, red and orange lines). However, the anomaly operation does not scale after 8 nodes (Figs. 1-b and 2-b, blue lines.)

We do not fully know why the anomaly operation does not show scaling beyond 8 nodes when using spatial chunking. We suspect that it is due to extra overhead or unnecessary communication or both. Further investigation is planned to understand this problem.

It is clear from the findings that the auto chunking scheme would be a suitable choice for general use cases on HPC.

Weak Scaling Analysis. The benchmark results for spatial and auto chunking scheme are shown in Figs. 3 and 4 respectively.

None of the operations studied, for either the spatial or auto chunking schemes, show a constant normalized run time as the number of nodes increases. Most operations show a deviation from ideal scaling over 1 to 16 nodes, ranging from roughly 10% to 40% when the ideal chunk size is used. However, the anomaly operation, when used with the spatial chunking scheme (Fig. 3-a), shows extremely poor scaling. However, the anomaly operation, when used with the auto chunking scheme (Fig. 4-a), shows better scaling, though not ideal. These results are consistent with the results in the strong scaling analysis.

For the auto chunking scheme, Figs. 4-c and d show that the spatial mean and temporal mean operations scale fairly well regardless of chunk size. However, for the anomaly (Fig. 4-a) and climatology (Fig. 4-b) operations, a chunk size of between 256 MB and 512 MB scales better compare to other smaller chunk sizes. Larger chunk sizes places more data on each Dask worker, therefore reducing the communication overhead. Dask's default chunk size for the auto chunking scheme is 128 MB. Note that a bigger chunk size requires more memory on the HPC node.

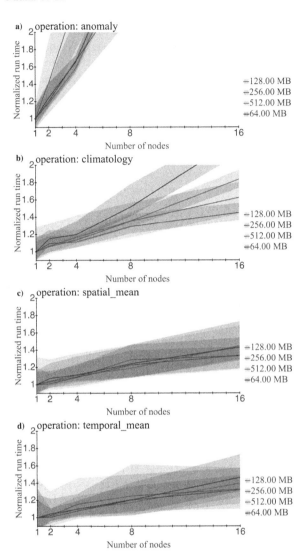

Fig. 3. This figure shows the weak scaling analysis results for the spatial chunking scheme. The x axis shows number of nodes used for each test. The y axis shows the operation run time normalized by the 1-node runtime. The red, blue, orange and green colors correspond to chunk sizes of 64, 128, 256 and 512 MB, respectively. The curves correspond to the medians of run time, and the shadowed areas show a single standard deviation from the mean run time. From the top, figures (a), (b), (c) and (d) show the anomaly, climatology spatial mean and temporal mean operations, respectively. (Color figure online)

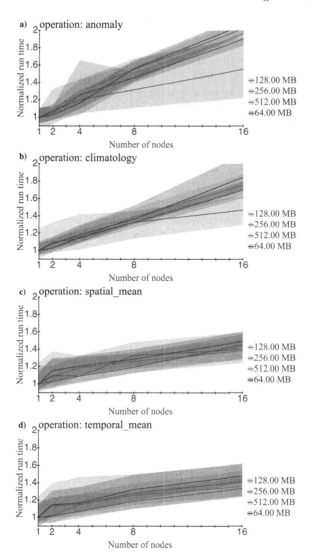

Fig. 4. This figure shows the weak scaling analysis results for the auto chunking scheme. The x axis shows number of nodes used for each test. The y axis shows the run time normalized by the 1-node run time. The red, blue, orange and green colors correspond to chunk sizes of 64, 128, 256 and 512 MB, respectively. The curves correspond to median run times, and the shadowed areas show a single standard deviation from the mean runtime. From the top, figures (a), (b), (c) and (d) shows the anomaly, climatology spatial mean and temporal mean operations, respectively. (Color figure online)

5   Conclusion and Further

The Pangeo community unites scientists and technologists together to make it possible to explore geoscience data using HPC or cloud in an interactive manner. Interactive usage gives a way for researchers to rapidly code and test their ideas [9], but our experiences suggest that it may also introduce some 'blind spots' due to its ease of use. For example, such an easy-to-use parallel platform makes it also easy for users to forget that they are dealing with Terabytes of data with hundreds of workers (*i.e.*, that their machine has real limits and that not all data sizes can easily be analyzed).

This benchmark study of the Pangeo platform shows that the best scalability was obtained with chunk sizes between 256 MB and 512 MB, and, compared to certain manual chunking schemes, the auto chunking scheme scaled well.

Compared to legacy parallel programming models (*e.g.*, MPI), users of Dask do not have to deal with the difficulty of coding their own parallelism. However, they still have to think about grid size and related issues, such as the chunk size and the chunking scheme most appropriate to the computation and the machine they are using. Fortunately, Dask's auto chunking scheme seems to scale quite well, and the knowledge of using a larger-than-default chunk size (*i.e.*, larger than 128 MB) is easy to communicate to users.

The benchmark code used for this paper is open source, and it is published on GitHub [23]. The development of the benchmarking suite continues, with the goal of this benchmarking suite being that user (or administrator of an HPC center) can run these benchmarks and find out what is the best chunk size, chunking scheme, workers per node, and threads per node for a given HPC cluster for geoscience applications. This will help both optimising the usage of the cluster for HPC administrators and optimise the time for HPC users.

Pangeo is still new to HPC platforms. HPC communities have a history of optimisation and parallelism using HPC platforms. For example, there is a history of automatic parallelism methods (*e.g.*, Fortran co-arrays) and the use of RDMA for communication between nodes [24]. These knowledge and specialization from the HPC community may help the development and optimisation of the Pangeo platform.

Acknowledgment. Dr. Abernathey was supported by NSF Earthcube award 1740648. Dr. Paul and Mr. Banihirwe were both supported by NSF Earthcube award 1740633.

References

1. Zender, C.S.: Analysis of self-describing gridded geoscience data with netCDF Operators (NCO). Environ. Model. Softw. **23**(10–11), 1338–1342 (2008). https://doi.org/10.1016/j.envsoft.2008.03.004
2. The NCAR Command Language (Version 6.6.2) [Software]. Boulder, Colorado: UCAR/NCAR/CISL/TDD (2019). https://doi.org/10.5065/d6wd3xh5

3. Nitzberg, B., Schopf, J.M., Jones, J.P.: PBS Pro: grid computing and scheduling attributes. In: Nabrzyski, J., Schopf, J.M., Weglarz, J. (eds.) Grid Resource Management. International Series in Operations Research & Management Science, vol. 64, pp. 183–190. Springer, Boston (2004). https://doi.org/10.1007/978-1-4615-0509-9_13

4. Yoo, A.B., Jette, M.A., Grondona, M.: SLURM: simple linux utility for resource management. In: Feitelson, D., Rudolph, L., Schwiegelshohn, U. (eds.) JSSPP 2003. LNCS, vol. 2862, pp. 44–60. Springer, Heidelberg (2003). https://doi.org/10.1007/10968987_3

5. Pangeo: A community platform for Big Data geoscience. http://pangeo.io

6. Robinson, N.H., Hamman, J., Abernathey, R.: Science needs to rethink how it interacts with big data: Five principles for effective scientific big data systems. arXiv e-prints p. arXiv:1908.03356, August 2019

7. Eynard-Bontemps, G., Abernathey, R., Hamman, J., Ponte, A., Rath, W.: The PANGEO big data ecosystem and its use at CNES. In: Proceedings of 2019 Big Data from Space, . Munich, Germany, pp. 49–52 (2019). https://doi.org/10.2760/848593

8. Abernathey, R., et al.: Pangeo NSF Earthcube Proposal (2017). https://doi.org/10.6084/m9.figshare.5361094.v1

9. Yu, X., Ponte, A.L., Elipot, S., Menemenlis, D., Zaron, E.D., Abernathey, R.: Surface kinetic energy distributions in the global oceans from a high-resolution numerical model and surface drifter observations. Geophys. Res. Lett. **46**(16), 9757–9766 (2019). https://doi.org/10.1029/2019GL083074

10. Rotary spectral analysis of surface currents and zonal average. https://github.com/apatlpo/mit_equinox/blob/master/hal/rechunk_rotspectra.ipynb

11. Kluyver, T., et al.: Jupyter Notebooks – a publishing format for reproducible computational workflows. In: Loizides, F., Scmidt, B. (eds.) Positioning and Power in Academic Publishing: Players, Agents and Agendas, pp. 87–90. IOS Press (2016). https://doi.org/10.3233/978-1-61499-649-1-87

12. Hoyer, S., Hamman, J.: Xarray: N-D labeled arrays and datasets in Python. J. Open Res. Softw. **5**(1), 10 (2017). https://doi.org/10.5334/jors.148

13. Met Office: Iris: A Python library for analysing and visualising meteorological and oceanographic data sets. Exeter, Devon (2010–2013). http://scitools.org.uk/iris

14. Rocklin, M.: Dask: parallel computation with blocked algorithms and task scheduling. In: Huff, K., Bergstra, J. (eds.) Proceedings of the 14th Python in Science Conference, pp. 126–132 (2015). https://doi.org/10.25080/Majora-7b98e3ed-013

15. Dask Development Team: Dask: library for dynamic task scheduling (2016). https://dask.org

16. Zaharia, M., et al.: Apache Spark: a unified engine for big data processing. Commun. ACM **59**(11), 56–65 (2016). https://doi.org/10.1145/2934664

17. Dask-jobqueue. https://github.com/dask/dask-jobqueue/

18. CNES: The Centre National d'Etudes Spatiales (CNES) is the government agency responsible for shaping and implementing France's space policy in Europe. https://cnes.fr/

19. Computational and Information Systems Laboratory.: Cheyenne: SGI ICE XA Cluster (2017). https://doi.org/10.5065/d6rx99hx

20. JupyterHub — JupyterHub 1.0.0 documentation. https://jupyterhub.readthedocs.io/

21. Jupyterhub/wrapspawner. https://github.com/jupyterhub/wrapspawner

22. Jupyterhub/batchspawner. https://github.com/jupyterhub/batchspawner
23. Benchmarking and scaling studies of the Pangeo platform. https://github.com/pangeo-data/benchmarking
24. Liu, J., Wu, J., Panda, D.K.: High performance RDMA-based MPI implementation over InfiniBand. Int. J. Parallel Prog. **32**(3), 167–198 (2004). https://doi.org/10.1023/B:IJPP.0000029272.69895.c1

Author Index

Printed in the United States
By Bookmasters